Significant Studies for Second Grade

Reading and Writing Investigations for Children

Karen Ruzzo and Mary Anne Sacco

HEINEMANN
Portsmouth, NH

Heinemann
A division of Reed Elsevier Inc.
361 Hanover Street
Portsmouth, NH 03801–3912
www.heinemann.com

Offices and agents throughout the world

Library of Congress Cataloging-in-Publication Data
Ruzzo, Karen.
Significant studies in second grade : reading and writing investigations for children / Karen Ruzzo and Mary Anne Sacco.
p. cm.
Includes bibliographical references and index.
ISBN 0-325-00512-5 (alk. paper)
1. Language arts (Elementary)—Curricula—New York (State)—New York—Case studies. 2. Second grade (Education)—Curricula—New York (State)—New York—Case studies. 3. Manhatten New School (New York, N.Y.)—Curricula—Case studies. I. Sacco, Mary Anne. II. Title.
LB1576.R68 2004
372.6—dc22 2003023397

Editor: Kate Montgomery
Production editor: Sonja S. Chapman
Cover design: Night & Day Design
Compositor: Publishers' Design and Production Services, Inc.
Manufacturing: Steve Bernier

Printed in the United States of America on acid-free paper
08 07 06 05 04 VP 1 2 3 4 5

To Jacqui Getz,
who inspired and guided us along this journey

CONTENTS

Foreword by Shelley Harwayne *vii*
Acknowledgments *xi*
Introduction *1*

PART ONE **Reading Work**

CHAPTER 1 Getting Started in the Reading Workshop: Combing Through the Library, Introducing Series, and Meeting Characters 10
CHAPTER 2 Understanding Dialogue: Investigation One 20
CHAPTER 3 Learning to Read Nonfiction: Investigation Two 73

PART TWO **Writing Work**

CHAPTER 4 Getting Started in the Writing Workshop: Writing About Memories, Introducing Picture Books, and Experimenting with Forms and Techniques 114
CHAPTER 5 Creating Setting in Writing: Investigation Three 122
CHAPTER 6 Content Area Research and Writing: Investigation Four 156

Appendices *213*
Bibliography *231*
Index *237*

FOREWORD

The first time I read *Significant Studies for Second Grade: Reading and Writing Investigations for Children* cover to cover was during the blackout of 2003. As many in the Midwest and Northeast will recall, it was a hot, muggy August afternoon. I had been stretched out on a lounge chair, reading on my back porch when the electricity fizzled out. I probably wouldn't have realized the loss, if my husband hadn't been watching television nearby. I stopped reading long enough to find batteries for a transistor radio and then listen to the coverage of the soon-to-become twenty-four hour inconvenience. Yes, I missed my air-conditioned bedroom that night, and cold drinks from the fridge, but most of all I missed having telephone service.

In the past, whenever I have been honored with the request to write a foreword for my colleagues' books, I have rushed to call them the minute I have finished their manuscript and then again the minute I have finished writing a draft of the foreword. The blackout of 2003 changed that pattern, and I decided that instead of belated calls to Karen and Mary Anne, I would simply write in this foreword what I would have said to them if I had been able to call.

So first, I want to thank you both for telling your teaching stories. You so graciously pay tribute to your students, their families, your colleagues, and your school community. I knew when I hired you both that you were gems, but I had no idea when I left the Manhattan New School that your professional collaboration would produce such rare treasure.

As I read your manuscript, construction workers were renovating and expanding the kitchen in my old house. They began by sinking large steel beams into the ground in order to support the new extension. In many ways, the teaching you describe served as support beams for your students' future elementary reading and writing challenges. What they learned in your second-grade classrooms about choice of texts and choice of topics, connecting their reading to their writing and vice versa, as well as the importance of deep study and meaningful practice of strategies will serve them well throughout their remaining years at the Manhattan New School as well as throughout their lifetimes as readers and writers.

Next, I want to thank you for teaching me so much about planning, especially the collaborative kind. Just as the public can easily picture two physicians talking about a patient, two lawyers discussing a case, or two architects discussing a building site, you have made it easy for your teachers to imagine the benefits attached to two teachers pulling together to regularly discuss their students. And your clear and consistent planning and implementation of those plans help readers appreciate that less is more. Rather than packing your teaching with fast-paced, ever changing courses of study, you do careful kidwatching and then carve out ample time, along with the change of seasons, to guide your children through well-designed and carefully planned studies, ones that are filled with deliberate challenges, preprepared packets of texts, appropriate and abundant supports, and finished products worthy of celebration. I have visited no other classrooms, in any part of the city, in which Henry, Pinky, Rex, and Nate seem like members of the class.

Then, too, I want to thank you for reminding me what beginning teachers and teachers new to literature-based workshops need. It is clear that your recent experiences as mentor teacher, staff developer, and even assistant principal have fed your thinking about the needs of teachers interested in strengthening their practice. By including the roots of your teaching as well as your reflective stance, you serve as powerful models for those new to the profession. Most of all, you remind new teachers not to be afraid to teach, to offer explicit information when the need arises. I also applaud your fresh feature of including your colleague Melissa's end-of-chapter comments. Hearing the voice of a new teacher makes this book more powerful.

I also found myself underlining the essential roles that you consistently cast for your young students. Your chapters are filled with gracious invitations, including asking children to rehearse for share time, join in the search for elements of craft, make and share unique discoveries, support their partners, sort classroom libraries, launch classmates on significant inquiries, and work like detectives. You also demonstrate how the ideas and actions of students on one day inform your teaching for the next. You each cast a magic spell in your classrooms, making your students fall in love with reading, writing, and paying attention to their worlds. No doubt, your students will always care about the quality of the dialogue and setting in the books they read or write and will remain committed nonfiction readers, writers, and bird-watchers. I wouldn't be surprised if they also kept memory collection notebooks for the really emotional moments of their lives.

In addition, I was thrilled to discover new works of children's literature and new ways of viewing familiar texts. I could so clearly picture you borrowing favorite books from the first-grade teachers in order that your students would feel at home during the beginning weeks of school. You have also eloquently elevated the role series books play for young readers and writers. And I appreciated how frequently you referred back to your dog-eared texts, helping readers understand that any one book can contain so many essential lessons. No doubt, I will be reading my own old favorites with new and informed eyes.

Karen and Mary Anne, you have written a book that calls out to be reread. I can easily imagine forming a study group around this text. A group of teachers could reread it searching for the role families can play, the importance of art in the life of readers and writers, the value of exercises for our youngest students, the need to follow students' leads, the way in which favorite texts can enhance student growth in the reading and writing workshop, and the range of genres that can emerge from an inquiry study.

Finally, thank you for helping me appreciate bird life in New York City. I recently read a column in the Metropolitan Diary section of the *New York Times* in which a parent sings the praises of her second grader's bird study at the Manhattan New School. The enthusiasm of her son was contagious, pulling in the entire family. So, too, for readers of this book. The description of your bird study will be contagious, inspiring teachers throughout the country to follow students' leads and design inquiry studies that make students' hearts beat just a little bit faster.

So congratulations are in order, dear Karen and Mary Anne. You wanted your readers to feel as if we are sitting on the rug and learning alongside you as you and your students unravel these significant studies, and we do. If every student in America were fortunate enough to call you teacher, there would be no need for any conversations about children left behind. You are gifts to the profession, and as soon as my new kitchen is complete, you must come for a well-deserved celebration party.

With pride, gratitude, and love,
Shelley Harwayne

ACKNOWLEDGMENTS

We would like to acknowledge and thank our colleagues at the Manhattan New School, P.S. 290, who are at the core of our professional community. They provide us the intellectual stimulation and support that allow us to grow as professionals. We feel honored to have become a part of the impressive group of Manhattan New School teacher-researchers who've authored books and raised the bar for literacy instruction in elementary schools around the country. Shelley Harwayne, our school's founding principal, has written a collection of professional books, including *Going Public* and *Writing Through Childhood*, that have inspired teachers, parents, and administrators; Joanne Hindley Salch's *In the Company of Children* invites us into her classroom, describing to us the inner workings of her reading and writing workshops. Paula Rogovin, in *Classroom Interviews* and *The Research Classroom*, shares her passion for research and guides us into understanding the important role inquiry plays in the classroom. Sharon Taberski's ability to reflect upon and refine her practice has made her one of the most clear and thoughtful teachers of reading we know. Her book *On Solid Ground*, an essential guide to the teaching of reading, is one we refer to and reference with many of the teachers with whom we work. Judy Davis and Sharon Hill's *No-Nonsense Guide to Teaching Writing* is our new favorite and a comprehensive guide to the teaching of writing. We thank you all for your inspiration and support as you watched us, so familiarly, juggle our teaching, consulting, writing, and personal lives.

We'd like to give a special thanks to Melissa Wigdor for helping us make sense of our work along the way. Melissa, you have been a joy to work with. We are proud to have your voice woven into each study in the book and look forward to hearing more of your professional voice. Thank you also for the tremendous editorial and organizational support in the final stages of writing this book. Without your final manuscript suggestions and meticulous care in composing the bibliography and organizing the charts, figures, and photographs, we would not have made our deadline. Thank you for your infectious energy for this project and for your enthusiasm for teaching and learning.

Thank you, Wayne Datz, copyeditor extraordinaire, who went above and beyond his duty as Karen's fiancé. For the vacation days and countless moonlighting nights you tended to our manuscript, we thank you! Not only did your keen editorial eye make our writing as accurate and as clear as possible, but your gift of humor kept us sane and laughing along the way. Although your lawerly skills were invaluable to the quality of this project, your genuine interest in the content of the project and the work of our second graders is what we appreciate most.

To Sara Scungio, educator, class parent, and a treasured friend from Australia, we want to thank you for helping us reflect and find our true voices. Your insightful comments and educational advice resulted in a much more thoughtful manuscript. Thank you for pushing us to ask ourselves *why* we do what we do. With each conversation we came closer to clarity.

A special thanks goes to Steven Jaffe, the technology guru of the Manhattan New School, for supporting us through computer glitches and crashes. We would also like to thank Peter Kornicker for his brilliant photographs and for taking the time to be so meticulous in the shooting of our work. To Tammy Swires Puch, Leslie Profeta, and Sara Scungio: thank you for capturing on film moments from our teaching lives; they inspired us and supported our writing.

Our colleagues at P.S. 290 provide us with daily laughter, compassion, and intellectual stimulation. They are part of our extended family, and we thank them for making coming to work at MNS every day a "teacher heaven." So to both those currently with us and those who have moved on to inspire the larger educational community, we thank you: Jill Marino Arens, Joan Backer, Isabel Beaton, Lauren Benjamin, David Bescanson, Jennifer Brophy, Ida Mae Chaplin, Regina Chiou, Dana Chipkin, Ann Marie Corgill, Neuza Costa, Dora Cruz, Beri Daar, Meredith Davis, Erica Edelman, Elissa Eisen, Doreen Esposito, Tara Fishman, Constance Foland, Jordan Forstot, Meggan Friedman, Caroline Gaynor, Mindy Gerstenhaber, Pam Godwin, Julie Greene,

Judith Hirschberg, Layne Hudes, John Keaveney, Judi Klein, Pam Kosove, Petrana Koutcheva, Jayne Kuckley, Diane Lederman, Anita Lee, Kristi Lin, Rachel Lisi, Jennifer Macken, Amy Mandel, Cheryl Melchiorre, Michael Miller, Lisa Elias Moynihan, Eve Mutchnick, Corinne O'Shea, Roberta Pantal-Rhodes, Kathy Park, Valerie Radetsky, Denise Rickles, Barbara Santella, Pamela Saturday, Marisa Schwartzman, Lorraine Shapiro, Lisa Siegman, James Smith, Mark Stein, Kevin Tallat-Kelpsa, Pat Werner, Melissa Wigdor, Debby Yellin, and Beatrice Zavala.

Thank you to Karen's parents, Clara and Ray Ruzzo, for allowing us to use their house when they were away and for stocking the freezer with soup, sauce, and meatballs. Being able to retreat to the peaceful calm of Rhode Island, away from the distractions and hustle and bustle of New York, resulted in very productive writing time. We thank you also for welcoming Booshie. Whether nestled in her bed, frolicking in the snow, or chasing birds at the feeder, Booshie was a quiet inspiration, always knowing just the right time for a break.

We are grateful to everyone at Heinemann for assisting us in moving this project from an idea to a book. Thanks to Leigh Peake, editorial director, for her initial enthusiasm in launching the book, and to Heinemann author Linda Hoyt, for her initial reading of and excitement for our book proposal. To Kate Montgomery, our editor, thank you for having faith in our work from the moment you took over this project and for cheering us on as we approached our final deadline. Your feedback and positive words gave us the energy necessary to write day after day. Thanks to Karen Clausen and Sonja Chapman for your quick responses and attention to detail.

Thanks to teachers and staff developers we've worked with in New York City at P.S. 111, P.S. 217, and P.S. 158 and to those we've worked with in Providence, Rhode Island, particularly Lucille Johnson, Deena Zook, and Daryl Mazza; Birmingham, Alabama, San Diego, California, Bend, Oregon, New Jersey, and Long Island, New York.

A very special thank-you to the students and families at the Manhattan New School, namely the 2004 graduating class—the stars of the book. They are the ones who made and continue to make our work worthwhile. Their enthusiasm for learning constantly pushed our thinking. A big thank-you also to their parents for their reliability and support and the connection they had to our work.

We are both extremely fortunate to have started our teaching careers in nurturing environments, surrounded by mentors and inspiring colleagues. Although we had unique and individual experiences, ironically we began our teaching lives in the same place—the Bronx, in New York City's District 10.

For Karen, it was principal Carolyn Jones and the staff of the Children's School (P.S. 257) that secured the solid foundation that supported all subsequent thinking in the area of teaching and learning. I thank you, Carolyn, for teaching me to appreciate tone and the role environment plays in instruction and for providing me with a model of teaching and learning that is forever embedded in my mind.

Karen would also like to thank her colleagues at the Bronx New School, at the Broad Street School in Providence, Rhode Island, particularly Joyce Binyon, at the Windmill School in Providence, Rhode Island, particularly Lucille Johnson, and at the Boston Renaissance Charter School, particularly Julie Lane. Thank you for your friendship, support, and guidance.

To Shelley Harwayne and Judy Davis, thanks for the fries and the warm welcome on that very first day I met you. I haven't regretted a day of my professional life since our lunch at Frankie's. I thank you both for the endless opportunities you've given me and for your friendship. Judy, knowing you are near provides me great comfort; thank you.

To my friend Christine Reiss, for always believing in me, and to Christopher Epps, who taught me to look beyond perceived limitations, thank you. To my mother, Clara, thank you for always making me a priority and offering love and support. To my father, Raymond, thank you for your resilience and insightfulness, thank you for keeping your eye on the ball and knowing what's important. I thank my sister, Susan, who for years now has been a sounding board for all that I do in life. Finally, to my husband, Wayne, who brought balance into *my* life and who each day makes me smile and reminds me of what's important—molto grazie, mi amore.

For Mary Anne, beginning in District 10 in the Bronx, it was the conversations around lunchtime tables with a group of fabulous teachers from P.S. 37. These conversations, led by staff developers from the Teachers College Reading and Writing Project, taught me about working in a community of teacher-learners. How lucky we were to have Elise Goldman, Donna Santman, Katie Wood Ray, and Lisa Ripperger supporting us as new teachers. While I was a study group member at the project, Laurie Pessah, our leader and codirector, brought me together with teachers from all parts of the city to constantly think, talk, and get better at my practice. Thank you to those initial colleagues for setting a foundation that remains the basis of my thinking today.

Thank you to Nina Bloom of P.S. 111 in District 2 with whom I worked as a staff developer in her new classroom. Thank you for recognizing and valuing the importance of a dialogue study in your reading curriculum.

Thank you to my parents, Lucy and John, for a lifetime of integrity and for instilling in me the work values I follow today. Thank you to my family and close friends for providing love, guidance, and great cooking on demand during this book writing process. My mother, Lucy, is the most reliable woman I know—thank you for making me who I am and for always trying to make my life as comfortable as it can be.

Thank you, Shelley Harwayne, for inviting me into the MNS community, for your support and inspiration for this book. *You're a gift to education!*

Thank you, Jacqui Getz, for your constant open door. Thank you for always being there to discuss "the book" or any matter, personal or professional, big or small, anytime and anywhere: in cab rides, or in the Jetta going across town, in between important meetings, or jogging down West End Avenue.

Finally, we want to thank each other. We both agree that this writing partnership was like a great marriage: every day, even during times of stress, we consistently brought out each other's best qualities.

INTRODUCTION

This book is about thoughtful planning and explicit teaching and their effects on student learning. In addition, it is a story. A story that takes place in the classroom, bringing, through the voices of our second graders, this planning and explicit teaching to life. As you read these pages you will hear us refer to "our classroom" and "our children" as well as alternate our names when bringing a minilesson to life in the classroom. As writers and for the sake of continuity, we chose to blend what was actually two classrooms and two teachers working across the hall into one. In many instances, however, we did operate as one class as we planned alongside each other and frequently combined our classes for lessons. As in an extended family, each class operated as a unit as well as a member of a team of learners sharing ideas and gaining insight from a larger support system. For us, as teachers, having a colleague across the hall with whom to brainstorm changed the way we viewed planning and subsequently instruction. It is our hope that you, our readers, will be inspired by our level of collaboration and its impact on our practice. This book is a result of that collaboration.

We are incredibly lucky to be working at the Manhattan New School, where, in 1991, founding principal Shelley Harwayne carved out a school culture where living and breathing reading and writing became second nature. She set the bar for all that school can be. In *Lifetime Guarantees,* Shelley speaks to the need for educators to create elementary schools that are as scholarly as universities. This belief, as well as her commitment to supporting teachers in their professional and personal growth as readers and writers, remains at our school's core.

When Shelley took her talents to lead New York's District 2, she left us in the very capable hands of Jacqui Getz, who brought a fresh look to our social studies curriculum, and who also shared Shelley's passion for reading and writing. As a way of getting to know the curriculum work of the Manhattan New School and as part of her expertise in planning and organization, Jacqui asked teachers to sketch out their yearlong plans in reading and writing workshop. She felt strongly that grade-level collaboration and planning would support teachers, particularly those who were new, as well as increase curriculum continuity. It was this push that initiated our process of developing yearlong plans in reading and writing workshop. The plans have been refined and reworked from those first meetings with our second-grade colleagues Kevin Tallat-Kelpsa and Regina Chiou. With the support of the professional writing community created by Shelley's and Jacqui's guidance toward thoughtful planning, this book came to be.

We imagine you are learners just as we are. When you want to get better at the teaching of writing, you read Katie Wood Ray's *Wondrous Words* or Shelley Harwayne's *Writing Through Childhood*. When you want a comprehensive look at reading workshop, you read Sharon Taberski's *On Solid Ground*. When you want a look at how to teach nonfiction in the writing workshop, you might pick up *Is That a Fact?* by Tony Stead. Mary Anne remembers as a new teacher how she sat for hours reading about and looking at the room arrangement and classroom environment described in Joanne Hindley's *In the Company of Children*. And Karen recalls back to her time as a Reading Recovery teacher, when she read and reread the pages of Marie Clay's *Becoming Literate* to gain an understanding of how children learn to read. Our shelves are lined with books that serve as resources to push our thinking and help us get better at teaching children.

Aside from the professional books that have shaped our teaching, the leadership and guidance of Shelley and Jacqui, and the brilliance of our Manhattan New School colleagues, we called upon our experiences as teachers and staff developers to support us as we wrote this book. We've learned alongside teachers and children over the course of our years of teaching kindergarten through fourth grade in public schools. As staff developers, we learned to clearly articulate our beliefs and practice in reading and writing instruction to teachers across the country in a variety of situations and settings. This book chronicles one year in our teaching lives. It is our hope that our wealth of experience is evidenced in the text and will provide you guidance to plan thoughtfully and teach explicitly.

What Is a Study?

In reading this book, you will come across the word *study* not only in our title but throughout the text. People are familiar with this term in different ways. For some, the word *study* refers to research based on the work of social scientists or psychologists who use control groups to develop statistical foundations. Among teachers, the word *studies* can be used when referring to theme studies, genre studies, or social studies. For us, the word *study* connotes a course of study or investigation into a particular topic, not necessarily a genre. For eight years now at Manhattan New School, we have been using *Investigations in Number, Data, and Space,* developed by TERC, to teach math. The writers of this math curriculum describe their investigations as emphasizing depth in mathematical thinking through ongoing, related lessons, rather than exposure to a series of fragmented topics. This idea of investigating topics in a constructivist nature, emphasizing in-depth thinking, was not new to us as teachers. We were used to inquiry work, digging deep in social studies and in our reading and writing workshops. Whether it be a specific topic in math, reading, writing, social studies, or even spelling, we followed the same investigative design, meant to help students construct their own understanding around a particular topic. In this design, children ask questions, investigate answers, form generalizations, test generalizations, and solidify understanding, all woven through practice. The studies in this book follow this investigative design. As you read this book, you will find we use the words *investigation* and *study* interchangeably and often. Our title, *Significant Studies for Second Grade: Reading and Writing Investigations for Children,* illustrates this method of teaching.

How to Read and Use This Book

The two reading studies found in Part 1 of this book, dialogue and nonfiction (Chapters 2 and 3), along with the two writing studies found in Part 2, setting and content writing (Chapters 5 and 6), are not intended to be genre studies but rather inquiries into particular topics in reading and writing that are significant in supporting our children as developing readers and writers. The four significant studies presented in this book are chronicled according to the number of weeks (between five and seven) in each study. As you read the book, we want you to feel as though you are sitting on the rug alongside our children, watching the study unravel as the students make exciting daily discoveries. In addition to the narrative of each study, we have provided you with an overview of each chapter titled "Study at a Glance." This feature outlines the goal(s), minilessons, literature needed, and student work plans for each week in the study. It is our intention that this feature will be a helpful tool for you and not a script to be used without consideration of your own classroom needs. As a way of laying the studies out systematically for the reader, we organized the goals and minilessons into neatly packaged weeks. In some cases, our children needed more time to practice the work presented and we adjusted our plans accordingly. As teachers, we know with interruptions such as field trips, weather-related releases, and vacations, there are some weeks when we are unable to deliver five focused minilessons.

These significant studies, in both reading and writing, occur within the structure of a workshop. In working with new teachers, we have found that there are many questions around the essentials of the workshop format, such as

How is the work time structured?
How much time is spent demonstrating a lesson?
How much discussion follows the lesson?
What are students doing during time spent on the rug?
What are children doing when you are conferring or working in a small group?
Does the workshop happen every day?

The following description of the workshop format is meant not only to clarify these questions and provide a basic understanding of the three parts of a workshop (applied to either reading or writing) but to help you better understand the supportive structure of the four significant studies outlined in this book.

Minilesson (10 to 20 Minutes)

A minilesson is a whole-group focused lesson where the teacher either demonstrates strategy work through text or models reading and writing behaviors. Minilessons are predominantly conducted on the rug through shared reading, where the teacher promotes interaction with an enlarged text. In *Significant Studies,* the shared reading enlarged text refers to either a big book, writing from a chart tablet, a transparency projected on an overhead, or an enlarged copy of a text. In some cases, our minilesson focus requires that children listen to text rather than view text. In this case, the minilesson is taught through read-alouds.

Student Work Time (30 to 45 Minutes)

After the teacher-led minilesson, children are given time to practice the work modeled in the minilesson. Children practice this work in one of three ways: independently, in partnerships, or through guided practice in small groups. As children work, the teacher is conferring with individual children or partnerships, or scaffolding the lesson to meet the needs of children in a small-group setting. Whether conferring or guiding a group, the teacher is taking notes that will later inform her teaching as well support her assessment of children. As teachers work with children, they look for specific examples of student practice that will serve as models for the whole class during share time.

Share Time (5 to 10 Minutes)

Students return to the whole group to discuss their application of the strategy, technique, or behavior learned during the minilesson. Having had a chance to practice provides children with a common experience and, therefore, a way into a conversation about what they learned about themselves as readers or writers. Although brief, and often skipped when a class is pressed for time, the share time is essential to the integrity of the workshop. It is here where children reflect on their progress as readers and writers, recapping what they learned, asking questions, and sharing discoveries. This time not only helps to reinforce and confirm lessons taught but also builds community and allows children to feel comfortable sharing ideas as part of a classroom of learners. In some cases in *Significant Studies,* you will notice that our children share with their partners prior to sharing with the whole group. It is our belief that providing even a couple of minutes for children to question and confirm in a comforting, established partnership helps them rehearse for the whole-group share.

In Part 1 of this book, you will be presented with an introduction to our fall reading work as well as two significant studies based in the reading workshop: dialogue and nonfiction.

Chapter 1, "Getting Started in the Reading Workshop," provides you with a glimpse into the foundations of the work that set the stage for the reading studies outlined in Part 1. Our goals for our fall reading work were to get to know our library, investigate book series, and familiarize ourselves with the characters we would live with throughout the year. This chapter provides the reader with a sense of how the year began without the same detailed road maps found in Chapter 2, "Understanding Dialogue: Investigation One," and Chapter 3, "Learning to Read Nonfiction: Investigation Two."

Chapter 2, "Understanding Dialogue," was designed out of a need to support our children as they began to read books with more sophisticated text. The dialogue study, our winter investigation, aims to provide children with the supports they need to navigate text with greater fluency and comprehension. In this chapter, along with the "Study at a Glance" feature (found in each of the significant studies), we provide you with a day-by-day plan to guide your reading and instructional planning. It is our intention that this feature will allow you to feel as though you are part of the specifics of our planning process; we hope you use this road map flexibly to meet the needs of your own classroom.

Chapter 3, "Learning to Read Nonfiction," our spring reading study, was designed out of a need to focus as deeply on the nonfiction portion of our library as we had on fiction through the investigation of how dialogue works. It is in this study that we teach our children to understand the varieties and variables of nonfiction, skills that eventually help support them as researchers and writers in the content study of birds (Chapter 6).

In Part 2 of this book, you will be presented with an introduction to our fall writing work as well as two significant studies based in the writing workshop—setting and content area research and writing.

Chapter 4, "Getting Started in the Writing Workshop," provides you with a glimpse into the foundations of the work that set the stage for the writing studies outlined in Part 2. In this chapter, our goals were to build community through memory writing, gain familiarity with the picture books we would revisit throughout the year, and try out different writing forms and techniques. It is through this work that the children gained a general understanding of looking at texts as writers and telling personal stories through writing. This chapter is about laying the groundwork that will be refined and built upon in Chapter 5, "Creating Setting in Writing: Investigation Three," and in Chapter 6, "Content Area Research and Writing: Investigation Four."

As the children wrote about memories that occurred in special places, we noticed the need for them to anchor their stories in particular settings. Chapter 5, "Creating Setting in Writing," grew out of this need to direct our young writers as they continued to write personal stories. This study is an extension of our work in writing personal stories that began in the fall. The intention for our winter study was to support the children as they moved beyond listlike writing and recollection of events and into using words to create vivid images in longer narratives. By focusing on establishing setting in writing and anchoring memories in time and place, we helped the children accomplish these goals.

Chapter 6, "Content Area Research and Writing," was our culminating study, focused around birds. In this study, children applied what they were learning about nonfiction in the reading workshop to this writing work. Using their knowledge about how nonfiction texts work, our children learned how to research information that would eventually support their nonfiction writing. In addition, children fused writing lessons learned from other studies along the way, such as using texts as mentors, establishing setting, and determining voice in writing, to create engaging, anchored nonfiction narrative pieces. We also show you how children synthesized what they had learned about birds and the writing forms learned throughout the year to produce writing across genres.

The following is a schedule of our reading and writing work for the year.

Yearlong plan in reading and writing workshop

	Reading Work (Part 1)	*Writing Work (Part 2)*
Fall	Getting Started in the Reading Workshop: Combing Through the Library, Introducing Series, and Meeting Characters (Chapter 1)	Getting Started in the Writing Workshop: Writing About Memories, Introducing Picture Books, and Experimenting with Forms and Techniques (Chapter 4)
Winter	Understanding Dialogue (Chapter 2)	Creating Setting (Chapter 5)
Spring	Learning to Read Nonfiction (Chapter 3)	Content Area Research and Writing (Chapter 6)

A New Teacher's Voice

Our colleague, Melissa Wigdor, is one of the most thoughtful new teachers with whom we've worked. Melissa came to the Manhattan New School as a student teacher from Bank Street College of Education. She had the fortunate experience of spending both her fall and spring semesters in Mary Anne's classroom, where she learned firsthand about the reading and writing studies described in this book. In many cases, student teachers come and go in six- to eight-week cycles, without enough time to either watch where a teacher is headed in her curriculum or understand firsthand from where she has come. In addition to having the opportunity to witness a year from start to finish, Melissa possessed a unique ability to gain perspective on the organics of reading and writing workshop. She wasn't as concerned by the children's book levels and published writing pieces as she was with their process as readers and writers. She watched closely at how we delivered minilessons and conferred with children, always noting how our questioning techniques led to authentic responses.

As teachers, we sometimes become absorbed in our day-to-day schedules as managers of our classrooms. We are responsible not only for the curriculum needs of our students but also for the details involved in managing a classroom of thirty students. Our colleague Doreen Esposito, a former television producer, reminds us of all we juggle. We've often heard her compare the job of managing a classroom to the job of producing a television show. The difference, she states, is that teachers not only produce but write, create, direct, and perform as host of a daily running show, all with only two commercial breaks.

With these demands, we often need to be reminded to slow down, become part of the audience, and take in the big picture. With her detailed questioning, Melissa forced us to step back from the depths of our work to view the production and articulate our practice.

Melissa's reflective nature and careful questioning guided her as she transitioned from being a student teacher to a classroom teacher at the Manhattan New School. Now, after her second year of growing and learning, she shares her experience as a new teacher with readers of this book. You'll find Melissa's voice at the end of each of the four studies, where she draws upon her experience as a student teacher and then as a new classroom teacher to reflect on our work. Through Melissa's eyes, readers will gain insight into what Melissa learned from each study as well as perspective on how to adapt the studies to fit individual classroom needs.

We invite you into our classroom to journey, as learners, alongside our children. We hope our studies inspire you to reflect on your own practice as teachers and guide you to plan for explicit work in your own reading and writing workshops.

CHAPTER 1

Getting Started in the Reading Workshop

Combing Through the Library, Introducing Series, and Meeting Characters

In November 2000, Mary Anne ran the New York City Marathon for the first time. As a casual runner, she needed to properly train for the big race. In the past when she went out to run, it was never for more than 3 or 4 miles; 26.2 miles was a long way. Mary Anne couldn't expect to face this challenge and simply finish the race without proper training. She learned that training was not only about increasing miles but also about increasing overall strength. Progress was gradual. Building up her fitness level to a point where she could enjoy the marathon experience and successfully cross the finish line without injury took a lot of hard work and training. The effort Mary Anne put into her marathon training is very similar to the work a young reader must do when transitioning into more sophisticated texts. If we, as teachers, do not fully prepare our students to face the difficulties of a longer read, just as a runner prepares for a longer run, they will not experience and enjoy success. Becoming a fluent and active reader is not as much about reading longer books as it is about preparing to do so. Stamina for reading requires active involvement in text, thinking, questioning, and thinking again. In preparing children for a longer read, we must empower them with strategies to negotiate the complexities of text.

In October of each year, Manhattan New School holds a back-to-school night, where parents meet their child's teacher and learn of the year's curriculum. One of the questions frequently asked of teachers on this night is How do I know my child's reading level and how can I support his or her reading at home? Without having the same knowledge of children's books and literacy instruction as teachers, parents are left to rely on age or grade-level notations assigned by publishers, who in many cases have different standards for assigning those levels. Outside of leveling notations, parents are left to judge books by their covers, which often misrepresent text and its various complexities.

It's necessary to explain to families that learning to decode text does not necessarily prepare children to take the leap from books with one hundred words to books with a thousand. As children begin reading longer books, they are required, among other things, to identify multiple characters and negotiate dialogue between them. We want parents to understand that reading involves more than decoding words and that our goal for their children is to make them think, to have them make predictions, create visual images, and use inference to understand text. In order for us to meet these goals, we need to teach our children to slow down and become thoughtful readers. It is not important for our children to sprint down the reading track. We want them jogging, so that we can help them process their reading and become active, engaged thinkers. We tell parents that we will not merely assign harder and harder texts to their developing readers. Instead, we will coach them through, explicitly teaching strategies necessary for handling more difficult text. This process of slowing down gives children time to refine strategies learned, enabling them to become more active and fluent readers.

Karen Szymusiak and Franki Sibberson, in *Beyond Leveled Books* (2001), capture precisely the role of teachers in supporting children as they move into reading more complex texts when they write:

> As children move beyond the early stages of reading, we should provide books that support them in moving toward more independent reading and complex comprehension skills rather than moving them higher and higher, and faster and faster, through advanced levels. Transitional readers need to broaden their reading strategies and improve their comprehension instead of simply reading books that are leveled higher than the last book they read. When we consider the skills transitional readers need, we worry that sometimes teachers are expected to concentrate on moving children to the next level rather than helping them learn and use the strategies they really need. (16–17)

Setting Goals for Reading Workshop

We believe that teaching plans should be well designed so that instruction can be both explicit and responsive to the individual needs of children. Although our goals for them as readers of fiction and nonfiction vary, the main goal, to help them become active and engaged readers, is constant.

Reading goals

Main goal for reading work: to become active and engaged readers

Fiction Reading	*Nonfiction Reading*
• to make smart book choices • to understand the predictability of books in series • to understand a character's role in a story and relationships between characters • to use table of contents, front and back blurb, and illustrations to make predictions (previewing) • to navigate dialogue in text • to understand narration or point of view and how it affects texts • to read with attention to fluency and expression • to question, wonder, and make connections and inferences • to sequence through retelling	• to understand the varieties and variables of nonfiction • to begin developing an understanding of different ways writers present nonfiction information • to develop an understanding of the features and structures of nonfiction • to use nonfiction features to locate information • to synthesize information • to question • to enter text with an understanding of purpose • to use prior knowledge

Getting Started in the Reading Workshop

Establishing Reading Habits

Starting the first day with the expectation that we all have reading identities, we began to lay the foundation for the classroom community that would be nurtured throughout the year. To help us understand our children's reading identities, we asked them questions pertaining to their lives as readers.

Do you have a favorite author?
Where is your favorite place to read?
What is your favorite book from first grade?
Who do you most love to read with?
Where do you keep the books you love the most?
What kinds of books do you most like to read . . . funny books, mysteries, poems?

With these questions, we began to build a community around our reading joys. We asked our children to share their personal preferences with other readers in the room. We sent the message that there was an expectation that reading was important and needed to be part of our daily lives both inside and outside of school. Before the start of the school year, we borrowed some favorite books from the first-grade teachers, knowing that these books would provide comfort to children on those first few days as we began to develop a new community of readers. We gave our children time to browse through their new classroom library. Some gravitated toward books they knew well, finding comfort in the familiarity, while others risked reading unfamiliar texts of interest. We watched as they began to develop relationships based on their reading interests. During these first days, we asked the children to think a bit more about their reading lives at home as we involved families in the homework through interviews and reflections (see Figure 1–1).

We asked the children to reflect on the things that made their home reading spot best for them as readers so they could locate places within the classroom where they could create a similar feel. In making their choices for a reading spot, we instructed the children to consider proximity to others and noise level so that each child would respect the other readers in the class. We wanted our children to be deliberate in their decision to select the reading spots they were to keep for an extended time. Giving children autonomy over decisions such as these supports the community as they become invested in the rituals and routines of the class. (See Figure 1–2.)

With the same attention we gave to selecting reading spots, we designed the classroom to support autonomy and independence. We created a meeting area where we gathered as a whole group. Worktables were spread out around the room so that student work time was

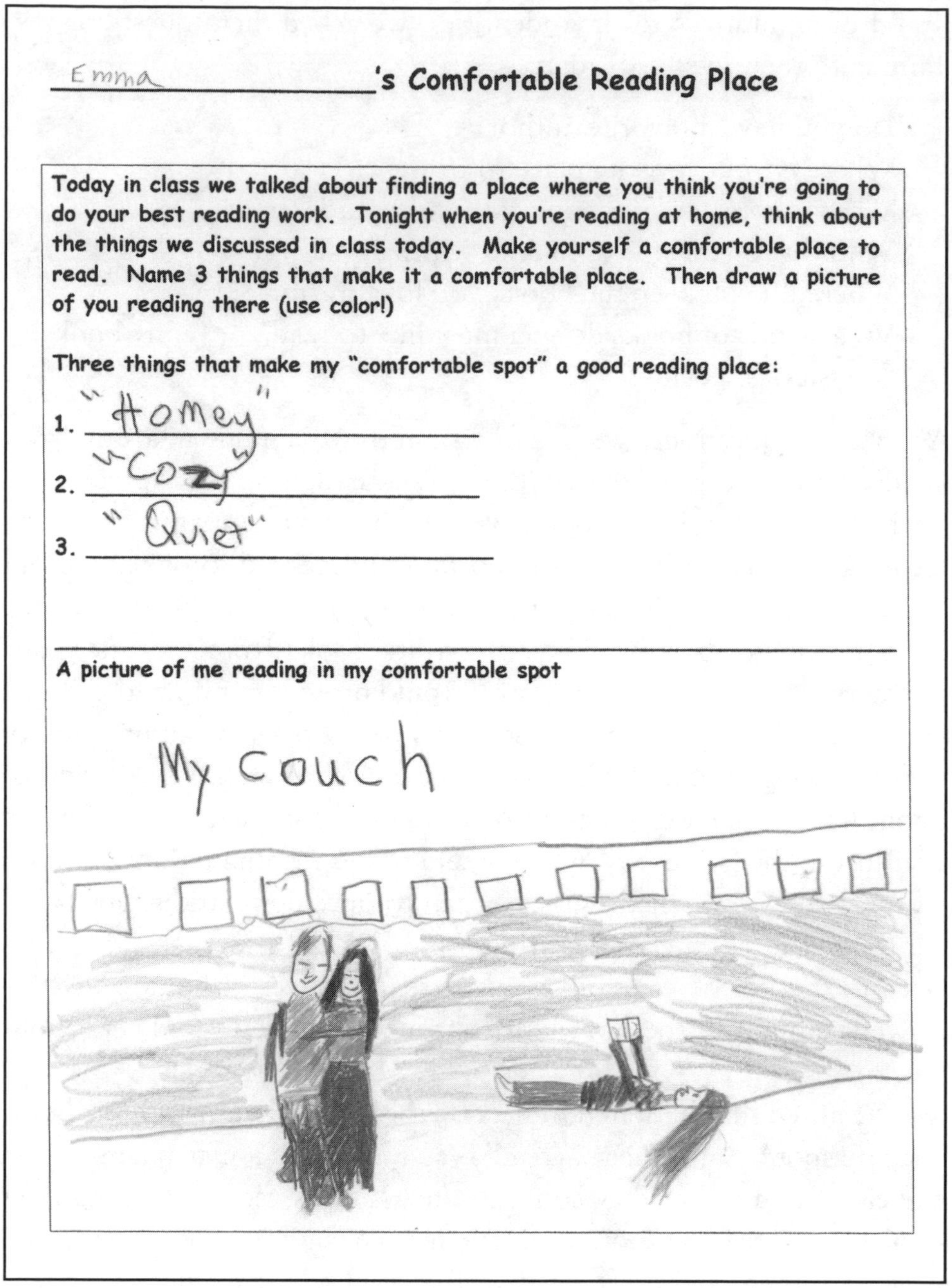

Emma 's Comfortable Reading Place

Today in class we talked about finding a place where you think you're going to do your best reading work. Tonight when you're reading at home, think about the things we discussed in class today. Make yourself a comfortable place to read. Name 3 things that make it a comfortable place. Then draw a picture of you reading there (use color!)

Three things that make my "comfortable spot" a good reading place:

1. "Homey"
2. "Cozy"
3. "Quiet"

A picture of me reading in my comfortable spot

My couch

Figure 1–1 *Emma reflects on her home reading spot*

manageable and our children had space in which to work. In addition, our children each had book boxes where they kept their independent reading books and reading logs. These boxes held the materials needed for reading time and were carried with each child to his or her comfortable reading spot. This avoided distractions for other readers as we encouraged purposeful work time. (See Figure 1–3.)

Figure 1–2 *Comfortable reading spots*

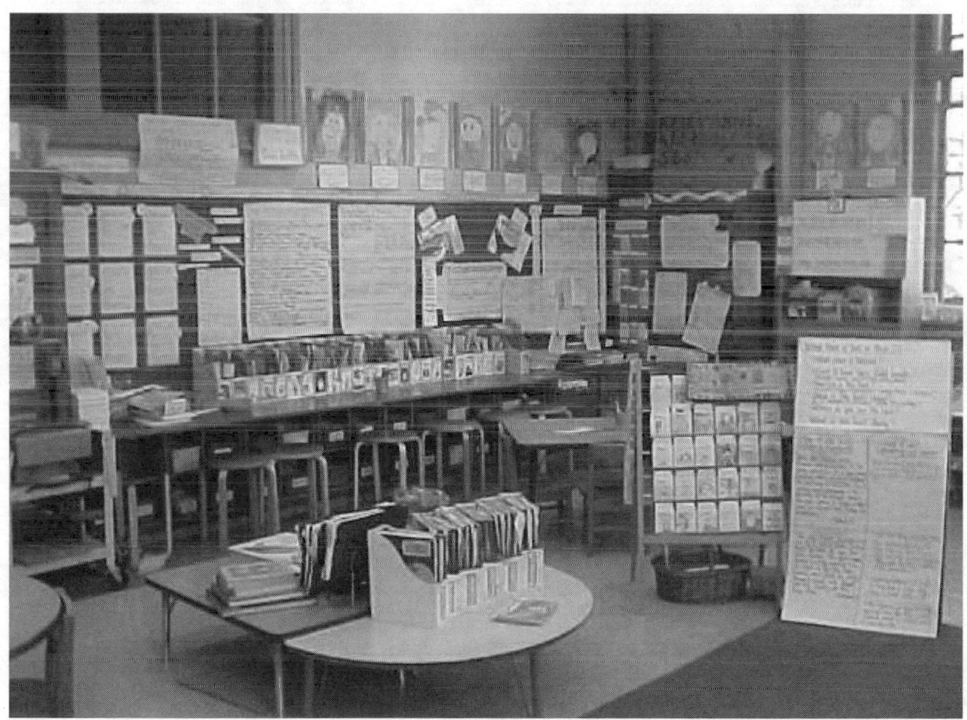

Figure 1–3 *A view of the classroom*

A quick look at planning for a ministudy in establishing reading habits

Ministudy	*Time Frame*	*Goals*	*Possible Minilessons*
Establishing Reader Habits	2–3 weeks	• developing reader identity • establishing routines for independent reading • developing home-school rituals • developing good reading habits and behaviors	• promoting conversation about reader identity through questioning • conducting partner interviews • conducting home-school interviews • modeling how to choose a reading spot • modeling how to select books and manage reading boxes

Getting to Know the Book Series in Our Classroom

Now that our children felt comfortable in the classroom and we had established routines, we were ready to look more closely at the books in our library. We had organized books in baskets, some by level, some by topic, and others by series. We wanted our library to be accessible to children and we were selective about the books with which we began our year. We wanted our children to feel comfortable with the books in the library before we added more to the mix.

As children became familiar with the library, they began to gravitate toward the series books; because of their predictability of characters and language, the kids found them comforting and supportive. Reading aloud one title in a series hooked children into reading others and provided enough support to get them started. As a way of continuing to support children as they read books in series, we began to look more closely at specifics such as chapter design, table of contents, reliable language, and setting. We read several books in the Mr. Putter and Tabby series and noticed common features among them. The following questions guided our thinking as we organized our findings and noticings. These questions also serve as a model for looking at and understanding the inner workings of any book series.

Questions (to be applied to any series)	*Answers (in reference to the Mr. Putter and Tabby series, by Cynthia Rylant)*
What do we notice about these books?	• We noticed titles can be used to make predictions. • There are three or four chapters in each of the books.
Is each chapter in a book an episode or one long story?	The book is one long story; each chapter does not stand alone.
Do the same characters appear in the books in this series?	• Mr. Putter and Tabby appear in all of the books. • Mr. Teaberry and Zeke appear in most but not all of the books in the series.
What have you come to learn about the characters (reliable content)?	• Mr. Putter drinks tea with milk and English muffins with jelly. He drives an old purple car. • Mr. Putter often thinks back to when he was a boy. • Tabby drinks tea with cream and English muffins with cream cheese.
What do we notice about the narrator of the series?	The narrator is a third person.
Are there any repeating phrases in the series?	• "Mr. Putter and his fine cat, Tabby" • "Mrs. Teaberry and her good dog, Zeke"
What do you notice about where the stories take place?	Most of the stories take place in or around Mr. Putter's house.
What do you notice about how much time goes by in each book in the series, and how does the author show the passage of time?	• The narrator uses phrases such as "the next day." • The narrator identifies season.
What do you notice about the conversations between characters in this series?	Mr. Putter thinks a lot in his head, and there isn't a lot of conversation between characters.

A quick look at planning for a ministudy in getting to know the book series in our classroom

Ministudy	*Time Frame*	*Some Goals*	*Possible Minilessons (modeled through one series as children children make connections and examine others)*
Getting to Know the Book Series in Our Classroom	2–3 weeks	• to notice reliable content and language • to understand chapter setup • to understand how time is marked in text • to begin to make generalizations about characters	• model through one series how to highlight reliable content and reliable language • examine text to determine if each chapter in a book is an episode or if each book is one long story • look for places in text that show transition between time (e.g., "the next day") • look for traits of different characters that exist across the titles in a series

Getting to Know the Characters in Our Classroom

After our children had acquired a basic understanding of the predictable features and inner workings of the series books in our class, we were able to focus in on one specific aspect of a book—characters. Friendships and partnerships developed through personal preferences for particular series. As children grew to know the other students in the class, they also grew to know the many characters they would live alongside in the second grade. Some felt protective over Mr. Putter as he creaked his way up ladders while others identified with his kidlike curiosity as he flew planes and made slingshots. Children found intrigue in the Sherlock Holmes nature of Nate in the Nate the Great series, by Marjorie Weinman Sharmat, while others were hooked on the sarcastic humor of Fox in James Marshall's Fox series.

As a way of supporting the connections children were making to the characters in their books, we designed a study around the characters to extend our children's thinking. We chose *Gooseberry Park,* by Cynthia Rylant, as a read-aloud to anchor our work. This was the first extended chapter book we read aloud. Although not part of a series, we chose this book for its strong characters and rich dialogue. This animal adventure is about a friendship among an unlikely threesome: a motherly squirrel, a protective Labrador, and a hysterical bat. We knew that the obvious and different traits of these three main characters would serve as a strong model for our children.

A quick look at planning for a ministudy in getting to know the characters in our classroom

Ministudy	*Time Frame*	*Some Goals*	*Possible Minilessons*
Getting to Know the Characters in Our Classroom	2–3 weeks	• to define attributes of a character • to make personal connections to characters • to compare characters within and among other books • to track character's behavior within one book or across series	• identify character traits • compare character traits with children's own personality traits • find similarities and differences between characters • identify relationships between characters • examine changes of a character from beginning to end of a book or across series

Now that our children had established reading habits, had grasped the value of reading books in a series, and had familiarized themselves with the characters in their books, they were ready to explore more deeply a complex reading strategy—understanding dialogue.

CHAPTER 2

Understanding Dialogue

Investigation One

In the fall, our second graders came to know the many characters they would live with through the year. They learned to compare, discuss the individual personalities of, and make personal connections to characters as a result of our fall reading work. While conferring with children during reading workshop, we discovered that although they had an awareness of characters—who they are and how they influence story—many were confused by the complexities of written conversations between them. We found that children became confused about who was talking when conversation shifted back and forth quickly between characters or if one character spoke through several sentences. We also found that children had a hard time keeping track of dialogue while reading and therefore had difficulty demonstrating comprehension when attempting to retell the story they were reading.

These findings, however, were not new. In previous years we had noticed children's difficulty negotiating dialogue but had not considered planning an investigative study of dialogue in text. The confusion about knowing who in a story was talking was an ongoing problem. It was clear that books like those in the Mr. Putter and Tabby series, which had less dialogue and more narration, were easier for children to comprehend and retell than books in the High Rise Private Eyes series, where dialogue makes up the majority of the text. Previously, we'd spoken with our children in groups and individually about the confusion written dialogue can present as they're reading a new book and instructed them to reread when fluency was interrupted or meaning compromised. Rereading as a sole strategy, however, didn't seem to sufficiently help our children understand how dialogue works. We knew that many of our second graders read word by word, in a staccato fashion that compromised their sense of fluency and phrasing. The running records we kept on our children informed us that they often omitted existing punctuation and/or inserted it where it didn't exist. We realized that we needed to instruct our children about punctuation and dialogue to enable them to read more fluently. It was clear that if we wanted our children to read fluently and deepen their comprehension, we needed to design an investigative study to specifically address written conversation—dialogue. So we took it on, searching professional books for guidance. While some books acknowledged dialogue and the difficulties it presented to young readers, none gave us the road map we needed to launch an in-depth investigation. We knew this work had to come from our own experience as teachers, so we examined texts and thought long and hard about how writers write dialogue and how we would instruct children to read it with greater fluency.

We began by revisiting the books in our classroom library. We looked specifically at the way authors construct conversation between characters. Our young readers had moved away from emergent books with one line of text per page and were now being asked to keep track of several lines of text and negotiate dialogue. Characters in books such as Pinky and Rex and Frog and Toad shift back and forth in conversation without much narrative support. In addition, our children were being asked, in many cases for the first time, to recognize who was talking in text even when the speaker was not identified.

Our goal was to teach our children how to be active and fluent readers. In the course of our planning, as we looked through the book series in our classroom, we realized that examining dialogue would lead us to consider other text variables such as voice of narrator, type of narration, and frequency of dialogue, or balance between dialogue and narration. We needed to instruct our children as to each variable so that our children would be able to approach new texts with the following questions in mind:

Who is telling the story?
How much of the story is told through narration?
How much of the story is told through dialogue?
What does the dialogue look like and how is it written?

	WEEK ONE	WEEK TWO	WEEK THREE	WEEK FOUR	WEEK FIVE
GOAL	to notice dialogue in text	to identify voice in stories and begin to name different styles of dialogue	to deepen understanding of how dialogue works	to deepen fluency and comprehension by developing and practicing reading strategies	to practice strategies in a book with first person narrative
LITERATURE	Henry and Mudge series, by Cynthia Rylant *Old Grizzly,* by Joy Cowley	Nate the Great series, by Marjorie Weinman Sharmat *Henry and Mudge,* by Cynthia Rylant	*Pinky and Rex and the New Baby,* by James Howe *Pinky and Rex and the Spelling Bee,* by James Howe	*Pinky and Rex and the Spelling Bee,* by James Howe *Pinky and Rex and the Dinosaur Game,* by James Howe	*Nate the Great and the Lost List,* by Marjorie Weinman Sharmat
MINILESSONS	facilitate conversation: What is dialogue? Do all books have it? examine books with dialogue to find words that mark dialogue	highlight differences between books told in first-person narration and books told in third-person narration highlight the various ways dialogue is written within a text organize various examples of dialogue found during the week	do a shared reading of the first conversation between Rex and her parents examine text for punctuation	revisit the names of the various dialogue styles reread dialogue, asking children, "Who's talking and how do you know?" record strategies to figure out who is talking in text	list what we know about Nate the Great as a character and what we know about the writing style underline dialogue where the character is not identified and ask students how they know who is talking
STUDENT WORK	examine and reread books in their independent book boxes, separating those with dialogue from those without dialogue use Post-its to locate places where the writer uses an alternative to *said*	search the class library for books told in the first person and books told in the third person locate with Post-its two places with dialogue	examine the various conversations between characters practice reading aloud the roles of Pinky and Rex, each taking on the voice of one character record with Post-its three places where they notice punctuation	practice the prereading strategies focused on during the minilesson record on Post-its "Who's talking and how do I know?"	highlight places where Nate is the narrator and places where he acts as a character underline places where a character is not identifed

Figure 2–1 *Dialogue study at a glance*

As a way of supporting our planning of this study, we asked our children the following question: "How do you know a character is talking?" We used the question to assess what kids knew about dialogue. Following are some of the children's responses:

> Most of them [characters] have loud voices.—Eli
> The author is telling you about Poppleton and what's going on in his mind.—Dakota
> Because it sounds different.—Emma
> It is a lot of expression. It makes you get into the story.—Max
> The writer writes down the names of who is talking and it's usually before.—Matthew
> If they are facing each other, I think they are talking to each other.—Nubia
> Because they kind of talk out loud.—Katie
> I know the talking stops when I see the period.—Stephanie

We thought about the children's responses, analyzing what they knew about dialogue and what they needed to know to become fluent, active readers. What they needed to know became the skeleton of our planning, helping us construct the weekly goals of this investigative study.

How student responses informed our planning

What They Said	*What They Know*	*What They Need to Know*
Most of them [characters] have loud voices.—Eli Because they kind of talk out loud. —Katie	Something sounds different when there is dialogue.	There is a distinction between character and narrator and visual information alone helps readers know when someone is talking.
The author is telling you about Poppleton and what's going on in his mind.—Dakota	Someone outside of the story talks about the character.	There is a difference between the narrator filling in information about Poppleton and the words Poppleton actually speaks.
It is a lot of expression. It makes you get into the story.—Max	Dialogue engages the reader.	Dialogue is about communication between characters.

What They Said	*What They Know*	*What They Need to Know*
The writer writes down the names of who is talking and it's usually before.—Matthew	Names in print give visual clues to the reader.	The *said* doesn't always come before the quote; there are many ways of showing who is talking.
If they are facing each other, I think they are talking to each other. —Nubia	Characters in books engage in conversation.	Readers rely on contextual and visual cues in writing rather than on pictures alone.
I know the talking stops when I see the period.—Stephanie	Periods indicate an ending.	Characters can talk through several sentences. The period does not necessarily indicate the end of talking—the quotation marks do that job.

Week One

Goal: to notice dialogue in text

In week 1 of the dialogue investigation, our goal was for our children to begin to notice dialogue in text. We knew this meant more than locating the quotation marks or noticing characters' names. It is important for children to extend their knowledge of dialogue beyond superficial noticings; they must understand the way dialogue works, which in turn will improve their overall fluency and comprehension. We knew from our initial reading conferences with our children that differentiating between narrator and character often confused them. We explored our library, looking for those books with dialogue and those without dialogue, sifting through books we came to know well during our investigation of series in the fall. On the first day of the study, Karen began her minilesson with the questions "What is dialogue?" and "Do all books have it?" Several hands went up and a murmur filled the room as the children turned to each other to share their ideas. When most hands were up, Karen called on Jenna.

"Yes," Jenna said confidently, "all books have dialogue because at least one person talks in every book!"

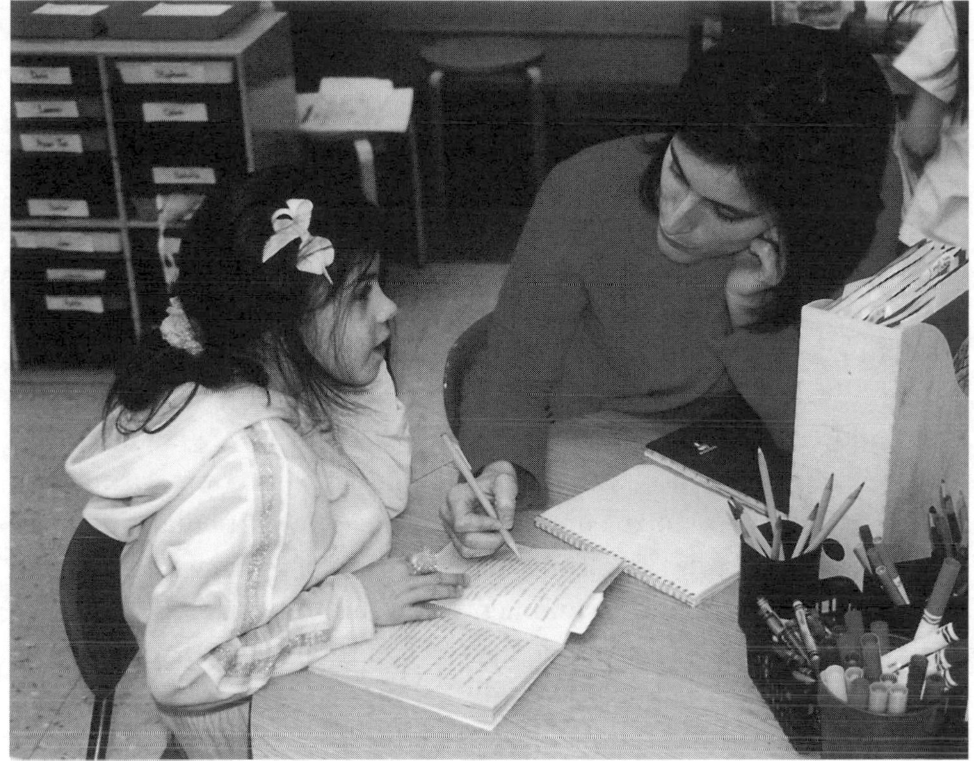

Figure 2–2 *Karen conferring with Diana*

"No," Nicholas responded, "I just read a book about eagles and no one talked."

The conversation continued, and Karen recorded the children's statements on a chart titled What Is Dialogue? Do All Books Have It? These comments were indicative of the beginnings of the children's understandings and misunderstandings.

Following the discussion, Karen turned to the accessible and familiar text *Gooseberry Park,* by Cynthia Rylant. We decided to use *Gooseberry Park* because our children were familiar with it as a read-aloud and because of its strong characters and rich dialogue. When Karen asked, "Does this book have dialogue?" the children overwhelmingly responded, "Yes." Jordana enthusiastically recalled Murray saying, "Find me a hamburger and I'll find fries." Diana, however, remembered that Professor Albert, Kona's owner and one of the characters often shown in pictures, rarely spoke at all in the book. She reminded us that we learned about him through the narrator and through conversations in the book that referred to Professor Albert, but that he spoke only with a neighbor in the book.

For two days, the children read through books in the classroom, making lists of those books with dialogue and those without. They noticed that most fiction books had dialogue and most nonfiction books did not. Some of our children, however, were eager to find exceptions to that generalization. At the end of the second day we had developed an extensive T-chart listing of books with and books without dialogue. Amanda came to the rug following independent reading time with a book held close to her chest. "I found a fiction book with *no* dialogue," she blurted out excitedly. Then she showed the class. The book was *Mr. Putter and Tabby Fly the Plane,* by Cynthia Rylant. The children had already noticed that books in the Mr. Putter and Tabby series generally have very little dialogue in comparison with other series, but Amanda's finding about this one particular title filled everyone with surprise. "Is it still fiction?" Devon asked with a puzzled look on his face. After a few moments, the children concluded that the character Mr. Putter was "made up" by Cynthia Rylant and that even without dialogue, the book was still fiction.

Karen decided to read *Mr. Putter and Tabby Fly the Plane* to the class, saying, "Let's see how *Mr. Putter and Tabby Fly the Plane* is different from fiction books with dialogue." The children made the following observations about *Mr. Putter and Tabby Fly the Plane*:

Mr. Putter is like Professor Albert from *Gooseberry Park*—neither character speaks.

Mr. Putter usually talks to Mrs. Teaberry, but she doesn't appear in this book (maybe because he was too busy with his plane).

Cynthia Rylant flashes back to when Mr. Putter was a boy, like she does in many Mr. Putter and Tabby books.

Mr. Putter doesn't actually say anything to Tabby, even though they spend a lot of time together.

Cynthia Rylant tells you that Mr. Putter cheered when his plane flew high into the blue sky, but you, as the reader, don't hear him cheer.

By the end of the book, the children wondered how Cynthia Rylant, as a writer, decided when to include and when not to include dialogue and why she chose to tell the reader "Mr. Putter cheered" rather than have him use words to describe his excitement. The children thought about what they might have said if *they* had finally succeeded in flying a temperamental toy airplane, like Mr. Putter had just done. "Yippee!" said Sara.

"Yes, all right!" Xanyani said, holding a tight fist to his chest.

"I did it, I did it!" Ethan said, bouncing his arms.

Not only were the children putting themselves in the role of the writer, inventing fun expressions for Mr. Putter, but they were using firsthand knowledge to define the role of dialogue and its impact on text.

The class discussed how the text would have looked and sounded different had Cynthia Rylant included dialogue. The next day, we focused on how the use of dialogue alters the reader's experience with the text. Karen started the day's reading workshop with *Henry and Mudge and Annie's Good Move,* by Cynthia Rylant. She read the book aloud, asking children to listen for places where they heard a character speaking. Children raised their hands when they heard the words *said Henry* or *Henry told Mudge*. This series is similar to Mr. Putter and Tabby in the sense that one main character is a person and the other is an animal. "The difference," said Stephanie, "is that Henry talks to Mudge a lot and Mr. Putter doesn't say much to Tabby."

"You're right, Stephanie; when we read *Mr. Putter and Tabby Fly the Plane,* we noticed that Mr. Putter didn't say *anything* to Tabby," Karen reminded the class.

To increase their familiarity with noticing dialogue and understanding its subtleties, we had our children practice reading books aloud to their reading partners, listening for places where they heard a character speaking. The children noticed that when reading dialogue, if they didn't change their voice when a character spoke in the text, then it sounded funny. They noticed that the words a character speaks in the text are "surrounded by talking marks." And they noticed that the writer tells you who is talking when she writes the word *said*. Lauren challenged that finding. "It doesn't always say 'said.' Hyunjoo and I noticed that it said '*asked* Bunny' in High Rise Private Eyes, not '*said* Bunny.'" Lauren and Hyunjoo had been reading The High Rise Private Eyes #2, *The Case of the Climbing Cat,* by Cynthia Rylant, in which Bunny and Jack, the main characters, are almost continuously engaged in a conversation that moves quickly back and forth with very little narration. Daniel showed us a place in *Fox Outfoxed,* by James Marshall, where he and Diana had read, " 'Keep your voices down,' *whispered* Fox." Noticing that writers use words other than *said* to tell the reader how a character said something turned out to be an important discovery of the day and was indicative of our children's growing understanding of the way dialogue works.

The focus for the final two days of the week was to find the many words writers use to show someone is talking in a book and to understand how these words influence reading. We decided to use the familiar big book *Old Grizzly,* by Joy Cowley, during the next two minilessons. So far, our minilessons during this week were read-alouds from *Gooseberry Park,* Mr. Putter and Tabby, and Henry and Mudge. Using a shared text allowed our children to read and examine dialogue in the text with us, providing them the opportunity to notice the way dialogue looks as well as the way it sounds. We also chose *Old Grizzly* because we knew the variety of verb choices (*grumbled, mumbled,* and *sighed*) used to illustrate the way Old Grizzy spoke would not only support the interpretation of text but add variety to our collection of *said* alternatives—a term our children used to name words writers use in place of *said*.

After reading the shared text *Old Grizzly,* Karen highlighted the words Joy Cowley used to describe the way Old Grizzly felt and acted. She asked the children what they learned about Old Grizzly from the words *grumbled, mumbled,* and *sighed,* which follow his talking. Karla responded, "The words tell about how Old Grizzly acts; when he grumbled, he was cranky, and when he sighed, he wasn't being patient."

Doris added, "And those words show us how Old Grizzly is feeling." Karen agreed, telling the class that words such as these help us interpret text and get to know the inner workings of characters.

Our children were then ready to try this work on their own, thinking about how the action words that follow a character's talking impact the meaning of the text. We gave each child two Post-it Notes and asked him or her to post two places in an independent reading book where the writer used a word other than *said* to clarify a character's words. We often use Post-it Notes as a way of being explicit about our expectations during independent reading time. Recording their findings reinforces thinking and holds them accountable for the work we expect them to do. The children were visibly excited with the prospect of using Post-it Notes. They quickly took their reading spots and began working. During partner share, Karla and Xanyani found they had both located *shouted* in their texts. Celine was excited to report that she had located the word *squeaked*. By the time the children came to the rug for whole-group share, they were bursting with eagerness at the chance to discuss their findings. Karen collected these findings, and together the class created a web. (See Figure 2–3.)

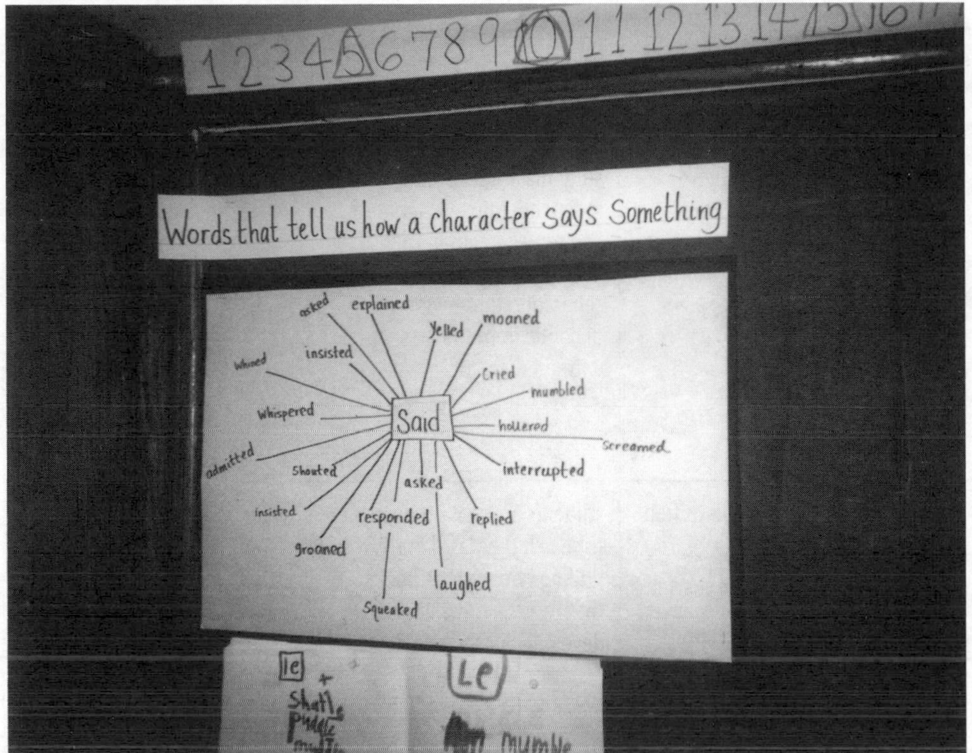

Figure 2–3 Said *web*

On the final day of the week, we reread *Old Grizzly,* discussing how the *said* alternatives impacted the meaning of the story. We thought about how different the book would have been if Joy Cowley had used only *said* to mark Old Grizzly's words. "Oh, it would have been boring if Old Grizzly had *said,* 'I'm having a bad day,' rather than *grumbled* it," Sara told us.

"Yeah," agreed Doris, "I wouldn't have been able to make a picture in my head of Old Grizzly grumbling."

We acted out the talking parts in *Old Grizzly*. The children excitedly grumbled, mumbled, and sighed their way through the text, then we sent them off with their partners to act out lines in their own reading books as if they were practicing for a play. At the end of reading workshop, we came together to discuss reading dialogue and how paying attention to the characters' actions and feelings helps a reader better understand the story. Noticing dialogue in text and learning to read it with an understanding of the way the character acts or feels empowered our children as readers, creating a new energy around independent reading.

GOAL: to notice dialogue in text

	OBJECTIVE	MINILESSON	STUDENT WORK	SHARE
DAY ONE	examine individual reading books, looking for those with dialogue and those without dialogue	• teacher reads one book with dialogue and one book without dialogue to the entire class • *discussion:* "What is dialogue? Do all books have it?"	students are sent off independently to examine and reread books in their independent book boxes, separating those with dialogue from those without dialogue	*partner share:* students meet in pairs to discuss and share findings *whole-group share:* chart students' discoveries begin a list of books that have dialogue and a list of books without dialogue
DAY TWO	use class library to continue to examine books with and without dialogue	• teacher shares findings from previous day • revisits and adds to chart from yesterday • *discussion:* "What have we learned about the differences between books with and without dialogue?"	students are sent off in pairs to search the class library, finding two to three books that test the theories developed during minilesson	*whole-group share:* • continue to share and chart findings • begin to make generalizations about the class library
DAY THREE	begin inquiry into books with dialogue	• teacher reads book with dialogue, e.g., Henry and Mudge • teacher rereads two pages, asking students to listen for places with dialogue	students are sent off in pairs to practice reading aloud and listening for places with dialogue	*whole-group share:* use T-chart to list what students notice about dialogue—both (visually) how it looks and (auditorily) how it sounds
DAY FOUR	find words writers use to show how a character is talking in a book	teacher uses a familiar big book such as *Old Grizzly* to demonstrate alternatives to *said*	• students are sent off independently with two Post-its to locate places where writers use an alternative to *said* • students will write one alternative on each Post-it	*partner share:* students meet with partners to discuss and share Post-Its *whole-group share:* teacher and students make a web showing alternatives to *said*
DAY FIVE	understand how *said* alternatives influence the reading of dialogue	teacher rereads *Old Grizzly,* discussing what the *said* alternatives tell us about the characters' interactions	students are sent off in pairs to act out lines from their independent reading books as if they were practicing for a play	*whole-group share:* class discusses how reading dialogue with attention to the way a character acts and feels impacts reading

Figure 2–4 *Day-by-day plan for Week 1*

Week Two

Goal: to identify voice in stories and begin to name different styles of dialogue

The first week of the dialogue investigation study passed, and, as with many investigations, the beginning stage proved exciting. Our children worked like detectives to make discoveries about dialogue—the way it was presented by writers and the way readers interpreted it. Discoveries led to generalizations that would be validated or invalidated through practice.

On Monday of the second week, the excitement was apparent. The children came into the room talking about the books they had read over the weekend. The children followed their normal routine of unpacking their book bags, putting notes in the teacher box, returning book baggies to their reading boxes, and spending ten minutes before reading workshop reading with their partners on the rug. The conversations on this particular Monday didn't have as much to do with the weekend activities as they did with dialogue. Our children returned from their weekends talking about books in a whole new way. Even before Liam took his book bag off his shoulders, he reported to Matthew on his weekend's discoveries: "I found *said* in my book twenty-two times last night. There was so much talking!" Pavel chimed in with excitement about how there was so much talking in his book too. He and his father had read *Frog and Toad Are Friends*, by Arnold Lobel, over the weekend and couldn't believe that their book was almost all talking. Allie reported that while she was reading *Cam Jansen and the Scary Snake Mystery*, by David Adler, she found the words *whispered, yelled,* and *explained* as alternatives to *said*. Our children's shared enthusiasm for this whole-class investigation made learning rich. As well as learning about the content in the books our children were reading, a whole-class investigation into dialogue provided opportunities for:

sharing perspectives and ideas
creating a common language
developing community
testing generalizations and theories
supporting peers

Our initial intention of getting students to notice dialogue in text was clearly working. Though we wanted our students to notice dialogue and become familiar with *said* alternatives, we did not want them to sacrifice meaning. While Liam's excitement over noticing *said* twenty-two times was proof of learning, we didn't want our children spending time being word counters. We wanted our children to synthesize their new learning of how to negotiate dialogue in text to support comprehension. We wanted them to read with an eye trained not only to stop and notice but to stop and think. While we were pleased with our children's initial noticings regarding dialogue, we knew they needed to dig deeper. Many times as teachers, we mistake initial understandings for mastery, but our experience as teachers and staff developers told us that this was not enough, that in order for our children to achieve mastery, they would have to understand the influence of this work on them as readers.

During the second week, we took a closer look at the inner workings of dialogue. The focus was to identify narration, or voice, in stories and eventually give names to the kinds of dialogue we found. We knew that after a week of examining the library for those books with and those without dialogue and noticing the *said* alternatives, the children looked at books differently. We knew we needed to begin getting the children to identify voice in a story, noticing and naming the different types of dialogue.

Record keeping is a crucial component of any investigation. It allows us, as teachers, to not only understand individual children but plan for explicit teaching tailored to the needs of the students. While looking back on her conference notes from week 1, Karen noticed that while Nicholas was reading *Nate the Great Goes Down in the Dumps*, by Marjorie Weinman Sharmat, with 97 percent accuracy, he was not always following the conversations. Nicholas asked Karen why there were no quotation marks around Nate's words. Karen explained to him that in this book, Nate was a character as well as the narrator; this was a different perspective than the third-person books we had focused on in week 1. Karen showed Nicholas how Nate uses the "I" voice to tell the story as the narrator and how when narrating, Nate is not in dialogue with any character.

This conference informed our teaching as we decided to examine books from the viewpoint of narration. In week 2 we began by reexamining our class library, highlighting the question Who is telling the story? We made a decision to read Nate the Great and Henry and

Mudge texts this week. These series were not only well known and well loved by our children but also provided a contrast in narration. While Nate the Great books are written in the first person with a character as narrator, Henry and Mudge texts are written in the third person with an unrelated narrator.

Week 1 began with the questions What is dialogue? and Do all books have it? After our initial examination of our class library, we were now ready in week 2 to examine books with dialogue, asking the question Who is telling the story? Focusing on this question, we separated books written in the first person and books written in the third person. Mary Anne planned to create a chart tablet of the children's comments about voice in text. She began by telling the class, "Today I'm going to read a short part from Nate the Great and a short part from Henry and Mudge. These are books we have read before. I'm going to read two pages from each book once without any interruptions. Then I will read the pages again and we can talk about who is telling the story." Mary Anne reminded the children about what to keep in mind while they were listening. "As I'm reading the first time," she directed them, "I want you to pay close attention to *who* is telling the story. I want you to listen for the words that might help you understand who is telling the story, words such as *I* and *said,* and remind yourselves of what you learned last week about how dialogue is written." Mary Anne read a short excerpt from both books.

When Mary Anne finished reading, Jordana said, "I can tell there is a difference between the books because in Nate the Great, Nate is talking *to* the reader."

Mary Anne wrote, "Nate is talking *to* the reader," on a chart tablet. Then she asked Jordana to say more about that. "Can you tell us a little more about what you mean?" she asked.

Jordana continued, "Well, I heard 'I said' in Nate the Great and 'he said' in Henry and Mudge." Jordana had noticed a quality of first-person narration—the use of *I* in the narration.

Mary Anne continued with the Henry and Mudge example. She read aloud the following line from *Henry and Mudge and Annie's Perfect Pet*: " 'And it doesn't have to be walked like a dog,' said Henry." She posed the question to the class, "Is Henry telling the story the way Nate told the story?"

Several hands went up. "No," noted Stephen. "It's very different! The narrator is telling us about Henry and Mudge's adventures. He's telling the story, but he isn't a character, like Nate."

As Mary Anne continued to read and question, the distinction between first- and third-person narration became clearer to these young readers. Mary Anne sent the children off to independent reading with a task. She directed them to pay particular attention to narration while reading and to ask themselves if the narration in their text was more like Nate the Great (first person) or more like Henry and Mudge (third person). They knew that when they returned to the rug they would be sharing their findings. As Mary Anne walked around the classroom taking notes, she heard partnerships making discoveries. Graciela and Emma noticed that in *It's Justin Time, Amber Brown,* by Paula Danziger, Amber Brown introduces herself on the first page, saying, "I, Amber Brown . . . ." This reminded them of the way the character Nate repeatedly introduces himself, "I, Nate the Great." They excitedly concluded that since Amber Brown uses *I* in the text like Nate, this book must be written in the first person. They continued reading to confirm their hypothesis. *What does this discovery mean for them as readers?* By knowing the perspective from which the story is told, Emma and Graciela can enter the text knowing what to expect in terms of voice. It is this expectation as well as others we planned to help our children internalize by the end of the study that would help them become more actively engaged in text.

When the class returned from independent reading, the children had plenty to share. Mary Anne was ready with a blank T-chart. She reported to the class: "I heard a lot of talk about 'I' voice while conferring with you and walking around the room today. Let's list those books written in the first person like Nate the Great and those books written in the third person like Henry and Mudge." Mary Anne reminded the children that another name for "I" voice was first-person narrative. She explained that first person is when the narrator (the person telling the story) is also a character and third person is when the narrator is removed from the story, or not one of the characters. Among the selections in the "I" voice column were Jigsaw Jones, Junie B. Jones, Nate the Great, and Horrible Harry books. In the third-person column there were quite a few more, including Pinky and Rex, Frog and Toad, M and M, and Cam Jansen books. We were beginning to discover that most of the series we had been reading from were written in the third person. (See Figure 2–5.)

The following day the children continued to search the class library for additional books with first- and third-person narration. Reminding the children of the discoveries they made the day before, Mary

Anne asked the children to distinguish between first- and third-person narration. Rebecca volunteered her thinking: "In Nate the Great, Nate is talking to the person reading the book *and* he is talking to Rosamond."

Max added, "In Henry and Mudge, Henry is *not* talking to the reader; he's talking to Mudge."

These familiar books were used throughout the investigation as a point of reference when referring to narration. The day before, the children examined their independent reading books with attention to

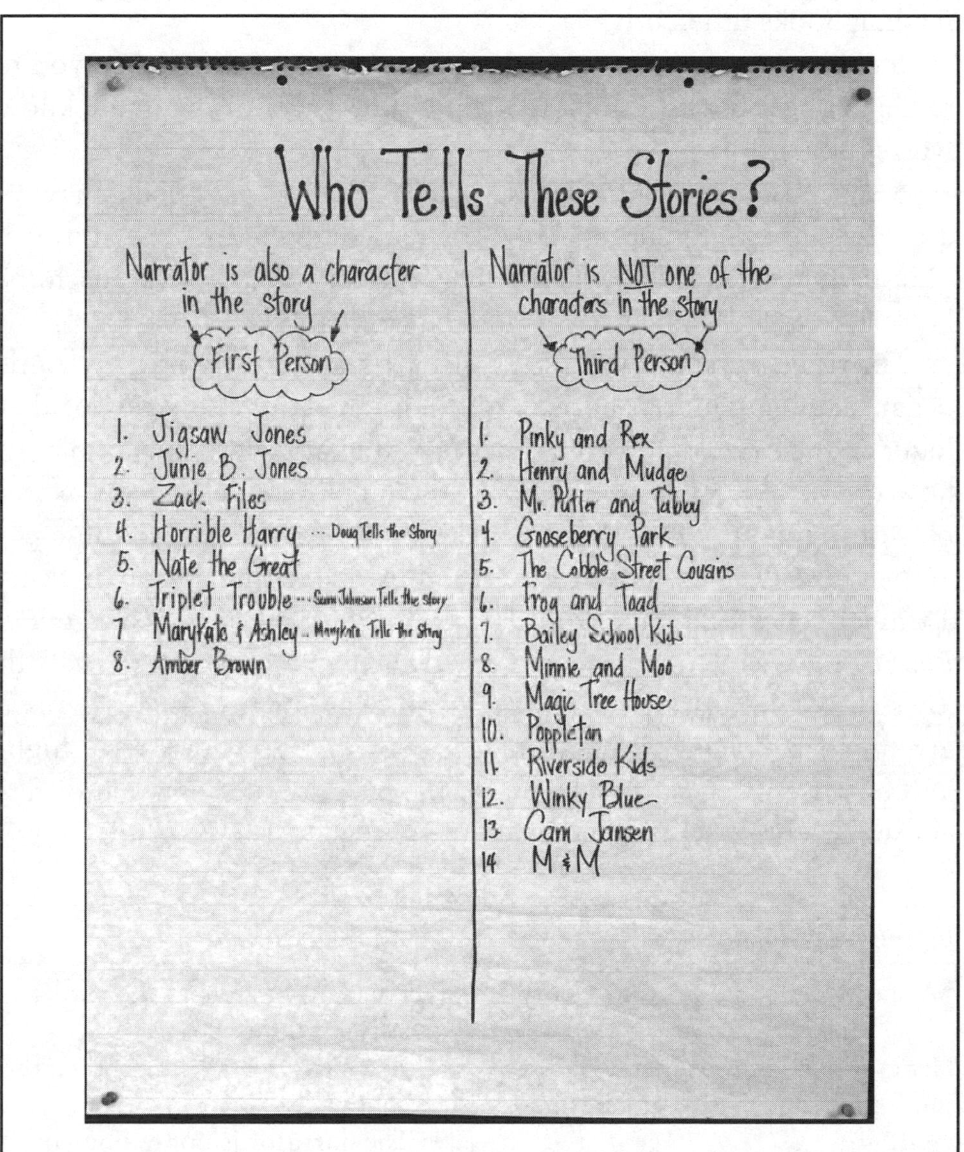

Who Tells These Stories?
Narrator is also a character in the story
First Person
1. Jigsaw Jones
2. Junie B. Jones
3. Zack Files
4. Horrible Harry ... Doug Tells the Story
5. Nate the Great
6. Triplet Trouble
7 MaryKate & Ashley
8. Amber Brown
Narrator is NOT one of the characters in the story
Third Person
1. Pinky and Rex
2. Henry and Mudge
3. Mr. Putter and Tabby
4. Gooseberry Park
5. The Cobble Street Cousins
6. Frog and Toad
7. Bailey School Kids
8. Minnie and Moo
9. Magic Tree House
10. Poppleton
11. Riverside Kids
12. Winky Blue
13. Cam Jansen
14 M & M

Figure 2–5 *First-person versus third-person books*

narration; that day, Mary Anne sent the children off to examine the entire class library, looking for those books written in first person and those written in third person. The children were excited not only to make new discoveries about the books in their library but to prove or disprove some of the discoveries made by their classmates during the previous day's reading time.

It is important for children to not only make discoveries but understand what these discoveries mean for them as readers. Mary Anne began a discussion, asking the class, "How might what you know now about how stories are told change the way you read a book?" Her purpose was to help the children begin to approach their independent reading books differently.

Stephen raised his hand. "I think it can be confusing when you're reading longer books. I think it might not be as confusing if you know who's talking."

Stephen's comment was clearly what Mary Anne was hoping the children would begin to understand. "You're right, Stephen," she affirmed. "But if you are aware of who is telling the story, you will approach the book differently. You will expect it to be written a certain way."

For three days following the talks around narration, Mary Anne began helping children notice and find names for the kinds of dialogue in their books. They began by looking at different examples of how dialogue is written. After the students looked closely at examples of dialogue, Mary Anne helped them find names for these examples. She decided first to focus on third-person narration, making a transparency of a page from *Henry and Mudge and the Snowman Plan* to use on the overhead projector. Displaying text in this way allows the entire class to participate and examine a text closely as a group. In the Henry and Mudge text example, Mary Anne highlighted several kinds of dialogue for the purpose of looking at different ways writers write dialogue.

Examples of Dialogue	*What We Noticed*
"A snowman contest!" said Henry.	The narrator is telling the reader who is speaking.
Henry looked at the chair. "Dad, I think that chair has been painting *you*!"	• The narrator talks first, then the character. • The narrator is not telling you who is speaking. • The narrator is telling you what the character is doing (action).

Examples of Dialogue	*What We Noticed*
"Hi Henry!" Annie said. "Hi Mudge!" "Mudge?" a relative on a swing said.	The dialogue goes back and forth and the narrator doesn't tell the reader who is talking.

After looking at Henry and Mudge, Mary Anne used a Nate the Great title. In a similar way, she highlighted some examples on the overhead. Here's what the children noticed about dialogue.

Examples of Dialogue	*What We Noticed*
Claude said, "I will walk with you." "Perhaps it blew away," I said. I dropped the map to the ground. "Don't get lost," I said, "or I will have two cases to solve."	The narrator (Nate) tells you directly who is speaking. The narrator (Nate) also speaks as a character to his friend Claude. The narrator (Nate) tells you in the middle he is speaking. Then he continues.

The children began to accumulate class lists of examples they would later use as reference. These examples supported them in naming and organizing the kinds of dialogue appearing in the texts the class examined as a whole, as well as the dialogue our children confronted in their independent reading books. During the share, the children added some examples they had found in their independent reading to this list. Our children created names for the different kinds of dialogue, helping them distinguish between dialogue examples. This naming helped our children recognize and refer to dialogue more easily in their own reading and gave us a common language that we would use for consistency. The names our children created to identify different kinds of dialogue were as follows:

simple dialogue—when the writer tells you who is talking immediately after the character's words
Example: "We're going to have a baby," Rex said.

no-said *dialogue*—when the writer does not tell you who is talking
Example: "Want to go for a ride on our bikes?"

continuation dialogue—when the writer tells you who is talking smack in the middle of the character's words
Example: "But that's neat, Rex," Pinky said. "It'll be fun having a baby around."

GOALS: 1. to identify voice in stories 2. to name different kinds of dialogue

	OBJECTIVE	MINILESSON	STUDENT WORK	SHARE
DAY ONE	examine individual reading books looking for those with attention to narration	• teacher reads excerpt from a book written in the first person (e.g., Nate the Great) and an excerpt from one in the third person (e.g., Henry and Mudge) • highlights some differences	students are sent off independently to read books, keeping in mind the question "Who is telling the story?	*partner share:* students meet with partners to discuss narration of book *whole-group share:* use T-chart to list books written in the first person and the third person
DAY TWO	use class library to continue to examine books with attention to narration	• teacher shares findings from previous day • *discussion:* "What have we learned about the difference between books told in first-person narration and books told in third-person narration?"	students are sent off with partners to search the class library for books told in the first person and books told in the third person	*whole-group share:* • continue to chart list of books in each category • *discussion:* "How might this new understanding change the way you read the book?"
DAY THREE	look at different ways writers write dialogue	teacher uses overhead to highlight the various ways dialogue is written within a text, e.g., Henry and Mudge (third-person narration)	students are sent off independently to read and locate with Post-its two places with dialogue	*partner share:* students meet with partners to discuss and share Post-its *whole-group share:* chart examples of dialogue found and discuss noticings
DAY FOUR	look at different ways writers write dialogue	teacher uses overhead to highlight the various ways dialogue is written within a text, e.g., Nate the Great (first-person narration)	students are sent off independently to read and locate with Post-its two places with dialogue	*partner share:* students meet with partners to discuss and share Post-its *whole-group share:* continue to chart examples of dialogue found and begin to name the different types
DAY FIVE	begin to organize the types of dialogue found over the past week	teacher and students organize various examples of dialogue found during the week	students are sent off independently to read and think about the discoveries they made about dialogue this week	*whole-group share:* continue to look at and organize week's collection of dialogue samples according to the names class has given each type

Figure 2–6 *Day-by-day plan for Week 2*

Week Three

Goal: to deepen understanding of how dialogue works

Our children had learned a lot about themselves as readers. They learned to look more closely at dialogue in stories, they learned the many words writers use to tell the reader who is talking, and they learned to identify the voice of the narrator. By the end of the second week, we were excited to see how the dialogue work our second graders had done during reading workshop would impact the way they read to their kindergarten reading partners.

On Fridays, we meet with Mindy Gerstenhaber's kindergarten children. Each second grader is paired with a kindergarten student in a reading partnership. Although there are times when the kindergarten children read to our second graders, the opposite is mostly true. On this particular Friday, we talked with our students about the importance of book choice. Some students complained that their kindergarten story partners had difficulty paying attention while they read. We told them that choosing books they knew well and could read with fluency was a good way to maintain their partners' engagement. Karen used Pinky and Rex to model how to engage students in story through fluent oral reading. She told them that had she chosen a random book from the shelf with which she was unfamiliar, she may not have read it with the same level of expression. She told them, "We want our story partners to pay attention to us while we read. We have to read like we're talking, as if we are putting on a play." The children remembered back to the beginning of the study when they practiced changing their voices in reading to enhance the actions of the characters in their books. Some of our children had already internalized this lesson, while others needed the reminder before going off to read orally to their kindergarten story partners.

Watching the second graders interact with their kindergarten story partners proved to be a perfect opportunity to assess the lessons our children had already learned from this investigative dialogue study. Leah, a second grader, chose to read *Sloppy Tiger and the Party,* by Joy Cowley, to Rachel, her kindergarten story partner. It was a book Leah had read several times and felt comfortable reading aloud. Karen sat down to listen to Leah read the book. She read:

I was going to Jim's party.
My sloppy tiger wanted to go, too.
"Promise you won't be sloppy," I said.

Leah turned to Karen. "Look, it's like Nate the Great. The girl in the story is a character *and* she is telling the story!" Leah then explained to Rachel that the girl in the story was talking as the narrator, telling the story to the reader. She also told Rachel that when the girl talks to her sloppy tiger, the writer uses quotation marks to show what she says. Leah also explained how the narrator includes *I said* when she speaks as a character. Rachel didn't seem to fully comprehend Leah's sophisticated understanding of how dialogue works in books written in the first person, but nonetheless, Karen noted that Leah had internalized lessons from the first two weeks of the study, meeting the goals we had set for the children.

As the third week of our dialogue investigation study began, we reviewed some of what we noticed during our reading partnerships with Mindy's kindergarten class. Karen started by sharing Leah's noticing about the first-person narration in *Sloppy Tiger and the Party*. She told the class how she saw Dakota pointing out all the dialogue in *Henry and Mudge and the Snowman Plan* to five-year-old Jake, noting that it was simple dialogue where the narrator tells the reader who is talking. And she told them how she saw Nicki reading *Mr. Putter and Tabby Fly the Plane* to Bebe, explaining to Bebe how the narrator, not a character, tells the story. "Mr. Putter doesn't say *one* word in the *whole* book," Nicki definitively told Bebe, "it's the *narrator* who's speaking to us." It was clear that many of our children were beginning to identify voice in stories and name different kinds of dialogue.

Karen introduced the enlarged copy of *Pinky and Rex and the New Baby,* keeping in mind that the focus for week 3 was to examine the different kinds of dialogue in one book series through shared reading. Although our children were familiar with the Pinky and Rex series from the fall, we knew that some of our children still confused these two characters' names. In addition, we knew that having an understanding of the qualities of these two characters would support our children as they navigated through the sometimes complex dialogue of the books in this series. Here's what our children told us about what they already understood about the Pinky and Rex characters:

Pinky

is a boy
likes pink
has a sister named Amanda
is in second grade
wears pink sneakers

Rex

is a girl
likes dinosaurs
has no brothers or sisters
is in the second grade
wears dinosaur T-shirts and yellow sneakers

Discussing Pinky and Rex as characters helped our students prepare to read and understand *Pinky and Rex and the New Baby*. We began reading the first pages of the text, noticing and keeping track of the conversation between Rex and her parents. Many early transitional series such as Poppleton, Mr. Putter and Tabby, and Minnie and Moo begin with the narrator providing the reader a description of the time and place of the story. This Pinky and Rex book does not, which proved particularly tricky for our young readers. In this text, James Howe begins by revealing Rex's internal thought, jumping directly into a conversation between Rex and her parents. The reader is left to monitor the conversation as well as figure out where the story takes place and what is happening. We knew that had our children been left to figure out this first page during independent reading without the support of a shared reading, their comprehension would be compromised. Together, however, we came to understand the following

This conversation was about Rex's mom having a baby.
This conversation took place in Rex's house.
Rex's action showed us that she was not happy about the news.

In addition, our children located the different kinds of dialogue we had named at the end of week 2. Although the conversation between Rex and her parents proved to be easy to follow, we took the opportunity to mark up the text as a model for what we wanted our children to practice in their partner reading that day. We sent the children off with an excerpt from *Pinky and Rex and the Spelling Bee* to read and asked them to notice the various conversations between characters and mark up the text according to what they noticed.

The following day, our children were excited to continue reading Chapter 1 from *Pinky and Rex and the New Baby*. As we began, Leah noticed the setting had changed. Rex was no longer at home talking to her parents about the new baby, but at Pinky's house telling him the big family news. After reading through Rex's conversation with Pinky, Karen asked the children what they noticed about the dialogue and narration. Amanda noted that there were quite a few lines at the end of the passage that were straight narration: "Well, the narrator tells you all about how Rex felt about Pinky's response to the big news."

Ethan chimed in, "Yeah, we don't learn about how Rex feels through her words; we learn about them through the narrator's words."

Our children were beginning to understand the relationship and balance between the narrator and the characters and the way the writer uses each to reveal the story line. We sent our children off that day to continue the work they began the day before—examining the text of *Pinky and Rex and the Spelling Bee*. We chose this text because of its similarity to the shared reading text we were using this week. We knew that examining two texts in the same series, with which they were already familiar, would allow our children to focus on the work of understanding different kinds of dialogue styles as well as the balance between dialogue and narration. (See Figure 2–7.)

The children had become quite familiar with both *Pinky and Rex and the New Baby* and *Pinky and Rex and the Spelling Bee*. When they returned to the rug for share time, Karen asked them about their understanding of the way the dialogue works in the Pinky and Rex series. She knew that developing some generalizations about the dialogue style in this series would not only support them in this particular series but serve as a model for the work we wanted our children to do during independent reading. Karen asked the children, "What do you notice about the dialogue and narration in the Pinky and Rex series?" Their responses told us that the children were beginning to make the following generalizations about dialogue and the way it works in the Pinky and Rex series:

The words of the characters don't give us all the details.
Action alongside the dialogue tells us what a character is doing and/or feeling.

The narrator adds to the conversations by giving the reader details and making transitions between settings.

The indentations can be used to guide the reader. They show us which character's turn it is to speak.

The writer uses a combination of simple dialogue (when the writer tells you who is talking) and continuation dialogue (when the writer interrupts the talking to tell you who is talking).

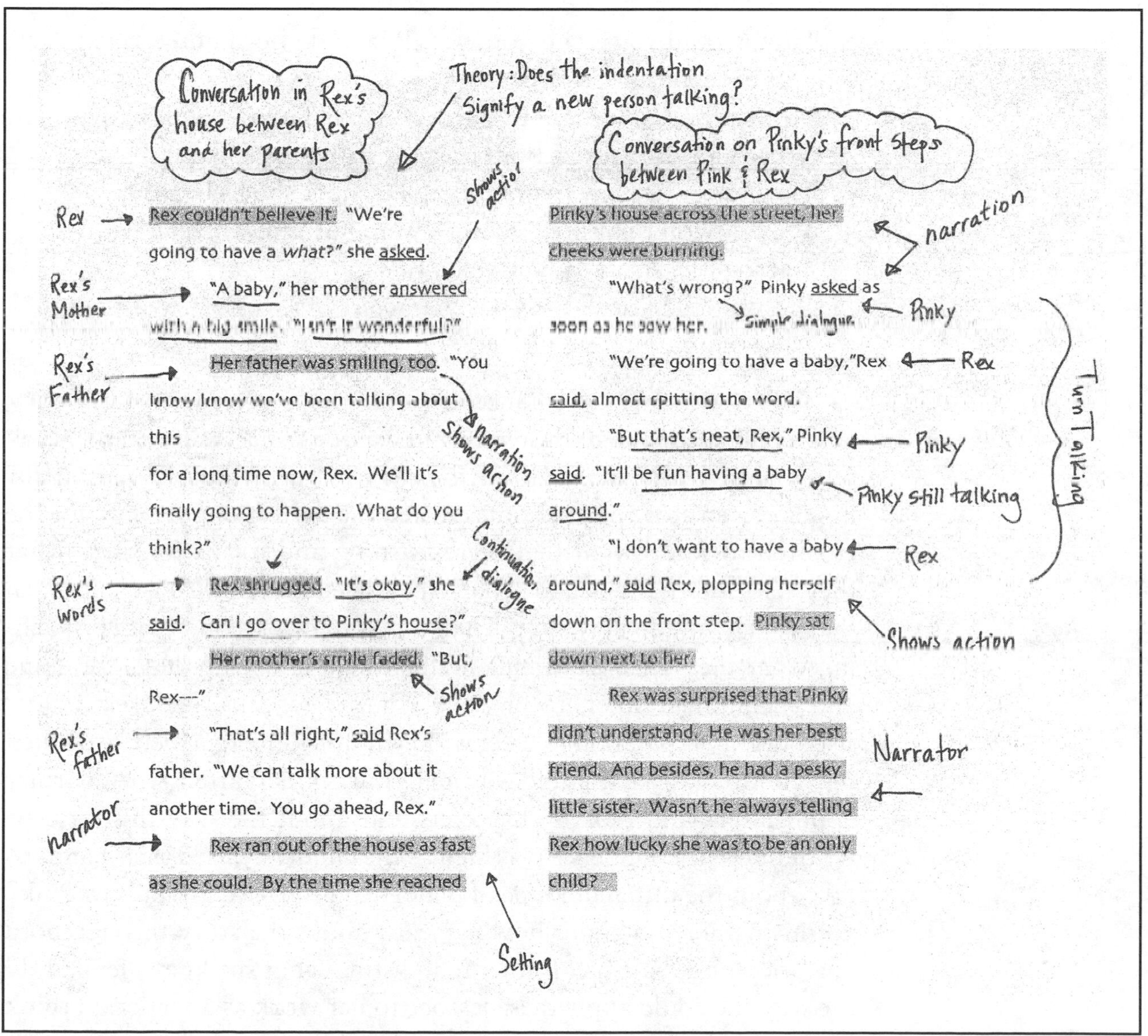

Figure 2–7 *Marked-up Pinky and Rex text*

Although we wanted our children to understand these generalizations about the way dialogue works, we didn't want them to lose sight of why we read—for meaning. So, before looking any further at dialogue and narration, we focused their attention back to story. We posed the following questions as a way of supporting our children as they made inferences about the story and connections between the text and their own lives. We designed these questions to promote conversation and lead our children to a better understanding of the story and their relationship to the text. Developing this relationship also served our children as they not only examined dialogue but looked for meaning clues to figure out who was talking in conversation.

How would you feel if you were Rex and your family were going to have another child?
How does Rex feel about the new baby? How do you know?
What does Rex do (action) to show us how she feels?
What does Rex say (words) to tell us how she feels?
Why do you think Rex's cheeks were burning when she ran across the street to Pinky's house?
What do we learn about the characters in this story and their interactions with each other?

We knew that we were meeting with our kindergarten story partners again at the end of this week and wanted to capitalize on the work our children had internalized thus far in the study. Preparing for kindergarten story partner time created the perfect opportunity for the children to recap what they were learning and for us to assess what they had internalized and where they needed help. You can't teach that which you do not know. The process of our second graders teaching what they were learning solidified new understandings for some and encouraged others to pinpoint what was tricky and seek out assistance. In preparation to meet with Mindy's kindergartners, we asked our children, "What could you tell your kindergarten story partner about Pinky and Rex as characters and about the way this series is written?" The confidence was high as the children raised their hands to talk about the different kinds of dialogue in the text, about how Pinky got his name, and about how we learn about the story through both narration and dialogue. Rather than listing what she knew, Jenna told the way she could apply these lessons to her work as a reader: "I think Pinky and Rex is a good book to read this Friday to my story partner because I know it really well and I can read it like I'm talking." Jenna was right in realizing that it is easier to make reading sound like talking when reading a book you know well. Together as a class, as if it were a script, we reread the first chapter of *Pinky and Rex and the New Baby*. The children then went off in partnerships to practice reading the work from *Pinky and Rex and the Spelling Bee* with a sense of fluency and phrasing.

The children were excited about acting out the text with their partners. They negotiated parts, practiced expressing feelings with actions and words, and learned to adjust their voices to accommodate the voices of the characters. This work forced the children to attend to punctuation, as it informed them about the characters' expressions. James Howe, the writer of the Pinky and Rex series, could obviously not be with us to tell us how he wanted the text read, but he informed us of this with commas, question marks, exclamation points, and periods. As we conferred with partnerships over the week, we noticed that some children overlooked the punctuation and therefore had difficulty with phrasing and intonation. Even those who did attend to the punctuation marks were not necessarily able to explain their function or name them.

This experience alerted us to the issue of punctuation. We watched transitional readers come to us from first grade not knowing how to attend to punctuation. It seemed that for some, this understanding came naturally, while for others, paying attention to punctuation had to be explicitly taught. We included instruction on punctuation as part of the dialogue study because of the interdependency between dialogue and punctuation. We knew that examining dialogue would force our young readers to appreciate the critical role of punctuation in story.

That day during shared reading, we wanted to focus on pointing out the punctuation surrounding dialogue and labeling it so that the children would have the words to explain what they were noticing. Karen began the minilesson by reading the first two pages of "Meeting Matthew," Chapter 2 in *Pinky and Rex and the New Baby*. The children were excited at the prospect of meeting Matthew—Rex's new adopted baby brother. Doris said, "I can't wait to see Matthew," to which Stephanie replied, "It's fiction. Matthew isn't *real*."

Karen found that interaction to be the perfect time to discuss the wonders of reading. She said, "Isn't it amazing how reading a book can take you somewhere and make you feel a part of a story? When we read about the Cobble Street Cousins, we feel like we're on Cobble Street, and when we read *When I Was Young in the Mountains*, it's like Cynthia Rylant takes us to West Virginia. Reading *Pinky and Rex and the New Baby* makes us feel excited about Rex's new baby brother, just as if we knew these characters personally." Just as reading can take you somewhere else, it's the dialogue that draws you into the characters' lives, allowing you almost to eavesdrop on private conversations. It plays an integral role in allowing the reader to feel like he's a part of the story, excited about its outcome. Naturally, having an accurate understanding of how dialogue works gives young readers the chance to enjoy this intimate experience.

After attending to story, Karen began reading *Pinky and Rex and the New Baby,* asking the children to notice the punctuation. We devoted the remainder of the week to noticing punctuation marks, discussing what punctuation marks look like, and talking about the function of each punctuation mark. In addition to examining the punctuation in Pinky and Rex during shared reading, our children read with attention to punctuation in their independent reading. By the end of the week, we had created the following chart as a way of organizing our findings and understandings of the names, looks, and functions of punctuation.

Name of Punctuation Mark	*What the Punctuation Mark Looks Like*	*The Job of the Punctuation Mark*	*Examples from Text*
period	It looks like a dot.	tells the reader to *stop*	"Lily and Tess giggled."—from *Cobble Street Cousins*
comma	It looks like a dot with a backward *c*.	tells the reader to *pause*	"But the next day, the dry skin was back."—from *Poppleton and Friends*
exclamation point	It looks like a rounded, lowercase *l* with a dot on the bottom.	tells the reader to "say it like you mean it"	"I have it!" said Mrs. Teaberry a few days later.—from *Mr. Putter and Tabby Toot the Horn*
quotation marks	They look like a pair of ears facing toward each other.	show the reader that someone is talking	"I was just feeding Poopsie," she announced . . . —from *Pinky and Rex and the New Baby*

Name of Punctuation Mark	*What the Punctuation Mark Looks Like*	*The Job of the Punctuation Mark*	*Examples from Text*
apostrophe	It is like a comma but it comes right above a word, not below.	allows two separate words to become one	"Finally, it's almost time for my party."—from *It's Justin Time, Amber Brown*
question mark	It is almost like a backward *S* with a dot on the bottom	tells the reader to use a questioning voice	"Why couldn't Kevin just go away?"—from *Pinky and Rex and the Bully*

Week Four

Goal: to deepen fluency and comprehension by developing and practicing reading strategies

Before determining reading strategies that would help our children accurately and fluently read dialogue, we took the time to review the different kinds of dialogue we found in *Pinky and Rex and the New Baby*. It is always important for us as teachers to provide opportunities for children to solidify concepts prior to asking them to apply their understandings to new learning. Knowing the importance of practice influences the work we give our children for homework as well as the amount of time we spend in class revisiting concepts learned. Although our children had named different kinds of dialogue in the previous week, we knew they needed time to process this learning through practice. We began this week reading the third chapter of our enlarged copy of *Pinky and Rex and the New Baby*. Our children had become quite familiar in week 3 with the story and the text as a script. So, in week 4, we began reading the following excerpt, reflecting back on different kinds of dialogue. Our children were able to highlight the characters' words with ease, recalling the names they had given to each kind of dialogue. (See Figures 2–9 and 2–10.)

> That night at dinner, Pinky asked, *"Is Rex adopted?" "No,"* said his mother. *"But Matthew is." "That's true,"* Pinky's mother said. She noticed Amanda slipping some string beans into the napkin on her lap.

GOAL: to deepen understanding of how dialogue works

	OBJECTIVE	MINILESSON	STUDENT WORK	SHARE
DAY ONE	examine dialogue within the context of a familiar book	• teacher introduces enlarged copy of *Pinky and Rex and the New Baby,* reviewing what children already know about the characters • shared reading of the first conversation	students are sent off with partners and excerpt from *Pinky and Rex and the Spelling Bee* to read and notice the various conversations	*whole-group share:* students share and generate a list of noticings
DAY TWO	continue to examine dialogue within the context of a familiar book	teacher continues reading the enlarged text, negotiating the dialogue between Pinky and Rex and paying particular attention to the clues within the writing that signal dialogue beginnings and endings	students are sent off with partners to continue reading Pinky and Rex text from previous day, marking the text to distinguish words between characters	*whole-group share:* students share their findings and form generalizations about how dialogue works
DAY THREE	think about meaning and the reader's relationship to the story—practice reading with expression	• teacher focuses on text meaning, using specific questions to promote conversation • teacher focuses on fluency, treating enlarged text like a script	students are sent off with partners to practice reading aloud the roles of Pinky and Rex, each taking on the voice of one character	*whole-group share:* students come back to report some of the successes and difficulties of reading text like a script
DAY FOUR	notice punctuation in text	teacher reads enlarged text of *Pinky and Rex and the New Baby,* supporting the children as they notice punctuation in text	students are sent off independently to read and notice punctuation and record with Post-its three places where they notice punctuation	*whole-group share:* • students share their punctuation noticings • teacher begins to create chart to organize the learning
DAY FIVE	notice punctuation in text; think about its function	• teacher continues to read from enlarged text, discovering punctuation • teacher reviews the punctuation noticings from day 4, working with class to define the punctuation terms and functions	students are sent off to continue their punctuation noticing and to think about how understanding the punctuation helps build fluency	*partner share:* students meet with partners and read aloud one page with lots of dialogue and punctuation *whole-group share:* teacher discusses and lists with students how noticing the punctuation helped them read more fluently • teacher adds to chart created yesterday

Figure 2–8 *Day-by-day plan for Week 3*

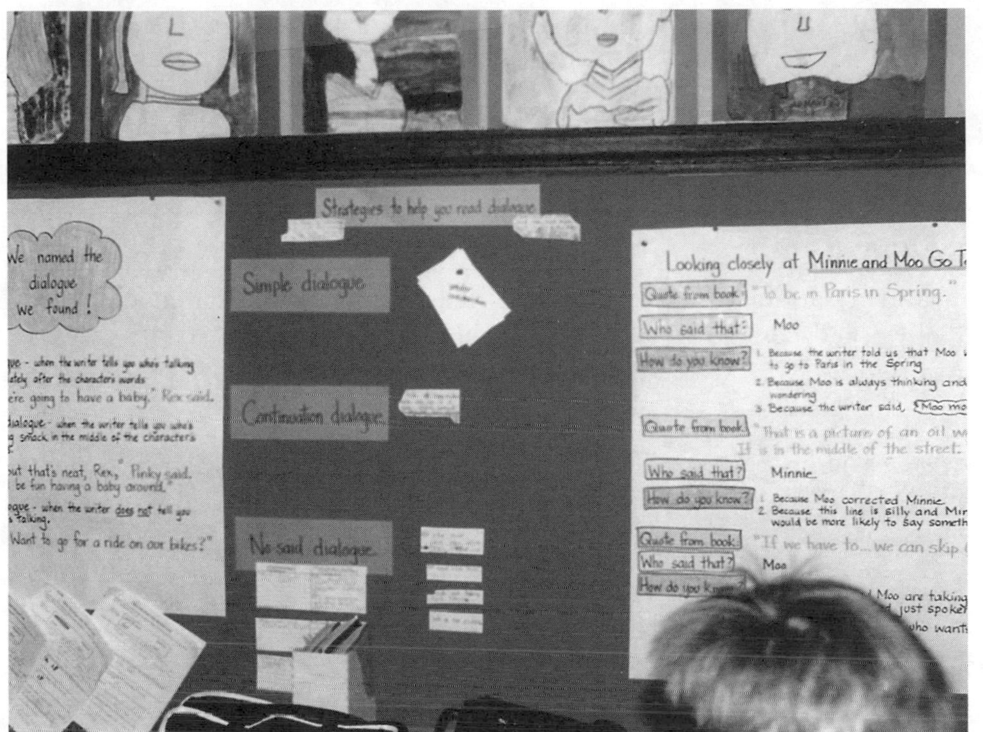

Figure 2–9
Bulletin board of dialogue work

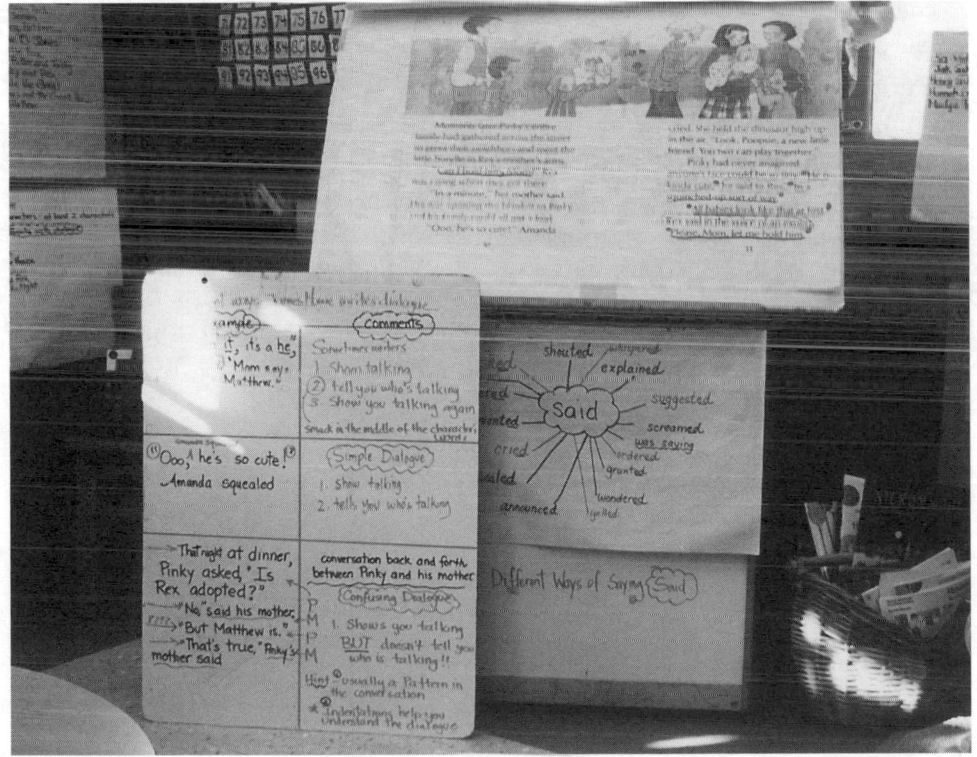

Figure 2–10
Charts demonstrating dialogue work

"Try eating them," she suggested. Amanda looked surprised. *"What? Oh, I was going to eat them. I was just, um, saving them for later. For a treat." "Right,"* said Pinky. *"Nothing like a few cold string beans while you watch TV."*

Dialogue	*What We Notice*	*What We Call It*
That night at dinner, Pinky asked, *"Is Rex adopted?"*	The narrator tells you directly that Pinky *asks* the words in quotations.	simple dialogue
"No," said his mother.	The narrator tells you that Pinky's mother (or "his" mother) *says* the word in quotations.	simple dialogue (where you have to figure out the *his*)
"But Matthew is."	The narrator does *not* tell you who is speaking.	no-*said* dialogue
"That's true," Pinky's mother said.	The narrator tells you directly that Pinky's mother *says* the words in quotations.	simple dialogue
She noticed Amanda slipping some string beans into the napkin on her lap. *"Try eating them,"* she suggested.	The narrator tells you that Pinky's mother (or "she") *suggests* the words in quotations.	simple dialogue (where you have to figure out the *she*)
Amanda looked surprised. *"What? Oh, I was going to eat them. I was just, um, saving them for later. For a treat."*	The narrator tells you in the sentence before that quotation who will be speaking.	no-*said* dialogue
"Right," said Pinky. *"Nothing like a few cold string beans while you watch TV."*	The narrator interrupts Pinky's words to tell you who is speaking.	continuation dialogue

At this point in our study, our young readers had become aware of the complexities of text. They knew punctuation around dialogue gives them clues about who is speaking, they knew identifying voice is important in following story, they knew writers use dialogue to reveal story lines and the inner workings of the characters, and they knew that dialogue is presented in different ways. Rather than breezing through text without considering conversation between characters or the balance between narration and dialogue, our young readers had learned to read more carefully, synthesizing their understanding of these text complexities and reflecting on how they affect their fluency and comprehension of story.

Now our goal was to develop reading strategies so that our readers could improve on their fluency and deepen their comprehension work. At this point in the study, our children came to the rug armed with an understanding about the balance between narration and dialogue and about how dialogue works. This week we planned to use an enlarged copy of *Pinky and Rex and the Spelling Bee,* a different title from our focus series, Pinky and Rex. During a shared prereading, Mary Anne used the actual book to read the title page, table of contents, and back cover blurb. She modeled for the children how readers preview a book to gather information before they actually read. She reminded the children of the amount of information they already knew about Pinky and Rex books and how this knowledge would help them make predictions and prepare them to enter the new book from that series with confidence. Mary Anne began with the questions "What have we come to know about the writing in the Pinky and Rex series?" and "What do we expect from this title—*Pinky and Rex and the Spelling Bee*?" The class organized a list of responses into the following two lists:

What Have We Come to Know About the Writing in the Pinky and Rex Series?	*What Do We Expect from This Title*—Pinky and Rex and the Spelling Bee?
• We know that Pinky and Rex are friends, so we know they will be talking to each other.—Eli	• We expect that there is going to be a spelling bee—like a contest.—Sara
• We expect that the characters will speak to each other and the conversation might get confusing because the narrator will not always tell us who is talking.—Eric	• We expect that the story is going to take place at school because that's where spelling bees take place and the cover picture shows Pinky and Rex at school.—Karla

What Have We Come to Know About the Writing in the Pinky and Rex Series?	*What Do We Expect from This Title*—Pinky and Rex and the Spelling Bee?
• We expect that the narrator is not a character who is in the story with Pinky and Rex.—Jordana • We know that some pages will have lots of dialogue and some have lots of narration.—Grace	• We expect that this book will be more about Pinky than about Rex because one of the chapter titles is called "Nervous Pinky."—Hyunjoo • We expect that Pinky is going to wear pink and Rex is going to wear a shirt with a dinosaur, because that always happens.—Petrit

Our children's expectations for this text were clearly articulated and very realistic, based on their prior experiences. It is important to note that prereading work is invaluable to the reading process. It prepares us to enter a text having some background knowledge about the story or writing style. When we look at the habits of our most proficient readers, we see children who naturally make connections between texts and look to the table of contents and the back blurb to make predictions and find information. As teachers, it is our responsibility to explicitly teach the natural habits of our proficient readers to those with less reading proficiency. The time that Mary Anne took to preview *Pinky and Rex and the Spelling Bee,* make predictions, elicit expectations, read the table of contents and back cover, and view the illustrations was well spent. For many of our children, it is the time taken to be explicit about reading behaviors and habits that remains with them as they move toward proficiency. With this in mind, we asked our children that day to review these prereading strategies during their own independent reading time.

The following day, Mary Anne began reading *Pinky and Rex and the Spelling Bee,* asking the children to think about who in the story was talking and how they knew. We knew we would be repeating this question over and over through the course of the week. "*Who's talking and how do you know?*" As a way of layering the learning, we wanted our children to articulate not only who was talking but how they came to determine that. Mary Anne read the following excerpt, reminding the children that sometimes there are clues that can help us figure out who is talking.

Pinky could hardly believe it. The big day had arrived at last.

"Slow down," Rex said, *"Why are you walking so fast?"*

"I can't wait to get to school," said Pinky. *"I've been getting ready all week."*

Max's hand went up immediately to answer Mary Anne's question of "Who's talking and how do you know?" Alexander, Emma, and Matthew also raised their hands with excitement over what they had noticed in this short reading. Their confidence was apparent. Mary Anne asked Max to share what he noticed.

"There's a comma," Max reported. "That's how I know that Rex is talking." Mary Anne encouraged Max to say more about what he meant. "Well," he continued, "there's a comma after 'slow down' and after 'Rex said' and a comma means a pause, not a stop. That's how we know Rex talks through that whole second line."

"So do you mean that Rex was not *finished* talking?" Mary Anne asked Max.

"Yes," he responded emphatically. "Yes. It was still her turn to talk and the narrator kind of *interrupted*."

Alexander reminded Max that this was what the class had called continuation dialogue earlier. "It's like when the narrator tells us who is talking right in the middle of the dialogue," Alexander added.

Mary Anne made Max's and Alexander's important observations public by circling the commas in question and jotting down in the margin of the enlarged text: "The commas tell us that Rex is not finished talking. It's a continuation of Rex speaking." A flurry of hands quickly went up.

"There's another line of continuation dialogue on that page," noted Eric. In this short passage, Eric saw an additional place where the narrator "interrupts" the talking to let the reader know which character is speaking. The children began to notice more continuation dialogue as Mary Anne read more of the text.

After the lesson, Mary Anne sent the children off with their partners and an excerpt from *Pinky and Rex and the Dinosaur Game*. Mary Anne directed them to read with attention to dialogue, asking themselves: "Who's talking and how do I know?" While the children read, Mary Anne conferred with Rebecca and Alexander, who noticed the many places dialogue is interrupted to inform the reader of who is talking. Alexander and Rebecca put a Post-it Note on one of these examples, explaining to Mary Anne the tricky nature of this dialogue style. "You have to be really careful when you read because if you don't look closely, you might not know that the character keeps talking." In the same book, Rebecca and Alexander made a point of highlighting a place where the narrator doesn't tell the reader who's talking but tells the reader about the character's action(s). "We knew that it was Pinky talking," explained Rebecca, "because the narrator is telling us what *Pinky* is doing and then what Pinky was saying."

During the share the children began to list ways they knew who was talking in the text. Mary Anne shaped that list into the following strategies:

> Look closely at the pictures.
> Look closely at the punctuation.
> Think about what you know about the characters.
> Read the line before and the line after.
> Make a picture of the story in your mind.
> Reread to keep track of who is talking.
> Look for the big clue *said* and *said* alternatives.

The children were able identify who was speaking and state how they knew who it was. Now Mary Anne wanted the children to think about strategies. Referring to the strategy list, Mary Anne told the students that on this day she wanted them to think about what they did as readers to figure out conversations in text when they approached difficulty. Mary Anne revisited the enlarged text of *Pinky and Rex and the Spelling Bee* and began modeling what she does as a reader to figure out who is talking. Mary Anne continued reading from the enlarged text, ready to reveal her own process as a reader to the class. She read the following excerpt without stopping to process so that the children could get a sense of the new developments in the story.

> Sitting down next to Rex, Pinky said, "So what if you're not good at spelling? It doesn't matter."
>
> "That's easy for you to say," said Rex. "You're not going to make a fool of yourself. I *hate* looking stupid. It's bad enough to make mistakes when you're all by yourself. But when you have to stand up in front of the whole class . . . I just know everyone is going to laugh at me, Pinky. They'll laugh and they'll say, 'That Rex is *so* stupid.' "
>
> "I won't laugh at you," Pinky told Rex. "And I won't think you're stupid either."

"You're just saying that because you know you're smarter than I am."

"Maybe in some things I am," said Pinky. "But you're smarter in other things. Like games. And you know lots more about dinosaurs than I do. You even know how to spell all their names."

This made Rex feel a little better. "Maybe you're right," she said. "But I'll tell you one thing. If everybody laughs at me, I'm moving to the moon."

When Mary Anne reread this passage, she processed her reading out loud so that the class could get inside her thinking. She said, "The first time I read the words, 'You're not going to make a fool of yourself,' I thought it was Pinky reassuring Rex not to worry about the spelling bee. But when I looked back to the text, I noticed that it was actually Rex talking to Pinky. Was anyone else confused by this?"

"No," James blurted out. "I saw the comma after the first part of Rex's words ["That's easy for you to say,"], which told me that the character was going to continue talking after the narrator interrupted to tell me who was talking."

Mary Anne pressed a little further, "Why do you think the narrator interrupted Rex's words?"

"Because he wanted to let you know who was speaking; they do that all the time," James said. Referring to the newly created strategy chart, Mary Anne pointed out that James had used the strategy of looking carefully at the punctuation to help him figure out who was talking in the text.

As Mary Anne reviewed the other strategies on the chart, she informed the class that aside from looking at the punctuation, she made a picture in her mind of the conversation between Pinky and Rex. Caroline told the class that she, like James, looked to the punctuation to help her navigate Pinky and Rex's conversation but that she became confused by the line, "You're just saying that because you know you're smarter than I am." Mary Anne asked Caroline what she did as a reader to figure out who was talking. "Well, I went back and read the line before. It told me that Pinky was talking, so I figured it was Rex's turn to talk. But then I also figured that it must have been Rex because she is more nervous about the spelling bee." Mary Anne turned back to the strategy chart, highlighting for the class that Caroline had used two strategies to help her negotiate the conversation. She had read the line before the tricky part and had thought about what she knew about Rex as a character.

Mary Anne told the children, "Today you're going to read with a partner, looking for places with dialogue and recording the strategies you use as readers." She then instructed the children to post places where they tried out one of these strategies or places where they discovered any new strategies that would help them as readers negotiate dialogue.

As a reinforcement of our class work, our children were reading a copy of *Pinky and Rex and the Double-Dad Weekend* at home with their families. We asked our children to practice the work of "Who said that and how do you know?" We created worksheets to give them a way to record some of their thinking. Using the text, we pulled some lines we believed would be tricky, asking our children to identify who was speaking and what strategies they used to figure it out. Figure 2–11 shows an example of one of the worksheets used for homework during week 4.

Figure 2–11 *Homework worksheet reinforcing strategy work from class*

Name Jordana

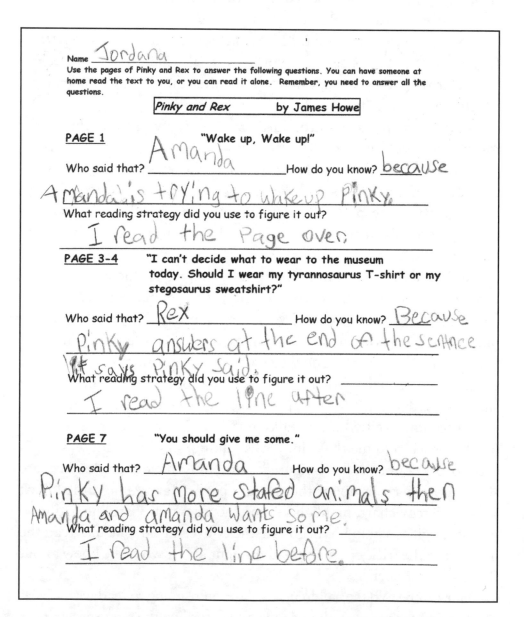

Use the pages of Pinky and Rex to answer the following questions. You can have someone at home read the text to you, or you can read it alone. Remember, you need to answer all the questions.

Pinky and Rex **by James Howe**

PAGE 1 **"Wake up, Wake up!"**

Who said that? Amanda How do you know? because Amanda is trying to wakeup Pinky.

What reading strategy did you use to figure it out?

I read the Page over.

PAGE 3-4 **"I can't decide what to wear to the museum today. Should I wear my tyrannosaurus T-shirt or my stegosaurus sweatshirt?"**

Who said that? Rex How do you know? Because Pinky ansuers at the end of the sentnce it says Pinky said.

What reading strategy did you use to figure it out?

I read the line after

PAGE 7 **"You should give me some."**

Who said that? Amanda How do you know? because Pinky has more stafed animals then Amanda and amanda Wants some.

What reading strategy did you use to figure it out?

I read the line before.

Our students finished the week making discoveries about the reading strategies they used during their reading. During their own independent reading, our children practiced naming and recording the strategies they used on Post-its (see Figure 2–12). As a way of valuing the strategy work going on in the classroom, we created a public chart titled Reading Strategies That Help Us Understand Dialogue. The chart became an interactive place where the children

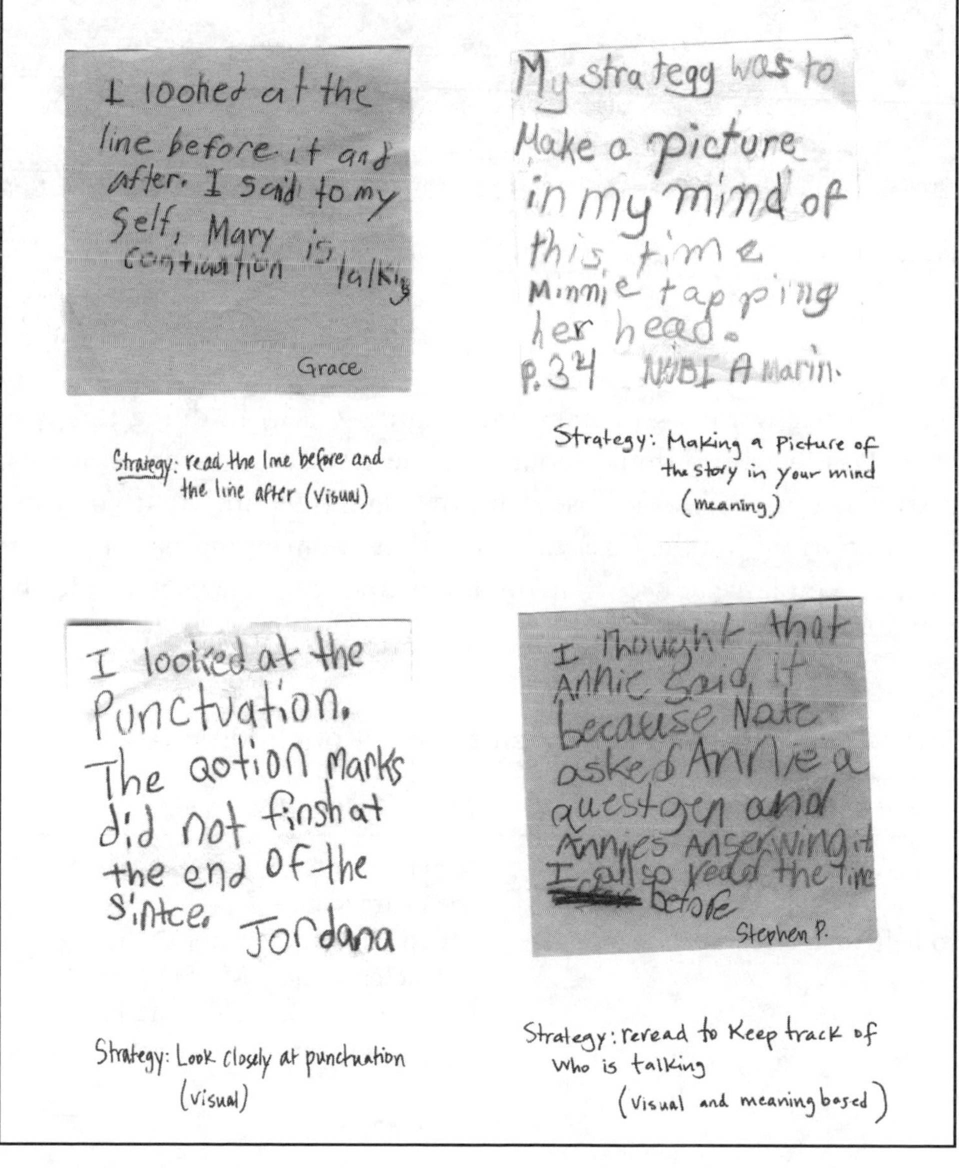

Figure 2–12 *Post-its that demonstrate strategy work*

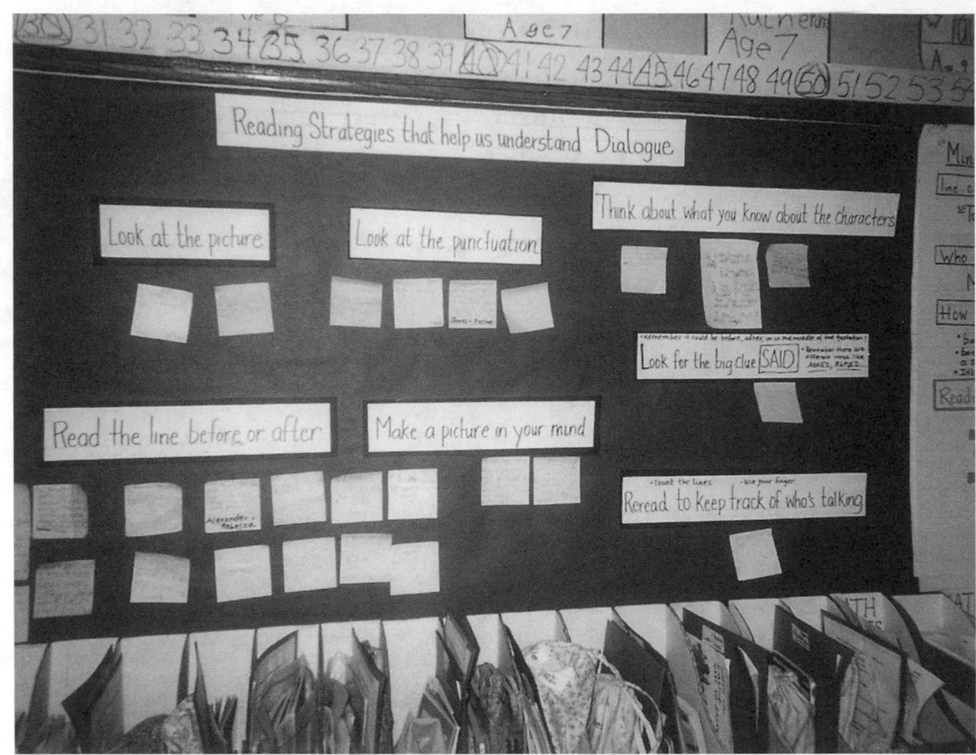

Figure 2–13 *Bulletin board of reading strategies that help us understand dialogue*

placed their written strategies. (See Figure 2–13.) In doing this, we, as a class, began to think about how these strategies worked for us, distinguishing between those that are visual (meaning that you look for support within the text) and those that are meaning-based (meaning that you have to use what you know about the characters and the story for support).

Strategies and evidence of their support for children

Visual Strategies	*Meaning-Based Strategies*
Look at the picture. I looked at the pictures to help me.—Rebecca	**Think about what you know about the characters.** I used what I knew about the character. I knew Mr. Sir would say that because he doesn't have to dig a hole every day.—Rachel

Visual Strategies	*Meaning-Based Strategies*
Look at the punctuation. I looked at the punctuation. The quotation marks did not finish at the end of the sentence.—Jordana	**Read the line before and the line after.** • I read the next line and it made sense.—Matthew • I thought that Annie said it because Nate asked Annie a question and Annie's answering it. I also read the line before.—Stephen
Look for the big clue *said* and *said* alternatives. I looked at the BIG CLUE. SAID.—Grace	**Make a picture in your mind.** It was kind of confusing the first time I read it. But the second time I read it, it wasn't confusing when I had a picture in my mind.—Lindsay
Reread to keep track of who is talking. (Combines visually looking to or counting lines for support or rereading and thinking about what makes sense.) I read the part before to see who was talking last.—Liam	

During a study such as this dialogue study, where children are asked to practice and refer to conversations that occur during mini-lessons, it is important for us as teachers to organize the thinking and discoveries that come from the children's work by rewriting and refining them through charts. These charts are then used to support children as they attempt independently the work they have done in a more supportive whole-group setting. The chart in Figure 2–14 recapped our strategy work, acting as a reference for the children during independent reading time.

As we read aloud the remaining pages of *Pinky and Rex and the Spelling Bee,* our children became drawn in by Rex's good nature and Pinky's insecurities. They began thinking about what would happen to Pinky the following day at school or that evening when Pinky was at home with his family. Would he tell his family the truth about the details of the day? Would he pretend he was sick so that he wouldn't have to face the kids at school the next day? We knew this was a perfect opportunity for our children to demonstrate what they knew about these characters as well as what they knew about the way dialogue works. We then sent the children off during writing time to imagine the story continuing. As writers some chose to write about the following day at school, while others chose to write about Pinky that evening at home.

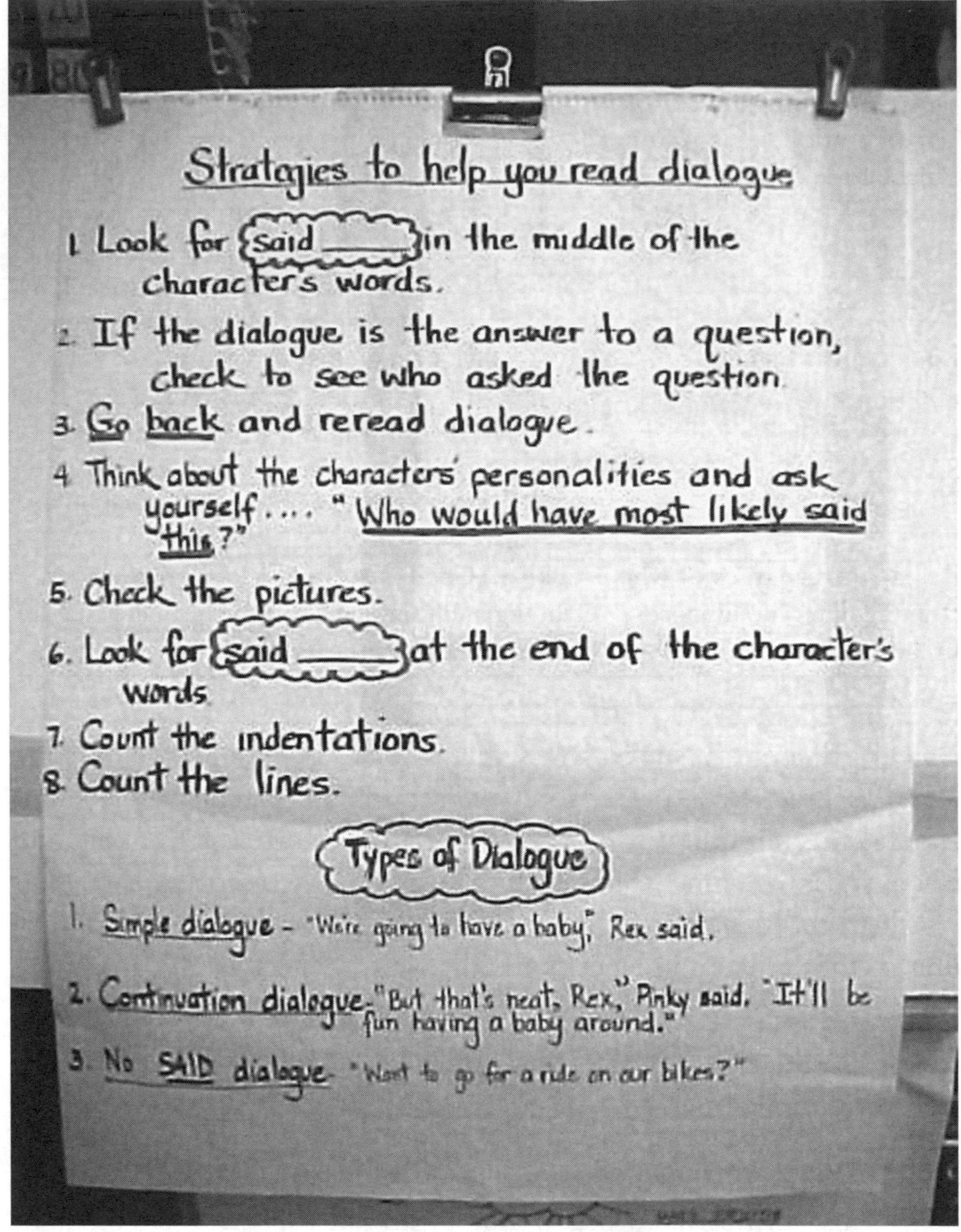

Strategies to help you read dialogue
1. Look for said ___ in the middle of the character's words.
2. If the dialogue is the answer to a question, check to see who asked the question.
3. Go back and reread dialogue.
4 Think about the characters' personalities and ask yourself.... "Who would have most likely said this?"
5. Check the pictures.
6. Look for said ___ at the end of the character's words
7. Count the indentations.
8. Count the lines.
Types of Dialogue
1. Simple dialogue - "We're going to have a baby," Rex said.
2. Continuation dialogue - "But that's neat, Rex," Pinky said. "It'll be fun having a baby around."
3. No SAID dialogue - "Want to go for a ride on our bikes?"

Figure 2–14 *Strategies to help you read dialogue*

Their writing proved to be a valid assessment of what they had internalized from the study:

- the conventions of print when writing dialogue (e.g., punctuation, capitalization)
- the balance between narration and dialogue and how they work side by side to reveal story and engage readers.

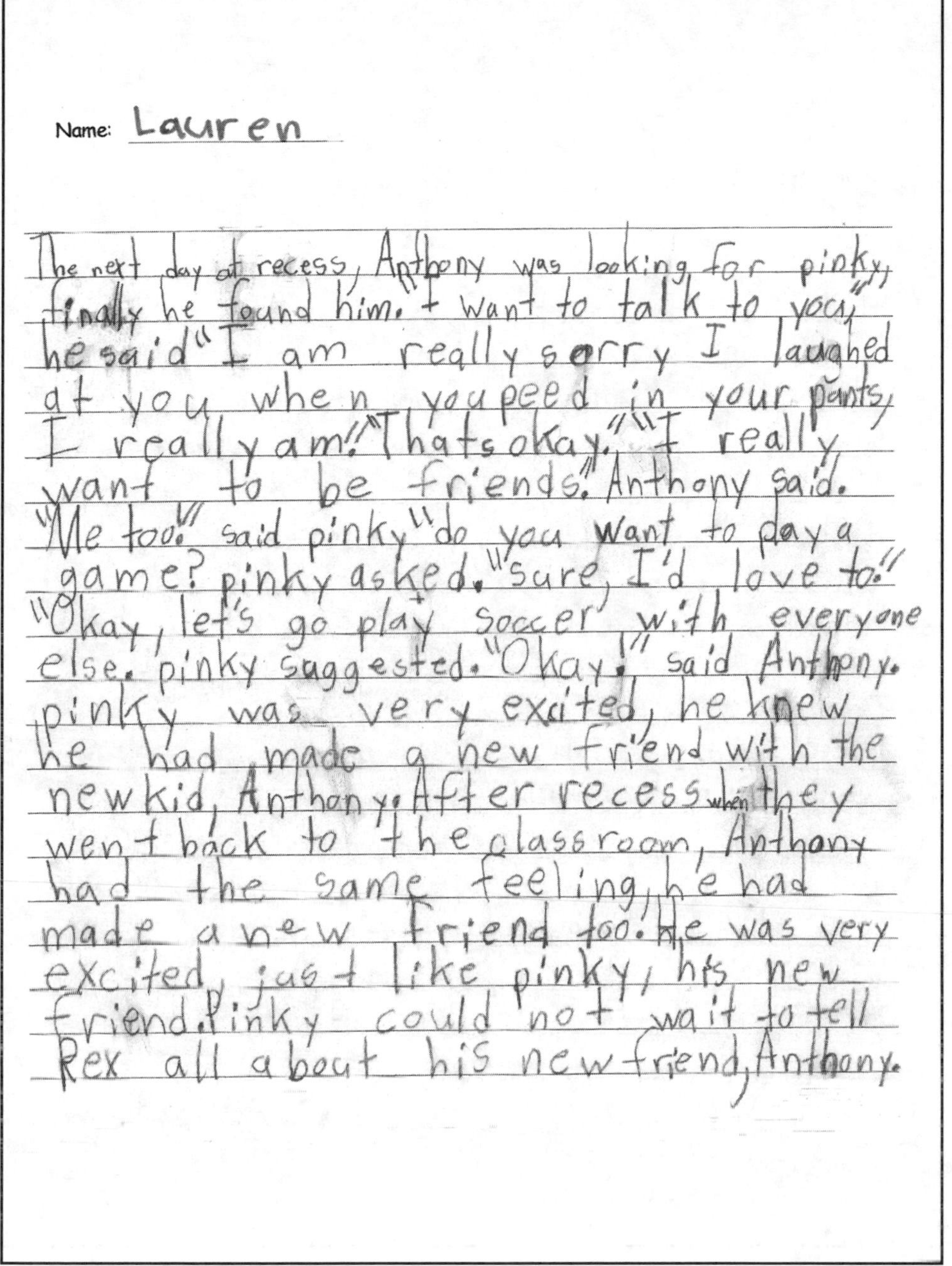

Name: Lauren

The next day at recess, Anthony was looking for pinky, finally he found him. "I want to talk to you," he said "I am really sorry I laughed at you when you peed in your pants, I really am!" "Thats okay." "I really want to be friends." Anthony said. "Me too." said pinky "do you want to play a game? pinky asked. "sure, I'd love to." "Okay, let's go play soccer with everyone else. pinky suggested. "Okay!" said Anthony. pinky was very excited, he knew he had made a new friend with the new kid, Anthony. After recess when they went back to the classroom, Anthony had the same feeling, he had made a new friend too. He was very excited, just like pinky, his new friend. Pinky could not wait to tell Rex all about his new friend, Anthony.

Figure 2–15 *Lauren's written conversation between Pinky and Anthony*

the attachment to the characters and the understanding of the inner workings of each

Figures 2–15 and 2–16 show two examples of this work.

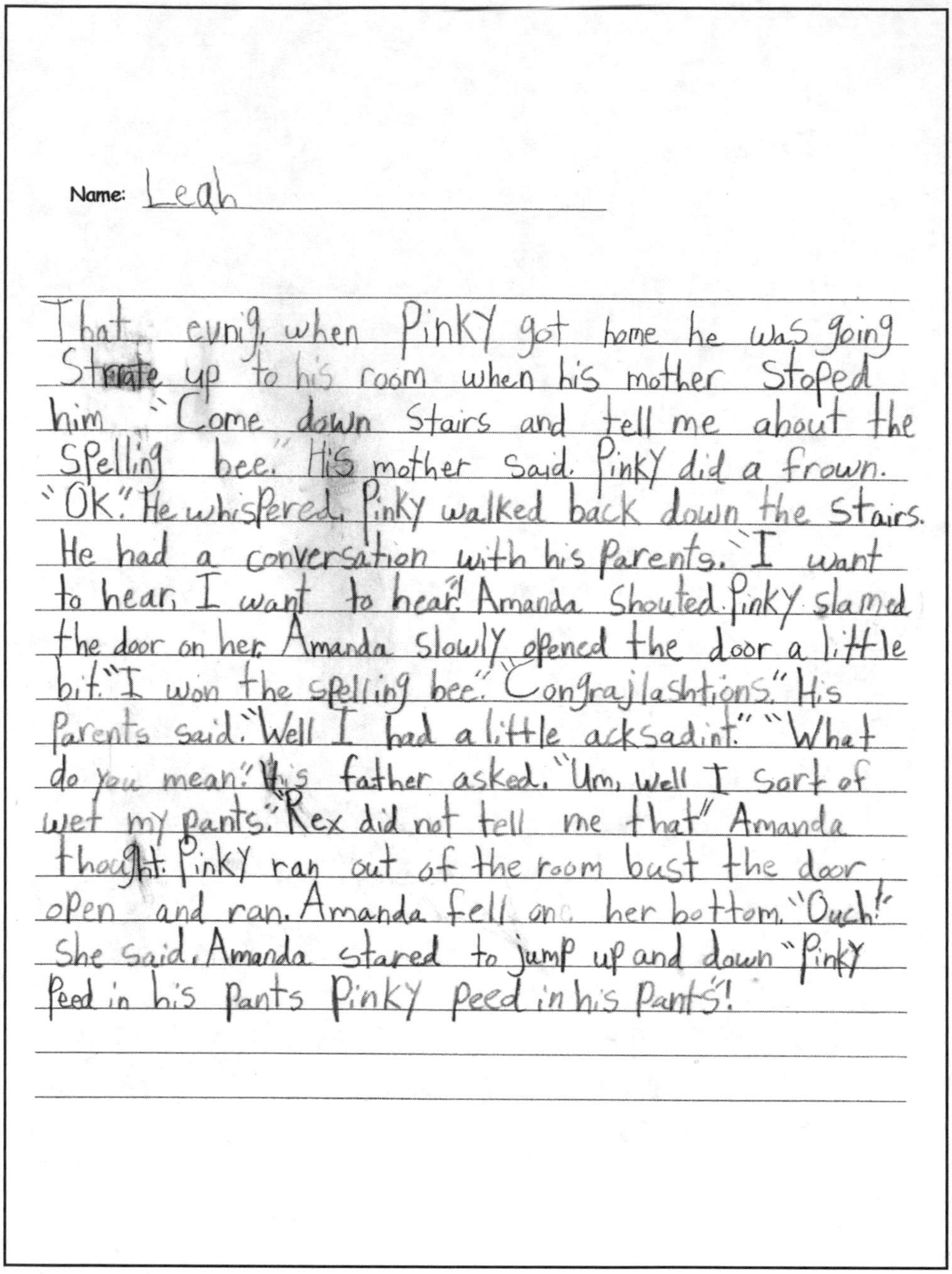

Name: Leah

That evnig, when Pinky got home he was going
Strate up to his room when his mother Stoped
him "Come down Stairs and tell me about the
Spelling bee." His mother Said. Pinky did a frown.
"OK." He whispered. Pinky walked back down the Stairs.
He had a conversation with his Parents. "I want
to hear, I want to hear." Amanda Shouted. Pinky slamed
the door on her. Amanda Slowly opened the door a little
bit. "I won the spelling bee." "Congrajlashtions." His
Parents said. "Well I had a little acksadint." "What
do you mean." His father asked. "Um, well I sort of
wet my pants." "Rex did not tell me that" Amanda
thought. Pinky ran out of the room bust the door
open and ran. Amanda fell on her bottom. "Ouch!"
She said. Amanda stared to jump up and down "Pinky
peed in his pants Pinky peed in his Pants!"

Figure 2–16 *Leah's written conversation between Pinky and Amanda*

GOAL: to deepen fluency and comprehension by developing and practicing reading strategies

	OBJECTIVE	MINILESSON	STUDENT WORK	SHARE
DAY ONE	revisit and highlight dialogue styles	teacher reviews underlined speaking parts of enlarged text and together with the children revisits the names of the various dialogue styles	students are sent off with Post-it Notes to read independently and look for various dialogue styles discussed during minilesson	*whole-group share:* share Post-it Notes from independent reading, making connections with the dialogue styles found during minilessons • chart findings to organize thinking and reinforce learning
DAY TWO	practice prereading strategies	teacher introduces enlarged text of *Pinky and Rex and the Spelling Bee,* reflecting on what the children already know about the series and looking to the table of contents, front and back cover, and illustrations to make predictions	children preview new books in own book boxes, practicing the prereading strategies focused on during the minilesson	*whole-group share:* students share their revelations as readers
DAY THREE	help children become more conscious of their process while reading dialogue	• teacher begins reading enlarged text of *Pinky and Rex and the Spelling Bee* • teacher rereads dialogue, asking children, "Who's talking and how do you know?"	students are sent off with partners to begin reading *Pinky and Rex and the Dinosaur Game,* underlining characters' parts, asking themselves and recording "Who's talking and how do I know?"	*whole-group share:* • share how students knew who was speaking in the text and what they looked for at confusion • begin shaping the children's reading behaviors for what they do at difficulty into strategies
DAY FOUR	pinpoint and name strategies used to read different styles of dialogue	teacher continues reading from this week's enlarged text, highlighting the dialoque and asking children: "Who's talking and how do you know?" and "What did you do as a reader to figure out who was talking?"	students are sent off with partners to continue reading *Pinky and Rex and the Dinosaur Game* to think about how they know who is talking while recording on Post-its what they did as readers to figure it out	*whole-group share:* share and begin to list strategies for what students did as readers to figure out who was talking in text
DAY FIVE	practice using strategies to read and understand dialogue	teacher continues reading enlarged text using strategies listed from the previous day regarding what students can do as readers to figure out who is talking in text	students are sent off independently to read, recording what they tried as readers on Post-its and marking those spots where they used a strategy	*partner share:* students meet with partners to share strategies used *whole-group share:* teacher collects Post-its on chart tablet and begins organizing them by strategy

Figure 2–17 *Day-by-day plan for Week 4*

Week Five

Goal: to practice strategies in a book with first-person narration

Among the many series books in our classroom library written in first-person narration, Nate the Great was one of the most widely read. Many of our children were familiar with this mystery series and continued to be engaged by its plot, hooked into unraveling the clues alongside its main character and narrator, kid detective Nate. But unlike the Pinky and Rex series, we hadn't examined Nate the Great for dialogue and narration. In addition, we knew that most of the Nate the Great books were written as one continuous story, without the support of chapter breaks. It's important to note that there are many variables to consider when determining the difficulty of text. Oftentimes publishers assign levels to their books, but it is our responsibility as teachers to look at the word choice, content, dialogue difficulty, chapter setup, page layout, and picture support to inform us about the books in our classroom libraries. We knew our children would need guidance and practice as they attempted to apply what they had learned about dialogue and narration in a third-person narrative series to this first-person narrative series. Nate the Great was a perfect and familiar way to expose them to this challenge.

In the same way we introduced the Pinky and Rex series to the class, we began talking about the Nate the Great series. The children quickly and automatically responded as if they knew Nate intimately, like a close friend. Answers were more detailed than simply stating that Nate was a detective. Nicholas raised his hand eagerly and responded, "Well we all know Nate *loves* pancakes!" Karen began a list of the children's responses. Some referred to story and character, while others referred to the writing style.

> Nate's always busy.
> Nate the Great books have no chapters or table of contents.
> Nate has a friend named Claude who helps him with some of his cases.
> Nate has a dog named Sludge.
> Nate always writes a note in script to his mother before he goes on a case.
> Nate always refers to himself as "I, Nate the Great."
> The sentences are short, like a poem.

Nate wears a detective coat and cap.
There are other characters that appear in this series—Annie with her dog, Fang, and Rosamond with her four black cats.

After briefly listing and discussing these qualities, Karen reminded the children of the previous week's work on determining strategies that would help them figure out who is speaking. One of the strategies, "Think about what you know about the characters," was used many times. This process of reviewing what they know about the character or the writing style of a series, along with previewing the cover blurb, table of contents, and illustrations, allows children to enter books with confidence and sets them up with the information necessary to make sense of the text. From this repeated process, our children learned the importance of prereading. We watched as they chose to practice this habit more and more on an independent level.

Practicing prereading work during the previous day prepared us to begin to enter *Nate the Great and the Lost List* armed with an understanding about Nate as a character and about the writing style of this series. The children were already aware from the work done earlier in this study that Nate was not only a character in the book but the narrator of the story. Over the next two days, Karen used the following excerpt to approach dialogue in a book written in the first person. She began by directing the children to listen closely for places where Nate played the role of a character and places where Nate played the role of the narrator.

> I, Nate the Great,
> am a busy detective.
> One morning I was not busy.
> I was on my vacation.
> I was sitting under a tree
> enjoying the breeze
> with my dog, Sludge,
> and a pancake.
> He needed a vacation too.
> My friend Claude
> came into the yard.
> I knew that he
> had lost something.
> Claude was always losing things.
> "I lost my way to your house,"
> he said. "And then I found it."

"What else did you lose?"
"I lost the grocery list
I was taking to the store.
Can you help me find it?"
"I, Nate the Great,
am on my vacation," I said.
"When will your vacation be over?"
"At lunch."

Our children's comments indicated that it was difficult not only to differentiate between Nate as a character and Nate as the narrator but to navigate the conversation between Nate and his friend Claude. Ethan referred to this when he said, "I think I know when Nate acts as the narrator, but I don't know when he is talking as a character."

Others agreed that it was difficult to negotiate the conversation between Nate and Claude. "This writer uses a lot of no-*said* dialogue," said Doris. "We really have to think about the story and the characters to figure out who is talking; there's no big clue *said* to look for." Karen agreed with Doris, highlighting the no-*said* dialogue examples in the text and reminding the children of the strategies that would help them when approaching this kind of dialogue:

Ask yourself: Who would most likely have said that? Use what you know about the story and the characters in the text.

Reread the line before and the line after the text. Characters in conversation take turns talking; knowing who spoke before or after the tricky part can clue you in to who is speaking the line in question.

Look closely at the punctuation. Punctuation gives you lots of clues about questions and responses and about when talking starts and stops.

Before the children went off to examine *Nate the Great and the Lost List* for themselves, Karen wanted to alert them to the difference between Nate speaking as the narrator and Nate speaking as a character. She asked, "Were you able to hear the difference between when Nate narrated the story and when he acted as a character?" Karla came up to the enlarged text to point out the difference between the first time and second time Nate said, "I, Nate the Great." She showed us how in one example there are quotation marks and in the other example there aren't. Ethan clarified, telling us that Nate speaks as the narrator for many lines until finally, when speaking to Claude as a character, he says, " 'I, Nate the Great, am on my vacation,' I said."

Karla seemed to understand. She told the class, "Nate uses *I* when he is sitting under the tree talking to us (the reader), and he uses *I* when he talks as a character to Claude."

Ethan thought back to the previous week's work and said, "It's easier to figure out who the narrator and characters are in Pinky and Rex books because most of the time the narrator tells you who is speaking and the narrator doesn't use the word *I* at all."

We asked our children in partnerships to review a few pages from *Nate the Great and the Lost List,* looking for places in the text where the writer does not alert the reader to who is talking (no-*said* dialogue). We asked them to use colored pencils to keep track of Nate's conversations and his narration of the story. Our children recorded their strategy work on a worksheet (see Figure 2–18).

We knew many of our children were familiar with the Nate the Great series from the beginning of the year and even from first grade. As a way of assessing their progress and helping them reflect on their reading habits, we spent some time during our conferring time focused on the question "In what ways are you reading differently than you did as a first grader?" Our children's responses demonstrated that they had become conscious of their growth as readers. Here are some of their replies:

> In first grade, I sounded like a robot. I skipped over quotation marks because I didn't know what they were. I didn't notice the periods as a first grader; I didn't stop and take a breath.—Devin
>
> The books are funnier. I act out the voice of Nate and his friends in the book.—Ethan
>
> When I was younger, I had no idea what the quotation marks meant and I went too fast and didn't understand.—Nicki
>
> I read better now because in first grade I didn't know anything about dialogue—now I use strategies. I notice the no-*said* dialogue and I ask myself, "Who would have most likely said that?" I reread when I'm confused.—Xanyani
>
> There's a lot of dialogue in Nate the Great. Writers should put more thinking (narration) into the books. The sentences are short. I like longer sentences because they tell me more about what is happening.—Dakota

Nate the Great and the Lost List

Pages 8, 9, 10 and 11 have MANY examples of No-SAID dialogue! Write down 3 examples of No-SAID dialogue and give two strategies for each example.

How would a reader figure out who's talking?

Examples of No-SAID dialogue. One example per box.	Strategies for figuring out who is talking. Two strategies per box.
"I lost my way to your house," he said. "And then I found it."	1. I knew his chariter and he's always losing things and then finding them.
"What else did you lose?"	2. I found out it was Nate's turn to speak.
"when will your vacation be over?"	1. It was claud's turn to speak.
"At lunch."	2. claud was aking him a question.
"No, he won't be home till lunch."	1. I read the line before
"Can you remember some of the list?"	2. I read the line after.

Figure 2–18 *Stephen's strategy worksheet*

It is important for us as teachers to set our children up for independence. Each week of this study, we watched our children develop more autonomy over their learning, and each week we expected that they would apply what they had learned to what was being taught. They were on their way to proficiency. They became more aware of the way books are written, noticing the balance between narration and dialogue; they became aware of the narrator's voice; they learned to use efficient strategies; and they developed a habit for prereading. So what did this mean for them as readers? This meant our children read with greater fluency; they were more actively engaged in reading, approaching text with expectations; and they monitored their understanding. Attending to the details of dialogue contributed to our children's improved comprehension, creating more careful and thorough readers.

In the last two days of this study, we scaffolded our children as they applied what they learned within the context of this supportive study to their independent reading lives. We gave our children the opportunity to practice their strategy work in some popular series books written in the first person. We referred back to the books listed on the T-chart we created in week 1, listing the first- and third-person narrative books (see Figure 2–5). Karen used *It's Justin Time, Amber Brown,* by Paula Danziger, and *Junie B. Jones Is a Graduation Girl,* by Barbara Park, to guide the children toward greater independence. In reading the first page of each book, the children made many connections to the lessons they had learned through this study. They noticed that both books are written in the first person. They noticed that Amber Brown introduces herself as "I, Amber Brown . . . ," just as Nate does in his books. They noticed the kidlike language of Junie B. Jones, written as though she were engaged in a conversation with the reader. They noticed that the balance between narration and dialogue in *It's Justin Time, Amber Brown* leans more toward narration and commented on how books with more narration and less dialogue are easier to read.

We had helped our children become inquisitive about characters and about the way books are written. They were well on their way to independence, and for the remaining days of this study, we allowed them to apply what they knew to their independent reading, making meaning of texts and new discoveries that would support them as they developed as readers.

Some of our children had grown to love practicing in writing what they had learned in this study. In our last assessment, we asked our children to invent a final conversation in writing between Claude and Nate. Figure 2–19 shows a creative example of Diana's understanding of story and the way dialogue is written. It demonstrates her control over punctuation, her understanding of the balance between narration and dialogue, her understanding of the characters in the Nate the Great series, and her ability to use dialogue as a device to reveal story.

Figure 2–19
Diana's invention of a final conversation between Nate and Claude

Nate the Great and the Lost List pages 26-48

In this book, Nate only talks to one character at a time. Put Nate's conversations in order. The conversations from pages 7-25 (last week's reading) are already listed.

First Nate has a conversation with... Claude
then... Rosamond
then... Annie (the first person Nate has a conversation with in part two)
then... Claude
then... Rosamond

On page 47, Claude comes to meet Nate the Great. Nate has been waiting a long time for Claude. Nate is holding the list when Claude comes around the corner. The writer, Marjorie Weinman Sharmat, chose not to include a final conversation between Claude and Nate. What do you think they would have said to each other? Who would have spoken first? Who would have spoken last? Use what you know about dialogue, and what you know about this story to write a final conversation between these two characters. "Hey claude where were you?" "oh I lost my way a few times." As Usual Claude was always Losing things. "Hey did you find my list?" "yeah" "Where?" "Well, Rosamond though it was a cat-pancake recipe then I talked herinto returning it. She said She will Keep the recipe in her head." "Now can I have my list Back?" "No I need it for something" I said "something very important" "Like what Nate?" "Nothing you need to know" I said "Will You rewrite it for me?" Claude Asked "Yes" I said. (on back →)

"bye" "I'll see You Soon Claude" I Said. I Knew I would see him Soon. I Nate the great Knew I would have to solve another case for Claude Soon!

GOAL: to practice strategies in a book with first-person narration

	OBJECTIVE	MINILESSON	STUDENT WORK	SHARE
DAY ONE	practice prereading strategies	teacher introduces enlarged text of *Nate the Great and the Lost List* and makes T-chart listing what children know about Nate the Great as a character and what they know about the writing style	children preview new books in own book boxes, practicing the prereading strategies focused on during the minilesson	*whole-group share:* students share their revelations as readers
DAY TWO	differentiate between character and narrator	teacher begins reading enlarged text of *Nate the Great and the Lost List,* asking children to listen for the differences between Nate as a character and Nate as the narrator	students are sent off with partners to read and highlight places where Nate is the narrator and places where he acts as a character	*whole-group share:* • discuss the balance between Nate as a narrator and Nate as a character • compare text with Pinky and Rex
DAY THREE	examine dialogue written without *said* or narrator's identification (*said* alternative)	teacher reads from enlarged text, underlining dialogue where the character is not identified, and asks students how they know who is talking	students are sent off with partners to read and underline places where a character is not identified	*whole-group share:* share how students knew who was speaking even though a character's name was not attached to the word
DAY FOUR	practice using strategies in other first-person-narrated texts	• teacher refers back to the chart created earlier in the study listing other first-person narrative texts • teacher reads first few pages of two other books written in the first person: *It's Justin Time, Amber Brown* and *Junie B.*	students are sent off in partnerships to explore first-person-narrated titles	*whole-group share:* share the discoveries of the day, comparing the narration and dialogue in the books they read to that in Nate the Great
DAY FIVE	apply lessons learned in the study to independent reading books	• teacher repeats lesson from day 4 using two texts written in the first person • students apply lessons from study to their independent reading	students read independently, applying lessons from study to their reading work	*whole-group share:* students discuss how the lessons learned from the study have moved them forward as readers

Figure 2–20 *Day-by-day plan for Week 5*

Through Melissa's Eyes A New Teacher's Voice

What I learned from this work

The work in this study, which I was fortunate enough to watch unfold as a student teacher, has taught me to look closely at the way children make sense of dialogue in text. As a new teacher, I never considered that children might have difficulty keeping track of conversations. I assumed that if children could decode, it meant they were reading and understanding. This work has empowered me as a teacher to look differently at kids as readers. Now I approach reading conferences with added questions for my students: "Who do you think is talking right here? How do you know?" Assessing their needs as readers in this way allows me to plan my reading work.

How I adapted this study to fit my classroom needs

Prepared with the day-to-day outlines and my assessments, I was ready to incorporate this dialogue study into my reading workshop. Teaching this study for the first time was a challenge. My children did not respond with the same sophistication that Mary Anne's and Karen's children displayed. As a teacher you want to build community around what your students are learning as readers, and by using a blown-up text of a Pinky and Rex book for shared work, along with providing multiple copies of the book for partner work, I was able to create this environment. The children were able to make discoveries about dialogue as I gave them time to practice the strategies I had taught. The children's responses reflected their deeper understanding of dialogue.

After teaching this work for one year, I approached the second year with more confidence. I saw how interconnected dialogue and fluency were, how you couldn't read fluently without switching voices for characters and paying attention to punctuation. Focusing on how to read fluently allowed my students to synthesize what they learned from the reading work we did earlier in the year on dialogue and apply it to read texts with expression and ease.

CHAPTER 3

Learning to Read Nonfiction

Investigation Two

As the second half of the year began, we entered a period when a substantial chunk of time would be devoted to teaching the reading and writing of nonfiction. This didn't mean that we would let the lessons from our fiction reading work fall by the wayside, depriving the children of a place to practice strategies learned. We knew our nonfiction work would be in the forefront of the reading workshop, and we appreciated the important status fiction held in our children's independent reading lives. We realized its role as a place for them to revel in the daily occurrences of the characters they came to know well. In addition, reading nonfiction affords our children an opportunity to practice essential reading strategies that will continue to move them forward along the reading continuum. We also knew that we would have to accommodate our children's need to read for longer periods of time. They needed to practice their work with understanding dialogue, continue to follow a favorite series, and have time to talk about fiction with their partners. We asked the question that many teachers ask: *How would we accommodate this new nonfiction work while maintaining an independent reading time, all within the constraints of a very busy school day?*

We needed to manage the flow of our day so that it included all of the subjects our children needed to cover daily to enable them to improve as readers. As we often do, we shifted the schedule a bit, making some changes in terms of placement and timing. We chose to shift our independent reading time to the morning and use our reading time for the nonfiction reading work. Essentially, our children were

	WEEK ONE	WEEK TWO	WEEK THREE	WEEK FOUR	WEEK FIVE	WEEK SIX
GOAL	to understand the difference between fiction and nonfiction	to begin developing an understanding of different ways writers present nonfiction information	to develop an awareness of the features and structures of nonfiction	to develop strategies for reading nonfiction	to deepen our understanding of nonfiction features	to reinforce and practice lessons learned from study
LITERATURE	• *Frog and Toad Together,* by Arthur Lobel • *It's a Frog's Life,* by Steve Parker	• *Phantom of the Prairie: Year of the Black-Footed Ferret,* by Jonathan London • *The Whales,* by Cynthia Rylant • *How the Whales Walked into the Sea,* by Faith McNulty	• *Salamander Rain,* by Kristin Joy Pratt-Serafini • *Wacky Plant Cycles,* by Valerie Wyatt	• *A Wood Frog's Life,* by John Himmelman • *My Favorite Tree: Terrific Trees of North America,* by Diane Iverson	• table of contents example from *Whales,* by Joan Short and Bettina Bird • glossary example from *How the Whales Walked into the Sea, Wacky Plant Cycles,* and *It's a Frog' Life*	*Whales,* by Gail Gibbons
MINILESSONS	• facilitate conversation to answer What is fiction? What is nonfiction? • examine the difference between fiction and nonfiction using frogs as a subject	• read *The Whales* for fiction and nonfiction qualities • read *How the Whales Walked into the Sea* and compare excerpt from this book with excerpt from the *The Whales*	• look closely at *Salamander Rain,* noticing and recording features and structures • use text to model the use of reading log • look closely at *Wacky Plant Cycles,* noticing and recording its features and structures	• create a list of some questions readers of nonfiction ask themselves when approaching a text • demonstrate the difference in approaching a book that demands a cover-to-cover read and a book that one can dip in and dip out of • create a list of questions readers of nonfiction ask themselves while reading a text	• examine table of contents from *Whales;* chart how we use those noticings as readers • examine glossary of contents from *How the Whales Walked into the Sea* • compare with Venn diagram the reasons for using table of contents versus index • examine the different ways writers write glossaries	• ask children what they know about Gail Gibbons and her collection of books • demonstrate one or two text features • ask children what they know about Joanne Ryder and her collection of books • demonstrate one or two text features
STUDENT WORK	• sift through class library, making categories of fiction and nonfiction • read and notice the difference between fiction and nonfiction text sets • complete questionnaire about their own reading lives • interview family members about their nonfiction reading lives	• examine *The Whales* for fiction and nonfiction qualities in partnerships • examine excerpts on one subtopic from each book • examine library for books that fit into "informational" fiction category	• examine nonfiction books, focusing on features and structures • record findings of features and structures on reading log	• examine nonfiction text with a list of questions readers of nonfiction ask themselves when approaching text • examine nonfiction text with attention to strategies to use while reading	• examine packet of tables of contents, marking up copies with noticings • examine packet of glossaries, marking up copies with noticings • examine nonfiction library to confirm generalizations • record how understanding each feature helped them in their nonfiction reading	• examine Gail Gibbons books for distinctive features and structures • examine Joanne Ryder books for distinctive features and structures

Figure 3–1 *Study at a glance: learning to read nonfiction*

receiving *time and a half* for reading! Here is a sample schedule of our day during the nonfiction reading study:

Sample schedule accommodating nonfiction work

8:30–9:00	Independent Reading Time
9:00–9:15	Read Aloud
9:15–10:00	Writing Workshop
10:00–11:00	Nonfiction Reading Workshop (minilesson, reading work, share)
11:00–11:50	Special (e.g., art)
11:50–12:45	Lunch/Recess
12:50–1:50	Math
1:50–2:15	Word Study
2:15–2:50	Social Studies/project time

Until this point in the school year, our reading workshop had revolved around reading fiction. We thought back to the organization of our class library. At the beginning of the year, we organized baskets by series. We later sifted, distinguishing between those series written in third person and those written in first person. We further sifted for dialogue style and chapter setup. We came to know those books that were short-story collections and those that were not. Within each series we came to know those that were to be read in number order and those for which it did not matter. We had started the year by looking superficially at our fiction collection and over the first half of the year came to dig deep and analyze many facets of fiction.

Our goal for the second half of the year was to investigate nonfiction with the same rigor and sophistication as we had with fiction. We began by using our knowledge of fiction and investigation as a springboard into the unknown—nonfiction. About the time of this transition, Karen heard Steph Harvey, author of *Nonfiction Matters,* report that 90 percent of the reading done by Americans is nonfiction. In thinking about investigating nonfiction, the question became, "How do we tap into kids' natural curiosity about the way the world works to get them as excited about reading and responding to nonfiction as they are about fiction?"

During the course of the year, we had come to know fiction and its predictable structure. Children knew that before reading a book they could make predictions, preview a book's front and back covers, and take note of picture and text clues. They knew they would experience characters, navigate through the dialogue, and come to understand setting. During our initial examination of nonfiction, we realized that there were more varieties and variables of nonfiction than of fiction and that nonfiction didn't provide the same predictability the children had experienced in fiction reading. In order for our children to read a nonfiction text successfully, they would need to understand its various features and structures. This understanding would allow them to approach a text with confidence and purpose.

Week One

Goal: to understand the difference between fiction and nonfiction

We began our nonfiction study by defining what we already knew—fiction. We thought back to one of our first read-alouds, *Gooseberry Park,* by Cynthia Rylant. We reminisced about the compassion we felt for our beloved Stumpy, Gooseberry Park's courageous and determined squirrel. We laughed as we thought back to Murray's outrageous antics: stealing Oreos from Professor Albert's kitchen and searching through Chinese restaurant garbage cans for duck sauce. Our children also spoke of the many books they had read during independent reading. They shared a common language and familiarity with our fiction library. In partnerships, our children reminisced about the cases from the Nate the Great mystery series and the relationship between go-getter Frog and laid-back Toad that they came to understand while reading the Frog and Toad series. They spoke of the characters they came to love and the predictability and comfort of reading books in a series. We wondered if nonfiction, an unfamiliar genre, could elicit similar reactions of engagement.

We began by listing what we knew about fiction, contrasting it to what we knew about nonfiction. As we often do, we designed a T-chart to illustrate our understanding and sort through our thinking about what we knew about fiction and nonfiction. (See our minilesson plan in Figure 3–2.)

We started by asking our children what they knew about fiction. Chelsea had recently finished *Poppleton in Spring,* by Cynthia Rylant, and was thinking about the Poppleton series when she responded,

Week 1—Minilesson 1

From known to unknown: What is fiction? What is nonfiction?

Needed: • prepared chart paper

Plan for Reading Workshop

<u>Minilesson</u>

Teacher facilitates conversation, defining terms *fiction* and *nonfiction*. Children think back to what they already know about each.

<u>Student Work</u>

Send children off in partnerships to sift through class library, categorizing books into fiction and nonfiction.

<u>Sharing/Reflecting</u>

Children share their findings. Teacher facilitates conversation and records thinking behind the classifications.

What Is Fiction?	What Is Nonfiction?

Figure 3–2 *Plan for first days of investigating nonfiction*

"Sometimes in fiction, characters are animals." She gave us the example of Poppleton the pig and his friends, Cherry Sue the llama, Fillmore the goat, and Hudson the mouse.

Our children agreed that very often, fictional characters are animals. Ethan chimed in, "Yeah, that's true for Stumpy, Gwendolyn, and Murray in *Gooseberry Park,* and Tabby in the Mr. Putter and Tabby series."

We spent a few minutes thinking back to the books we knew well, moving on to further define our understanding of fiction and nonfiction. The following chart shows our initial understanding.

Chart of children's answers to questions: What is fiction? What is nonfiction?

What Is Fiction?	*What Is Nonfiction?*
• Sometimes in fiction, characters are animals. • In fiction, animals wear clothing. • In fiction, there's often dialogue between characters. • In fiction, a narrator tells the story. • In fiction, quotation marks are used when a character talks. • In fiction, some characters are more important than others. • Fiction books are funny. • Sometimes fiction books have episodes like cartoons.	• Nonfiction is real. • Nonfiction is true. It can happen. • Nonfiction could have happened in the past. It's history. • Nonfiction can be world news. • Nonfiction answers questions.

The children's responses confirmed what we thought was true: their understanding of nonfiction was far less sophisticated than their understanding of fiction. It was evident that they needed to develop a deeper understanding of nonfiction. They didn't comment on how varied nonfiction reading can be or how readers approach nonfiction differently than they do fiction. They didn't comment on the features and styles of nonfiction or the reasons they might approach a nonfiction text. We knew our children needed lots of experience reading and examining nonfiction. That day, we sent the children off in partnerships to sift through the class library and asked them to make two distinct piles: one fiction and the other nonfiction. It was this work that would allow us to switch the focus of the class library and the reading workshop from fiction to nonfiction, and we set out to design a study that would allow our children to achieve this goal. The work we had our children do in this unit of study would eventually be a steppingstone into the work of writing nonfiction (Chapter 6).

As a way of bridging the gap between fiction and nonfiction, we put together several text sets for the children to examine (see Figure 3–3). Each set included a familiar fiction book and a nonfiction book on the same topic. It was our intention that children, in partnerships, while investigating the differences between these fiction and nonfiction

Topic	Fiction	Nonfiction
frogs	*Frog and Toad Together,* by Arnold Lobel	*It's a Frog's Life,* by Steve Parker
whales	*The Whales,* by Cynthia Rylant	*How the Whales Walked into the Sea,* by Faith McNulty
birds	*The Bird House,* by Cynthia Rylant	*Birds, Nests and Eggs,* by Mel Boring
chameleons	*A Color of His Own,* by Leo Leonni	*Chameleons Are Cool,* by Martin Jenkins
spiders	*Miss Spider's Wedding,* by David Kirk	*Spiders,* by Gail Gibbons
opossums	*Possum Magic,* by Mem Fox	*Opossums,* by Lynn M. Stone
caterpillars	*Charlie the Caterpillar,* by Dom Deluise	*Where Butterflies Grow,* by Joanne Ryder
wolves	*Red Riding Hood,* by James Marshall	*Look to the North,* by Jean Craighead George
apples	*Johnny Appleseed Goes A' Planting,* by Patsy A. Jensen	*The Life and Times of the Apple,* by Charles Micucci
trees	*The Birthday Tree,* by Paul Fleischman	*My Favorite Tree: Terrific Trees of North America,* by Diane Iverson
music	*Music, Music for Everyone,* by Vera B. Williams	*Making Music: Six Instruments You Can Create,* by Eddie Herschel Oates
space	*Floating Home,* by David Getz	*All About Space,* by Ian S. Graham and Geriant H. Jones
pigs	*Poppleton in Spring,* by Cynthia Rylant	*Pigs,* by Gail Gibbons

Figure 3–3 *Sample fiction-nonfiction text sets*

books, would deepen their understanding of each. As a class model, we chose to highlight *Frog and Toad Together,* by Arnold Lobel, and *It's a Frog's Life,* by Steve Parker. We chose *Frog and Toad Together* because it was one of the books from the Frog and Toad series we had come to know and love. We wanted the children to spend more time comparing the qualities of fiction and nonfiction than getting to know individual stories. *It's a Frog's Life* was new to the class, so we read it through for enjoyment and to gain familiarity. The following day we compared the two texts. Here's what the children discovered.

Comparing fiction and nonfiction

Frog and Toad Together, *by Arnold Lobel*	It's a Frog's Life, *by Steve Parker*
• Toad is always acting lazy. • There are characters and dialogue. • The illustrations help me get a picture in my mind.	• The frog is talking to us about real frogs. • There is so much information about frogs. • There are lots of words I don't know. • There is a lot on one page: words, boxes, illustrations, titles. • Is this a true story?

It was time for children to examine fiction-nonfiction text sets within their partnerships. Leah and Amanda went off with a zip-top bag containing the fiction text *Stellaluna,* by Janell Cannon, and the nonfiction text *Bats,* by Elizabeth Russell. Ethan and Devin went off with *A Color of His Own,* by Leo Leonni (fiction), and *Chameleons Are Cool,* by Martin Jenkins (nonfiction). As the partnerships settled in, they began to read the paired books. Several children, as they sat down to work, decided they would assign roles to each other. Leah and Amanda decided that Leah would read the fiction book and Amanda would read the nonfiction book. Ethan and Devin had a different arrangement. They agreed that one would read while the other listened and then they would switch roles for the second book. The room was buzzing with all kinds of discoveries as the children settled in to do the work at hand. They worked on these text sets for a few days, eventually recording their findings. Leah and Amanda noticed some fictional features from *Stellaluna,* such as the use of dialogue and the idea that animals presented as characters talk to one another. They commented, "Mother bat comes back," referring to the happy ending of *Stellaluna,* a common quality of fiction. Leah and Amanda read their nonfiction title, *Bats,* by Elizabeth Russell, making an immediate connection to Murray, the fictional bat they remembered from *Gooseberry Park*. Reading that bats are nocturnal in a nonfiction book confirmed Murray's repeated reference to himself as nocturnal. This taught them that sometimes animals in fiction books behave in factual ways. They also made reference to the question-and-answer format of

Week 1—Minilesson 2

Examining the difference between the fiction and nonfiction books

Needed:
- prepared chart paper
- fiction/nonfiction text sets
- recording sheets for kids modeled after chart

Plan for Reading Workshop

<u>Minilesson</u>

Read *Frog and Toad Together,* by Arnold Lobel, and *It's a Frog Life,* by Steve Parker, noticing and recording the differences between fiction and nonfiction.

<u>Student Work</u>

Send children off in partnerships with text sets to examine differences between fiction and nonfiction. Children should read books and use chart to record—same as modeled lesson.

<u>Sharing/Reflecting</u>

Children share their findings. Teacher facilitates conversation and records their findings.

Name: ______________________

Fiction	**Nonfiction**
author: ____________	author: ____________
title: ____________	title: ____________
What do you notice about your **fiction** book?	What do you notice about your **nonfiction** book?

Some example text sets

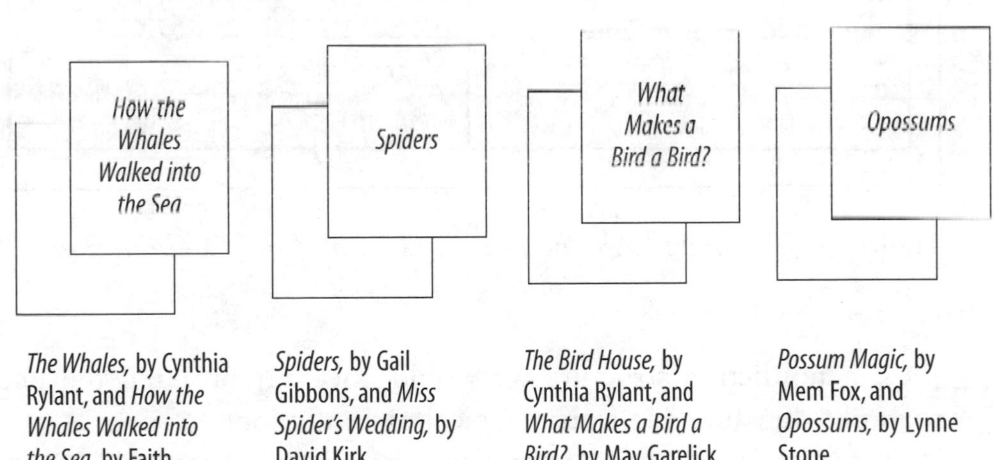

The Whales, by Cynthia Rylant, and *How the Whales Walked into the Sea,* by Faith McNulty

Spiders, by Gail Gibbons, and *Miss Spider's Wedding,* by David Kirk

The Bird House, by Cynthia Rylant, and *What Makes a Bird a Bird?,* by May Garelick

Possum Magic, by Mem Fox, and *Opossums,* by Lynne Stone

Figure 3–4 *Plan for comparing fiction and nonfiction*

Names: Leah and Amanda

fiction: author Janell title Stellaluna	nonfiction: author Elizabeth title Bats
What do you notice about your *fiction* book?	**What do you notice about your *nonfiction* book?**
• menchon names of bats like a furtie bat • She meshoned that mother bat would carry Stellaluna clutched to her breast • dioloe • bats exercis their new wings • Bats hing upside down • The illosrashos are painted • It defnly has to be fiction because bats don't talk • Mother bat comes back!	• qushens • Bats are nocturnal just like Marry said • Bats are the only mammals that can fly • On one page it asks You a quashen and on the other it anwsers for You. • On the top is says the main thing and on the bottom it tells You about it. • The chapter titles are qushens. • The words dicribs it better then the picter shows You. • Photograhs

Figure 3–5 *Leah and Amanda's comparison of books about bats*

Bats, a nonfiction structure we would later explore, and the photographs they found, a feature typical of nonfiction.

Before the week ended, we designed homework that would support our children in their new nonfiction work. We wanted the children to examine their home libraries as well as involve their families in this new investigation. We began with a questionnaire for the children

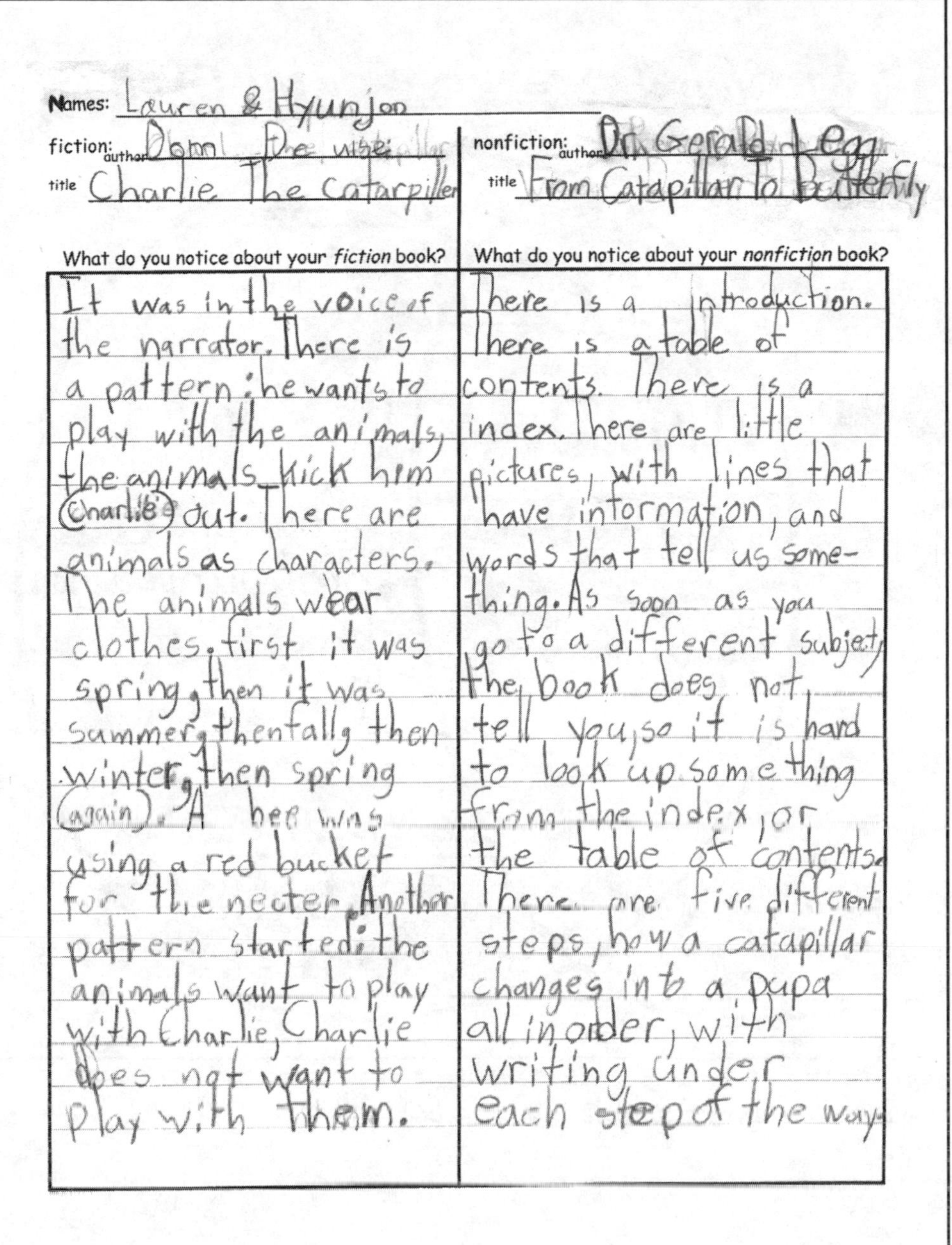

Names: Lauren & Hyunjoo

fiction: author Dom De wise title Charlie The Catarpiller	nonfiction: author Dr. Gerald Legg title From Catapillar To Butterfly
What do you notice about your *fiction* book?	What do you notice about your *nonfiction* book?
It was in the voice of the narrator. There is a pattern: he wants to play with the animals, the animals kick him (Charlie's) out. There are animals as characters. The animals wear clothes. first it was spring, then it was summer, then fall, then winter, then spring (again). A bee was using a red bucket for the necter. Another pattern started: the animals want to play with Charlie, Charlie does not want to play with them.	There is a introduction. There is a table of contents. There is a index. There are little pictures, with lines that have information, and words that tell us some-thing. As soon as you go to a different subject the book does not tell you, so it is hard to look up something from the index, or the table of contents. There are five different steps, how a catapillar changes into a pupa all in order, with writing under each step of the way.

Figure 3–6 *Lauren and Hyunjoo's comparison of books about caterpillars*

about the books they had at home. We asked them what kind of nonfiction they read, why they read it, and what they learned from reading it. (See Figure 3–8.)

In addition, the children went home to interview family members about their nonfiction reading lives (see Figure 3–9). Their answers

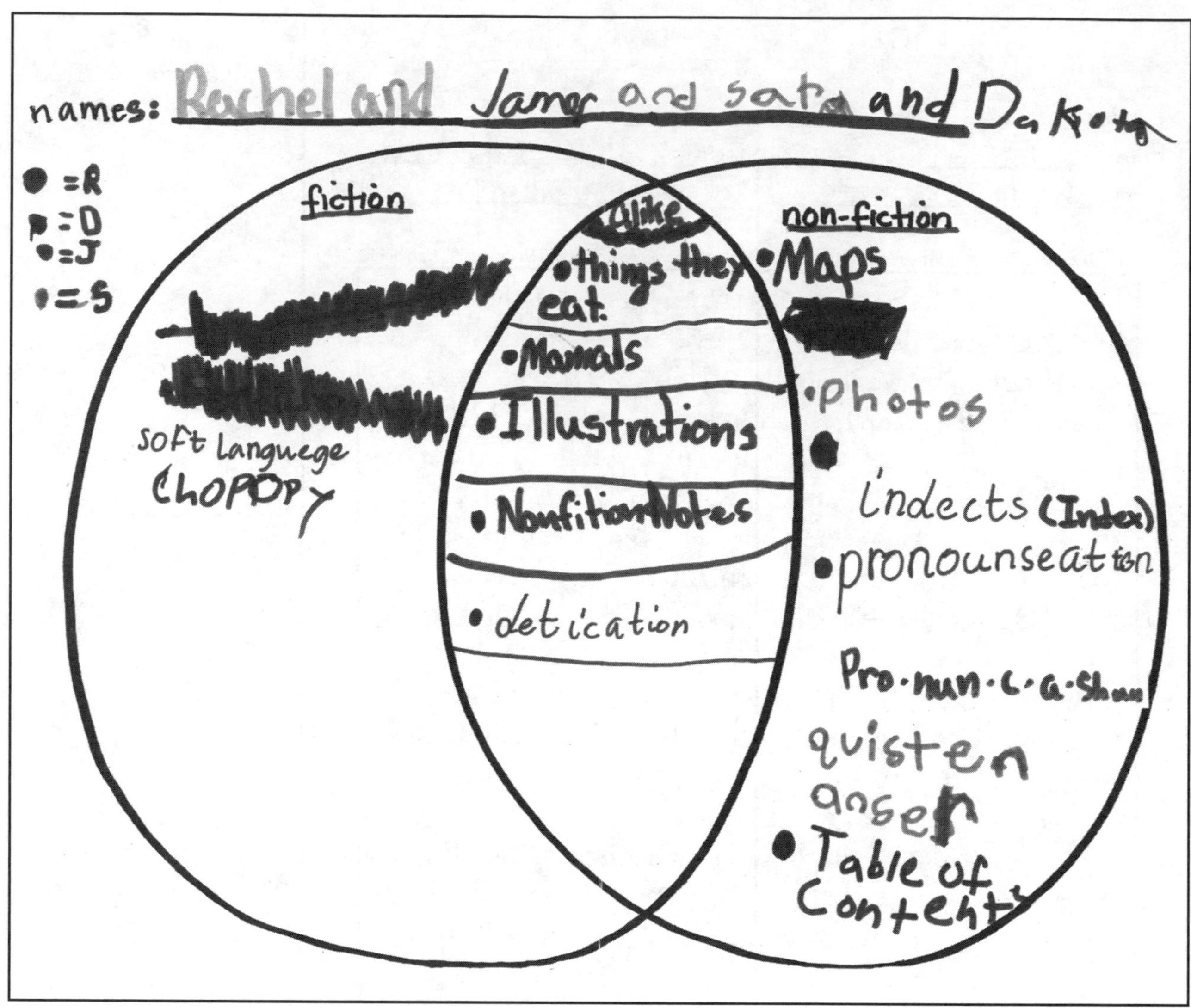

Figure 3–7 *Venn diagram: an alternative response to text sets*

enlightened our thinking about nonfiction reading while supporting the notion that people read nonfiction daily and for various purposes. The quantity and variety of nonfiction reading materials taught us a lot. The children were surprised to learn that recipes, a subway map, and a pamphlet describing a vacation spot are all examples of nonfiction reading. We put our children's interviews of their family members on a bulletin board labeled "Some Things Our Interviews Taught Us About Nonfiction." The family interviews helped children sort and classify nonfiction into categories (diaries, brochures, recipes, magazines, menus, etc.) and provided them with an opportunity to learn about the reading lives of

Name: Daniel date: ______

Questions about your own non-fiction reading

1. Do you have more fiction or non-fiction books in your home library? More fiction

2. List your three favorite non-fiction books.

Baseball Almanac
great dinosuar Atlas
Dictionary

3. Other than books, what non-fiction reading materials do you have in your house?

newspapers	Bank acount statements
computer manuals	Lego instructions
bills	News on t.v.
recipes	Labels

4. Think about one non-fiction book/piece you read this week.

What was it? Great dinosaur Atlas

Why did you choose to read it? because I wanted to know more about Dinosuars

What did you learn from reading it? I learned that there are a few more plant eaters then meat eaters.

5. Make a list of all non-fiction materials you read this week while out of school. This may include materials at home, at the doctor's office, on the bus, etc.

I read a eye chart at the doctor's office	sports section in newspaper
one way sign	Lego instructions
great Dinosaur atlas	Adress on a letter
read words on crisp ix cereal	read Label on shampoo bottle.

Figure 3–8 *Daniel's questionnaire about his own nonfiction reading*

their family members. We learned Marcelino's father read the newspaper to learn about events in Mexico, his home country. We learned that Eric's father had read a map for directions on how to get somewhere by subway, and Matthew's baby-sitter had read a recipe to learn how to make cornbread. We learned that Rachel's mother read the *New York*

Name Rachel **Date** ________

Person I'm interviewing Mommy

<u>Nonfiction Reading Interview</u>—We've begun our study of nonfiction this week. We'd like to learn about what kinds of nonfiction reading materials you used today.

Question #1

What are three nonfiction things you read today?

1. New york times
2. Articals for work
3. part of a dictionary

Question #2

Choose one of the nonfiction reading materials you read today. Why did you read it?

She read the dictionary Because, She wanted to know if a word was used right.

Question #3

Did you learn something you didn't know before from reading something nonfiction today? What was it?

She learnd more about Gorge bush's tax cut plan.

Figure 3–9 *Rachel's nonfiction reading interview*

Times for current news about George Bush's tax plan, and that Allie's baby brother read a nonfiction book about cars, a toy he loves to collect! The children ended week 1 of our Learning to Read Nonfiction study with a developing understanding of the various forms of nonfiction as well as the various purposes for reading it.

Week Two

Goal: to begin developing an understanding of different ways writers present nonfiction information

By the end of week 1, each partnership had examined many fiction-nonfiction text sets. In doing so, they developed some questions about the generalizations of fiction and the generalizations of nonfiction. These questions guided our discussions and helped us clarify what we knew about the two.

Do all nonfiction books have photographs?
Do only fiction books have dialogue?
Do all nonfiction books have questions and answers?
Does a nonfiction book have to be read from cover to cover?

We began to think deeply about the differences between fiction and nonfiction, looking more carefully at the fiction and nonfiction piles we had developed during week 1 of the study. We came to notice the varied use of illustration in nonfiction texts, dispelling the myth circulating the classroom that photography existed in all nonfiction books. We also noticed that some nonfiction books have dialogue while most, but not all, fiction books do. Lastly, we noticed how the structure of some nonfiction books demanded a cover-to-cover read while others offered the choice of dipping in, grabbing information, and dipping out.

In our attempt to separate fiction from nonfiction, we realized that several books straddled the fiction-nonfiction line. Did Jonathan London's *Phantom of the Prairie: Year of the Black Footed Ferret,* the life cycle story of the black-footed ferret, one of North America's most endangered species, belong in the fiction pile or the nonfiction pile? We relied on books like this to further the conversation and develop a deeper understanding of the elements of fiction and nonfiction. The children developed arguments for both sides as though they were preparing for the debate team finals. Devin and Ethan argued that *Phantom of the Prairie* was fiction. Devin said, "Phantom is the character's name, and in nonfiction the animals never have names."

Ethan continued, "When we read it, we all worried about the kits. In 'real' nonfiction, you're not supposed to worry about the animals."

Alexander countered the thinking of Devin and Ethan: "No, it *is* nonfiction because we learned a lot about the black-footed ferret. Before we read this book, I didn't know that ferrets call their young 'kits' or that they spend six weeks inside their mother before they're born."

A similar problem occurred when examining *The Whales,* by Cynthia Rylant. Doris, who adored the work of Cynthia Rylant, could not conceive of her writing a nonfiction book. "Cynthia Rylant is a fiction writer," Doris said. "She's written all my favorite series, including Cobble Street Cousins." Alexander was determined to prove that *The Whales* was nonfiction. He told the class how he'd learned a lot about whales when reading the book and how it even had a whale picture glossary in the back. Our students read and reread *The Whales,* some arguing that the words Cynthia Rylant used sounded more fictionlike while others located facts imbedded in the text. Here's what some children said after Mary Anne read *The Whales* aloud:

> It's nonfiction but in a fictional way.—Liam
> I think it's half fiction and half nonfiction because she's telling you about whales, but the idea is fiction.—James
> Cynthia Rylant puts a little bit of fiction in the story.—Caroline
> I learned from her writing that whales aren't so rough, they're gentle.—Rachel
> The picture glossary looks fake, not real like when authors use photos.—Grace

Investigating this book closely led to the discovery that not only had Cynthia Rylant written *The Whales,* she'd illustrated it, adding a whole new dimension to the allure of Cynthia Rylant. Was our beloved fiction writer an illustrator and perhaps the author of nonfiction? The children were whistling with the possibility. They looked to our Cynthia Rylant book basket to see if they could find other books she had either illustrated or written in a more nonfiction-like style. Doris, an artist herself, was excited to find that Cynthia Rylant *had* illustrated other books: *The Bookshop Dog, The Cookie Store Cat, Cat Heaven,* and *Dog Heaven.* Thinking that perhaps these too were written in a nonfiction way, Alexander searched them, looking for picture glossaries and imbedded facts about dogs and cats, to no avail. Alexander relented, stating that although Cynthia Rylant's other books were fiction, this book, *The Whales,* was certainly nonfiction.

To help focus our children's understanding of the difference between fiction and nonfiction, we gave each partnership a typed-text copy of *The Whales,* and we asked them to reread the text, highlighting the parts they considered fiction and the parts they considered nonfiction. This was a task they settled into quickly, hoping to uncover something that would definitively point to either fiction or nonfiction. Doris and Caroline decided to underline the fiction parts in purple and the nonfiction parts in yellow. Others thought this was a great idea and followed suit. As we listened in to Doris and Caroline's conversation, we heard them talking about the fiction qualities of the book, questioning the line "And under the Red Sea, their dreams are in color." "It has to be fiction," cried Doris. "How would Cynthia Rylant know if whales are dreaming?"

Caroline agreed, "You're right, she makes it seem like whales are human."

The question remained. The next day, Mary Anne read Faith McNulty's nonfiction text *How the Whales Walked into the Sea.* This book, new to the class, caught the children's attention. "It looks like the whales are ready to jump out at you," Pavel commented about the cover illustration.

"That's because they are more real looking," said Grace, "This book is probably more nonfiction than *The Whales.*"

As a way of demonstrating the difference between these two texts, Mary Anne compared an excerpt from Faith McNulty's *How Whales Walked into the Sea* with an excerpt from Cynthia Rylant's *The Whales* on the same subtopic—baby whales.

How the Whales Walked into the Sea, *by Faith McNulty*	The Whales, *by Cynthia Rylant*
Baby whales are born under water. The newborn quickly swims up for a breath of air.	Whales love their children, and when they are born, the babies are gently pushed to the top of the water where they take their first breath and see their first sky . . . .

Mary Anne read these two excerpts about baby whales, and the children began to notice some differences between the writing styles of Faith McNulty and Cynthia Rylant. "*How Whales Walked into the Sea* is more like scientific writing," Matthew said. Mary Anne led the children to consider the scientific versus storylike qualities of the two texts. She said: "Doesn't it sound like Faith McNulty used shorter, fact-like sentences?" Some children agreed, determining that Faith McNulty's style of writing about whales had a more scientific bent than Cynthia Rylant's.

"It feels like she's really trying to teach us about whales," commented Lindsay.

"But Cynthia Rylant teaches us, too. She names all the kinds of whales," Alexander rebutted.

Mary Anne called their attention back to the two excerpts, asking the children to identify what they learned from Faith McNulty's writing. "I learned that baby whales are born under water and after they're born, they swim to the top of the water for a breath of air," Jordana said.

"Cynthia Rylant is teaching us the same thing!" said Alexander. Nicholas agreed, stating that the only difference was that Cynthia Rylant used the word *children* to talk about the baby whales and Faith McNulty used the words *baby whales*. Even Alexander agreed that it would be unusual for an author writing a nonfiction text to refer to baby whales as *children*.

We began to see these two pieces differently, noticing how an author's choice of words can affect a reader's perception of the text. Mary Anne supported the children as they commented on the details and poetic nature of the writing in *The Whales* excerpt and the short, fact-filled sentences in the excerpt from *How the Whales Walked into the Sea*. Mary Anne sent the children off that day to further examine the writing in these two books, this time using excerpts from each book again about the same topic—the thoughts of whales.

By the end of the week, everyone had agreed that *How the Whales Walked into the Sea* was certainly more nonfiction in nature than *The Whales*. We started to rethink the latter book's classification, going back to something James had said the first time we read *The Whales:* "I think it's half fiction and half nonfiction because she's [Cynthia Rylant] telling you about whales, but the idea is fiction." Reviewing this comment was very supportive. We started to think about names other than *fiction* or *nonfiction* to label the writing that James referred to as "half fiction, half nonfiction." Before finally settling on *informational fiction,* our children went through lots of possibilities: *narrative nonfiction, imaginative nonfiction, storylike nonfiction, learning fiction,* and even *faction*. Once we named this fiction-nonfiction hybrid, we sent the children off to find others that could easily fit into this category. We were surprised to find so many. Here's a sample of some of the books they found that easily fit into the category of informational fiction.

Honey Paw and Lightfoot, by Jonathan London
Baby Whale's Journey, by Jonathan London
Growing Frogs, by Vivian French
Two Orphan Cubs, by Barbara Brenner and May Garelick
Bumblebee at Apple Tree Lane, by Laura Gates Galvin
The Moonflower, by Peter and Jean Loewer
Pond Year, by Kathryn Lasky
Where Butterflies Grow, by Joanne Ryder
Welcome to the Greenhouse, by Jane Yolen

By the end of week 2, our children were becoming aware of and identifying the many ways in which writers could present nonfiction information.

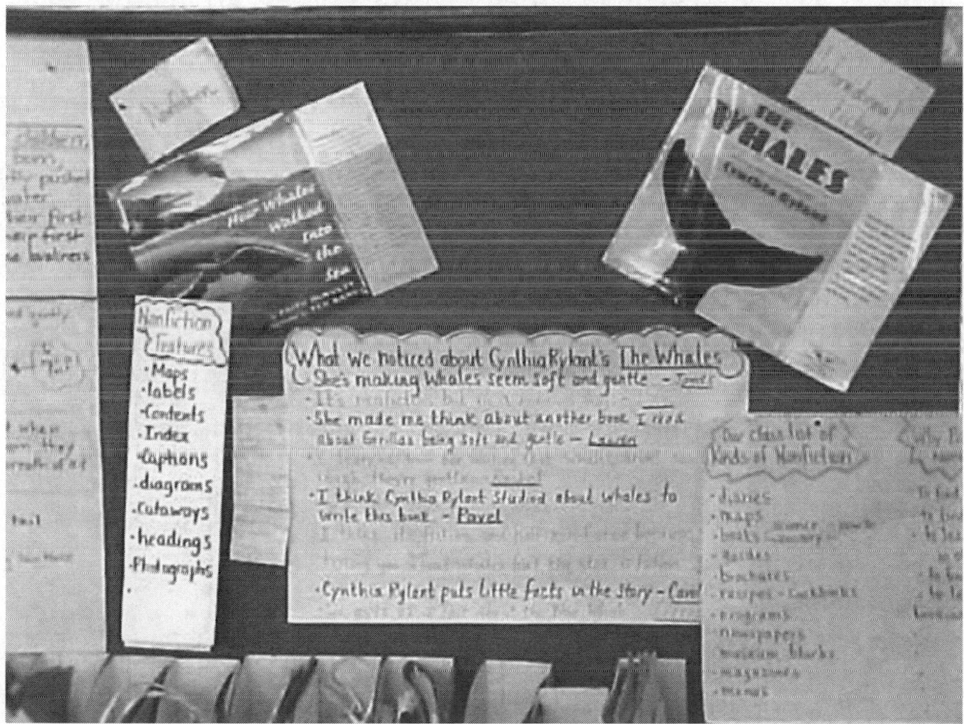

Figure 3–10 *Bulletin board display of fiction versus nonfiction study using books about whales*

Week Three

Goal: to develop an awareness of the features and structures of nonfiction

In the first two weeks of the study, our children developed an understanding of the differences between fiction and nonfiction and some of the ways in which writers present nonfiction information. Now it was time to look more closely at the features and structures of the nonfiction books in our library. In preparing for this next stage, we gathered nonfiction books of various genres and topics and put them into assorted baskets, rejecting the temptation to organize them by subject, author, or structure. These were discoveries we wanted the children to make.

We began with the journal-like nonfiction book *Salamander Rain: A Lake and Pond Journal,* by Kristin Joy Pratt-Serafini, to model the work we wanted the children to do in their partnerships. We chose this book because it contained many nonfiction features and structures that the children had yet to examine and because the colorful pages made ideas easy to share. During the initial reading, we asked the children to look at the feature-filled pages to see which features grabbed their attention. Chelsea excitedly reported that the borders around the pages gave us lots of information. Ethan talked about the field guide quality of the book, while Dakota focused in on the index cards containing main character Klint's journal entries. After the initial read, Jenna noticed that the journal entry writing started in the spring and took us through each season. The list of features grew as some commented on the bold print, website and bibliography lists, question-and-answer trivia, newspaper clippings, and font styles. Other children noticed the various writing structures: editorials, feature articles, scientific field guide information, fun facts, and more. As a way of helping the children distinguish between features and structures, we sorted their noticings into two categories on our chart: Supportive Text Features, which helped us locate information, and Supportive Writing Structures, which dictated how to approach the text as a reader.

Features and structures in *Salamander Rain: A Lake and Pond Journal*

Supportive Text Features	*Supportive Writing Structures*
• journal entries • border illustrations	• journal entries • first-person narration—"I" voice

Supportive Text Features	*Supportive Writing Structures*
• author's note • bold print • fact boxes • postcards • bibliography • websites • captions • newspaper clippings • illustrations • labels	• question-and-answer section • editorials • feature articles • fun facts • postcard writing • how-to/instructional writing • lists

Before sending the children off on their own to examine the features and structures of the books in our nonfiction library, we modeled the reading log they were to use during this week. Karen placed a transparency of the reading log on an overhead projector and recorded the noticings the class made during the initial read of *Salamander Rain: A Lake and Pond Journal*. She wove the children's responses into her model of how to write a short paragraph. It was this style of recording the children would need to do this week in their partnerships.

The following day we repeated the minilesson using *Wacky Plant Cycles,* by Valerie Wyatt. We also chose this book for its variety of features and structures. We knew the conversation would be enriched by the contrast between the parallel informational narrative voice that taught us about the cycle of plants and the fictionlike quality of the book's main character, who also taught us about the cycle of plants. Following two voices in the text had the potential to be tricky; however, we were confident that exposure to various nonfiction texts from the previous weeks would prove supportive.

Karen read a few sections of the text first through the voice of the narrative writing and then through the voice of the character. She knew the children would pick up on the different writing structures as well as the different text features. The text proved engaging. Stephanie immediately noticed the cartoon character featured alongside the sciencelike, labeled photographs. Diana also noticed the book's features when she commented on the diagrams and bold print within the initial pages of the text. After listing some of the children's initial noticings, Karen addressed the children's comments while she shifted their thinking toward writing structure. "Your findings have mostly to do with what you *see* in the text. Listen again to what you *hear* as I reread the first couple of pages." As Karen reread, she called their attention to the differences in writing styles between the two parallel texts. Similar to the discoveries they'd made when comparing the writing in *The Whales* with the writing in *How the Whales Walked into the Sea,* the children commented on the contrast between information presented in a scientific way and information presented in a more entertaining way. They were clearly more taken by the entertaining voice of the character in the text.

"The character sometimes speaks into a bubble, like in a comic book," said Devin.

"It's like he is talking to us, like he wants us to answer," Nicholas suggested. Nicholas was referring to the way the character engaged him with the question "Do you like peanut butter sandwiches? Peanuts are actually seeds. So is the grain used to make the bread. How many other seeds can you find in your kitchen?"

The children spent the week developing an awareness of the features and structures of nonfiction. Just as we had examined the texts of *Salamander Rain* and *Wacky Plant Cycles,* noticing and recording the features and structures important to each text, the children did the same with other books in our library. Stephen and Xanyani noticed the storylike structure of *Winter Solstice,* by Ellen Jackson, while Allie and Sara noticed the picture glossary and the "fakelike" illustrations in *World Water Watch,* by Michelle Koch (see Figure 3–11). Rachel commented on the many nonfiction features she noticed in *Birds,* by Jill Bailey (see Figure 3–12), and Lauren wrote about the surprise of finding dialogue in her "storylike" nonfiction text (see Figure 3–13).

Week Four

Goal: to develop strategies for reading nonfiction

Now that our children had developed an awareness of the features and structures of nonfiction, we needed to provide them with the strategies they would need to successfully and independently navigate through a

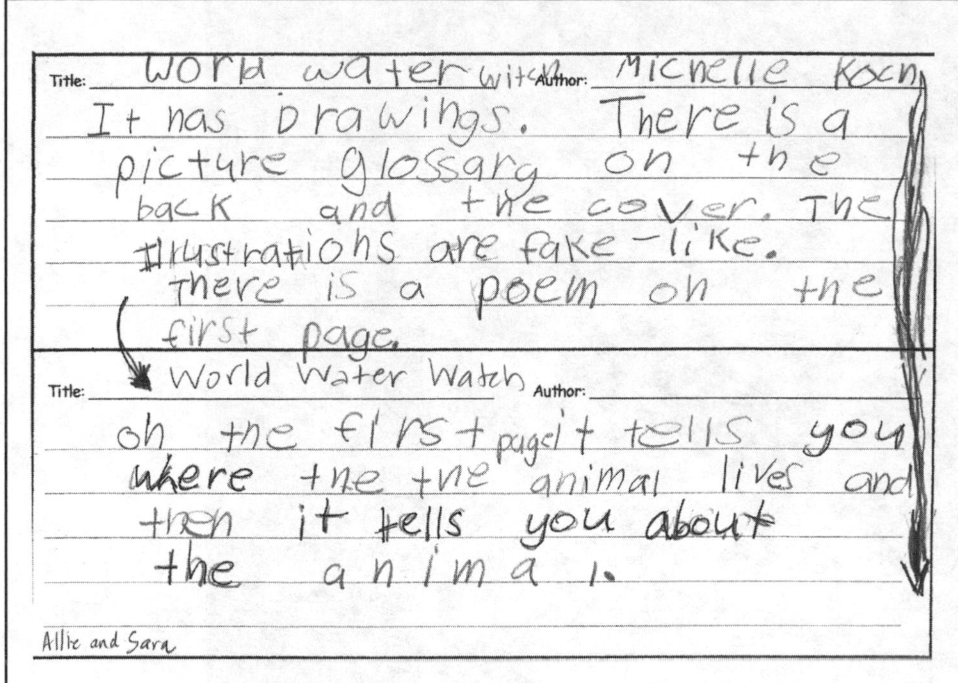
Title: World water witch Author: Michelle Koch
It has Drawings. There is a picture glossary on the back and the cover. The illustrations are fake-like. There is a poem on the first page.

Title: World Water Watch Author:
on the first page it tells you where the the animal lives and then it tells you about the animal.

Allie and Sara

Figure 3–11
Allie and Sara's log of nonfiction features and structures

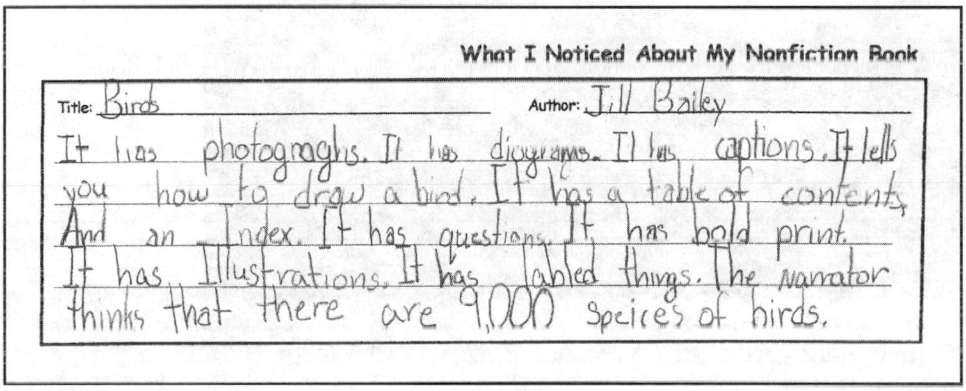

What I Noticed About My Nonfiction Book

Title: Birds Author: Jill Bailey
It has photograghs. It has diagrams. It has captions. It tells you how to draw a bird. It has a table of contents And an Index. It has questions. It has bold print. It has Illustrations. It has labled things. The narrator thinks that there are 9,000 speices of birds.

Figure 3–12
Rachel's log of nonfiction features and structures

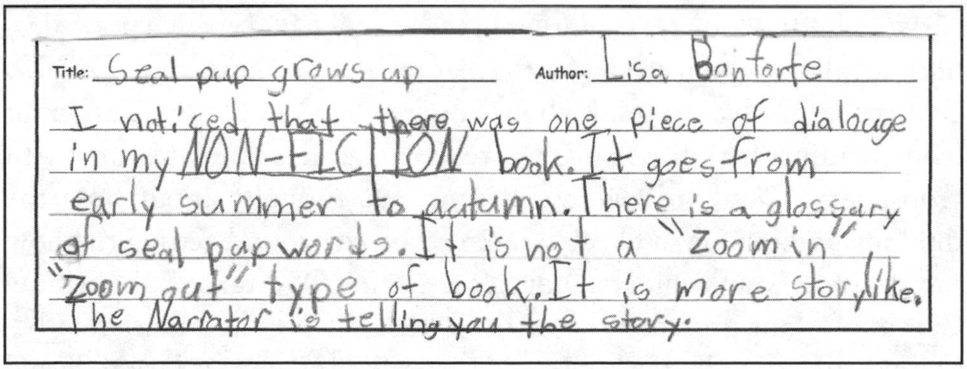

Title: Seal pup grows up Author: Lisa Bonforte
I noticed that there was one piece of dialouge in my NON-FICTION book. It goes from early summer to autumn. There is a glossary of seal pup words. It is not a "Zoom in" "Zoom out" type of book. It is more story like. The Narrator is telling you the story.

Figure 3–13
Lauren's log of nonfiction features and structures

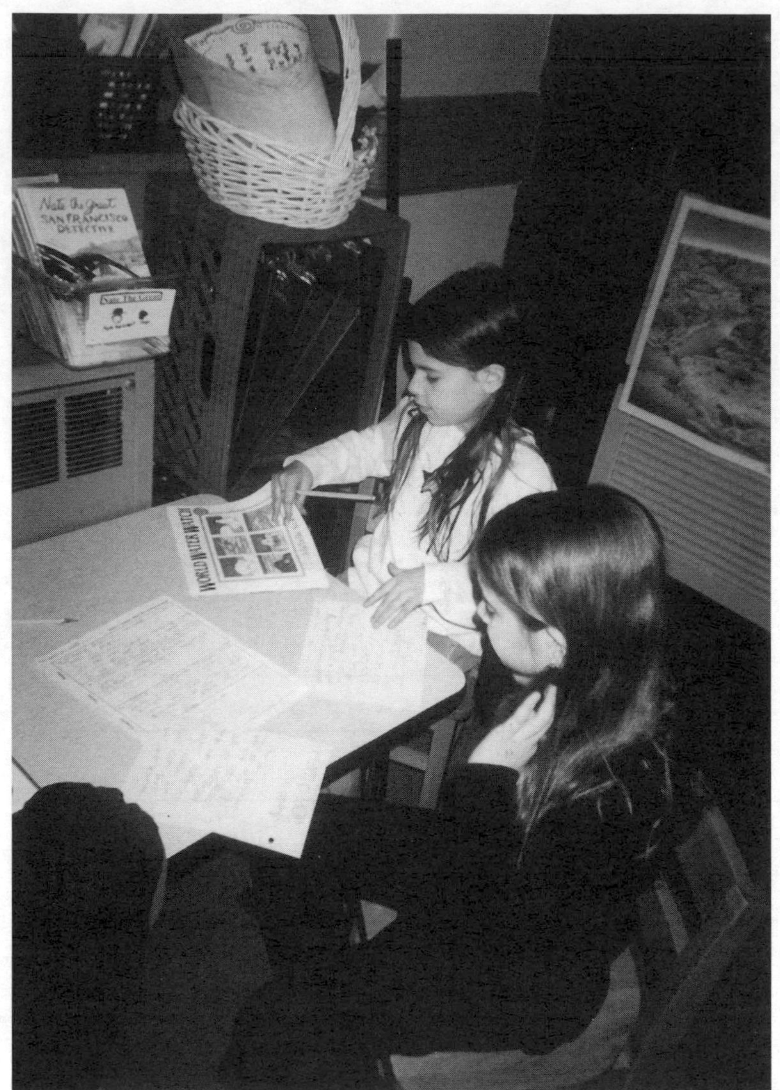

Figure 3–14 *Allie and Sara examine* World Water Watch

variety of nonfiction texts. Earlier in the year, we had spent a good deal of time talking about strategies for reading fiction. This study led us to challenge ourselves to think about how reading nonfiction is different from reading fiction. Again, we relied on our shared history with *Gooseberry Park,* by Cynthia Rylant. We thought about how the thinking and talking in the classroom revolved around getting to know the characters and understanding the setting. We talked about how Cynthia Rylant provided the reader with a setting that alternated between Professor Albert's house and Gooseberry Park, and we reflected on Kona's relationship with each of the characters in the story.

Over the course of this study, it was clear that the children were approaching nonfiction in a different way than they had fiction. Although they were enthusiastic and answering self-generated questions on topics of interest, we knew they weren't as equipped for success as they had been when reading fiction. Our young readers entered second grade with an understanding of the way fiction works. Read-aloud choices tended to be fiction both at home and at school. In addition, we deepened our children's confidence as fiction readers as we studied series and examined dialogue. They came to understand story elements and the predictability of fiction. Nonfiction, however, was less familiar and less predictable. We knew in order to set the children up for independence and success in reading nonfiction, we had to teach strategies for approaching an unfamiliar nonfiction text with an unfamiliar layout and structure. We also knew that we would have to show our children how those elements could support them as readers.

Karen began with *A Wood Frog's Life,* by John Himmelman, and *My Favorite Tree: Terrific Trees of North America,* by Diane Iverson, to demonstrate how different structures suggest a different type of read. Although unfamiliar with *A Wood Frog's Life,* some of our children had previously read *A Dandelion's Life* and *A Salamander's Life,* books from the same series by John Himmelman. "I know what to expect from this book because I read one just like it about salamanders," said Nicki.

Ethan agreed that the salamander book was from the same series, noting, "This book will probably show us the wood frog's life cycle, just like the salamander book taught us about the salamander's life cycle. I also know there is a big picture of the author in the back next to the glossary." It seemed that knowing the work of an author was supportive when approaching another text by the same author. We knew that since Ethan and Nicki would not have to work hard to figure out the layout of this text, they could concentrate on the content information and learn a bit about the wood frog.

Before reading *A Wood Frog's Life,* Karen browsed the pages with the children and asked if they thought this book would be one she would need to read from cover to cover or one of which she might dip in and dip out. Devin said that he hadn't read any of the others in the series but that it looked more storylike and, therefore, would probably need to be read from cover to cover. Ethan chimed in, "Well, I read the others just like it, and I *know* you can't just turn to the middle of the book to find information. You have to start at the beginning if you want to understand the wood frog's life cycle."

Karen read the text confirming that, indeed, the structure suggested a cover-to-cover read. Karen led the children to think about all the questions they might ask themselves before approaching an unfamiliar nonfiction text. After generating a list of questions as a class that the students were to use during reading time, Karen sent the children off to approach unfamiliar nonfiction. Here are the questions they kept close at hand:

What is the layout?
How is the information presented?
What are the specific features?
What questions do I have that might be answered in this book?
What is the structure of this text?
How will I read this book—cover to cover or dip in and dip out?
Do I know this author? If so, what have I come to expect from him or her?

The following day, we chose to highlight *My Favorite Tree: Terrific Trees of North America,* by Diane Iverson, a nonfiction book with a different structure than *A Wood Frog's Life*. Before browsing the pages of this text, Karen reviewed the previous day's questions about what to keep in mind when approaching a nonfiction text. In a wondering tone, she modeled the thinking behind those questions. "I'm not familiar with this author's writing or the way she likes to present information. I see from the title that this book is about trees, but I don't know if the book is storylike, suggesting a cover-to-cover read, or more reference-like, allowing me to dip in and out. What do you think?"

"I think the little girl on the front cover is going to tell about her favorite tree," said Amanda.

"It looks almost like fiction; even the pictures are fake-like," Sara said.

As Karen browsed through the pages of *My Favorite Tree,* the children noticed the nonfiction qualities of each right-hand page and the fiction qualities of each left-hand page. Leah called out as Karen approached the page devoted to oak trees. She noticed the sign that hung from the gambel oak tree, "No boys allowed." This caused a stir, as it seemed the girls on the left-hand page of the text had a secret tree fort, claiming the gambel oak for themselves. As we looked to the right, we noticed many nonfiction features. We easily located information pertaining to the tree's habitat, height, leaves, and bark as well as some interesting facts and information about oak trees and the wild companions they host. The children recognized this book as a field guide. "It tells us about all different kinds of trees. I bet it has a table of contents that shows which tree is on which page," said Nicholas. And it did; Nicholas was right. After reading parts of the book, Karen referred to her initial questions and wonderings about how to read the text and what the layout might look like, leading the class to determine that *My Favorite Tree* was more like a field guide and wasn't necessarily meant to be read from cover to cover. The children also noticed differences between the photolike illustrations on the right-hand pages and the scenic, "kidlike" illustrations on the left-hand pages. These differences allowed them to discover facts through illustration while imagining themselves as the child in the text sitting by the tree. We concluded that this book would be great for someone studying trees who wanted to dip into the text, locate what she needed, and dip back out.

Our children were now comfortable approaching a nonfiction text. They knew it was important to understand how the book worked before reading it. Many referred to the chart of questions each time they approached a new nonfiction text while others internalized the questions. Now our children were ready for strategies that would help them monitor their comprehension of nonfiction, supporting them in their successful negotiation of nonfiction texts. Although some strategies they'd learned as readers of fiction could be easily transferred to nonfiction, our children would need additional strategies in order to successfully negotiate the complexities of nonfiction.

Here's a list of those strategies we taught our children, along with the ways they would implement them in their own reading.

Some nonfiction strategies

Strategy	*Ways Children Would Implement Strategy*
Compare information in book with what you already know about a particular topic. Process and synthesize information.	Ask yourself: "How does this fit in with what I already know about . . . ?" • Stop to think and rethink what you are learning while reading a book.

Strategy	*Ways Children Would Implement Strategy*
	• When the format allows, read in chunks. • Reread difficult parts or parts you want to remember. • Listen to internal voice that says: "Wow, that's surprising!"
Question to layer what you know with what you want to know.	Develop lingering questions: "I wonder . . . ."
Critique book for accuracy or for contradictions with other books.	Ask yourself: "How is this different from what I learned when I read . . . ?"
Move between pictures and text to make sense while reading.	Ask yourself: "What do the pictures and the writing have to do with one another? How are they related?"

By the end of week 4, our children had developed strategies for entering a nonfiction text and monitoring their understanding. With this new self-assurance, our children felt as confident in their nonfiction reading as they did in their fiction reading. They were excited for reading workshop to begin and disappointed when it ended. At the end of the week we reflected back on our nonfiction reading work and asked the children how they felt when reading nonfiction. The following comments were indicative of the confidence and excitement they now carried with them into their nonfiction reading lives.

> I feel like I'm learning so much [that] I want to read more.—Lindsay
>
> It depends on what kind of nonfiction book I'm reading. If it is a biography, sometimes it makes me sad because somebody could kill somebody. If it is a book that explains something, I want to read more of the book.—Sara
>
> I feel smart because nonfiction gives me information about nature, animals, space, bugs, and mammals. I know what to call the animals because some are labeled.—Nubia
>
> When I read nonfiction books, I feel that I am learning more about the subject and I am more interested in the book, which makes me want to read more.—Aldin

Week Five

Goal: to deepen our understanding of nonfiction features

We ended week 4's work secure that our children's understanding of nonfiction strategies would help them not only enter a text with confidence but also monitor their own understanding as they negotiated the varieties and variables of nonfiction. We were uncertain, however, about the depth of their understanding of how to use nonfiction features to locate information and support reading. We looked back to the chart we started in week 3, and expanded on the nonfiction features we found.

table of contents
tables
cutaways
bibliography
italics
illustrations
graphs
titles
websites

distribution maps
borders
color print
glossary
clippings
fonts
labels
captions

boldface print
index
cycle maps
diagrams
author's note
bullets
photographs
fact boxes

It was time to take a closer look at the features that would most support their reading. The features that stood out the most to us were the table of contents, the glossary, and the index. Knowing the basic purpose of these features was not enough. We knew that developing an understanding for *how to use* these three nonfiction features would give our children autonomy over their reading and eventually over their research. We set out to design three ministudies to deepen their understanding of these important features. This week would be spent exposing our children to this trio through a series of minilessons.

We came to understand and develop strategies for managing the unpredictable nature of nonfiction structures. We realized that one of the ways of dealing with an unpredictable text was to understand the infrastructure of the book—the table of contents, the glossary, and the index. In week 4, when commenting about the layout of *My Favorite Tree,* Nicholas stated, "It tells us about all different kinds of trees. I bet it has a table of contents that shows which tree is on which page." Without knowing so, Nicholas was referring to the integral role the table of contents plays in helping one locate information and successfully navigate text.

We began by examining the table of contents feature, one with which we were familiar from our study of fiction series. In the fall, our children learned how a table of contents helped readers make predictions about what was going to happen in a story. We remembered back to our examination of the *Pinky and Rex* series and discussed how the chapter titles listed in the table of contents helped us make predictions and supported our understanding of the story. Understanding how to use a table of contents in our fiction texts served as an entryway into the work we would do to understand this feature and its purpose in nonfiction texts.

As in all of our studies or inquiries, we wanted to know what the children knew about the subject we were to study. Mary Anne asked, "What is a table of contents?"—a big question that revealed their current understanding.

Eric responded, "A table of contents helps you know what you are going to find before reading the book."

Katie made a connection to the fiction book she was reading when she stated, "Just like in *Cobble Street Cousins,* by Cynthia Rylant, the table of contents in nonfiction tells me what the chapters are going to be about."

Stephen answered, "A table of contents page tells us where to go to find the information we are looking for to answer our questions." Stephen's response was different. He addressed *why* nonfiction readers would use a table of contents, an understanding we hoped all the children would own by the end of week 5's ministudy.

In our planning, we searched our nonfiction books, looking for a good variety of table of contents pages. We found some that simply listed the contents in a straightforward way, some that listed subcategories and used bold print to highlight main categories, and others with clever chapter titles that left us wondering exactly what each chapter was about. The marked-up copy of one table of contents page in Figure 3–15 illustrates the thinking behind our planning.

We used this example in our first minilesson to demonstrate the workings of a table of contents. It was a perfect first example because while it is rather straightforward in design, it has variables such as different font styles and subcategories to negotiate. Mary Anne placed a blank version of this contents page on the overhead projector. The children noticed some of its obvious visual qualities. They noticed the

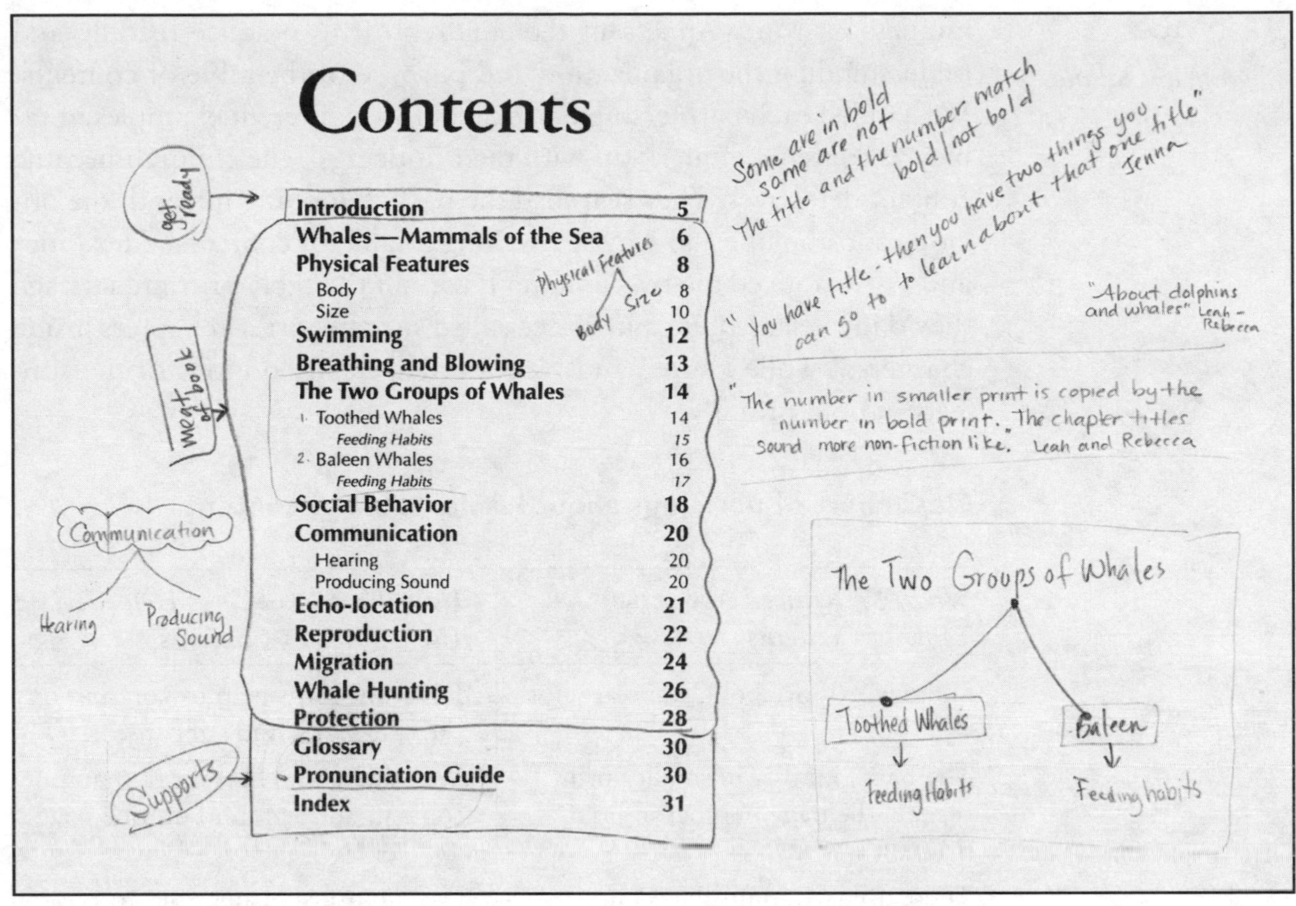

Figure 3–15 *Marked-up table of contents from* Whales, *by Joan Short and Bettina Bird*

indentation under certain categories, such as "Physical Features" and "Communication," where more specific information could be found. These noticings addressed the variables of this particular table of contents and were recorded on the class chart we made (see page 104). We looked beyond the list of noticings, stretching ourselves to think about *how* these noticings helped us use the table of contents. For example, when Eric noticed "some words are bold, some are not," Mary Anne asked the children why they thought the information was presented to the reader that way. Sara thought that perhaps the writer wanted us, as readers, to be clear about the "important," or "main," information in the book. Leah brought up the fact that the page number in smaller print sometimes repeated the number in bold print. She was referring to how some pages were divided into subcategories. This would help a reader zoom in to locate very specific information. After the minilesson, Mary Anne sent the children off to practice reading and understanding the organization and purpose of the table of contents. We handed each partnership a packet of three different examples of tables of contents to mark up with their noticings. The children became content detectives. They searched the packet, looking for both the obvious and the unusual ways of writing a table of contents. Alexander and Katie noticed the two-column layout of the table of contents page they'd investigated. Eli and Grace called subcategories "chapters inside chapters," while Lauren and Nubia called them "options of the subjects in bold print."

Class chart of noticings about *Whales* table of contents

What We Noticed About the Table of Contents	*How These Noticings Help Us Use a Table of Contents*
Some words are bold, some are not.	Different fonts help us zoom in on the categories and subcategories.
The page number in smaller print repeats the page number in bold print.	We understand that more than one topic might be found on one page.
There are two minisubjects underneath the title "Communication," where you learn more about it.	We can use subcategories to find more specific information about what we are looking for.
I notice other features, like the index and glossary, are listed in the table of contents.	We can look to the table of contents to help us locate other supportive features within the text.

Over the next few days, our children used their newly developed understanding of the workings of a table of contents to help them confront the table of contents pages in their own nonfiction reading. We continued our ministudy of features and shifted the focus from examining tables of contents to examining glossaries. Just as we did with the table of contents, we chose a few good examples of glossaries of varying style and form. Fortunately, we didn't need to look far. Our nonfiction library provided us with many inviting glossary examples. We were surprised at the variety and creativity authors used in designing them. *It's a Frog's Life* contains a glossary that includes illustrations and is written in the same catchy "I"-voice writing as the rest of the text. We found straightforward picture glossaries and more complicated ones. We even found a glossaried index, which essentially combined two features into one.

Asking the children the familiar question What is a glossary? led to basic responses. "A glossary tells about the important words in a book," said Jeanine.

"A glossary is a list of words at the end of a book," Diana added. "It describes the words."

The children had some understanding that a glossary is included in many nonfiction books. They didn't understand its purpose, structure, or how the reader might use it. Mary Anne began by putting the glossary from the familiar book *How the Whales Walked into the Sea* on the overhead projector. Immediately the children noticed the pictures alongside the words and the bold print woven into the writing labeling each whale. Mary Anne read about the humpback and the bowhead, the first two glossary definitions listed. Diana was puzzled. She had noticed that some other glossaries were alphabetized, and this one was not. "Why would Faith McNulty put the humpback before the bowhead?" she asked. James remembered that the humpback was the first whale pictured in the book. Clearly, we needed to better understand the organization of a glossary.

The children went off in partnerships with a packet of three glossaries from different books. We asked them to investigate whether or not a glossary followed the order of the contents of a book, like the one from *How the Whales Walked into the Sea*, or was alphabetized like Diana had mentioned. The classroom was buzzing over this question. The children were intent on determining if their glossaries had the same orderlike quality of Faith McNulty's glossary or if they were alphabetized. Victor and Jeanine quickly noticed the words in the glossary in *Wacky Plant Cycles* were listed in alphabetical order. They marked "ABC" on the top as way of recording their thinking as they moved on to one of the other glossaries in the packet. Diana excitedly made this same discovery, announcing to her partner, Karla, "I knew glossaries were in alphabetical order. I don't understand why Faith McNulty wouldn't have put the whale names in alphabetical order, too!" Karla noticed the glossary from *Wacky Plant Cycles* looked like a dictionary with a boldfaced word, a colon, and a definition.

Alexander and Nicholas were focused on the glossary from *It's a Frog's Life,* by Steve Parker. They weren't as interested in the alphabetical order or unusual title of the glossary, "Difficult Words I've Learned from Know-It-All Newt," as they were in the voice of the writing. They giggled as they realized that the frog himself was defining the difficult words from the text. Starting with *a*, Nicholas read the definition for *amphibian:* "A creature that can live in water and on land (like me!)."

Alexander scanned from *a* down to *d*, locating and chuckling to Nicholas as he read the definition for *dung:* "Newt says this is waste stuff that comes out of your rear end. Deer make mountains of it near the Pond!"

When the children returned to the rug, they were eager to share their findings. Diana was proud to announce that all of the glossaries they had examined were organized in alphabetical order. She suggested to the class that perhaps Faith McNulty's "glossary" was not actually a glossary. Stephen agreed. He noted that although the *Whales* glossary provided information like a regular glossary, it was organized in order of contents, making it a mixture of a table of contents and a glossary.

We followed the same process of inquiry for the study of indices. By the end of the week, the children had deepened their understanding of the three nonfiction features that would support them as readers and, eventually, researchers of nonfiction. The minilessons and practice packets we had provided allowed them to develop generalizations about tables of contents, glossaries, and indices. On the last day of this ministudy, the children searched through our entire collection of texts, looking to support their theories and generalizations. We also provided them the time to think about how these three features helped them as readers. Figure 3–16 shows an example of the log Stephen kept that demonstrates how each of the three features helped him as a reader of nonfiction.

Week Six

Goal: to reinforce and practice lessons learned from study

Over the course of this study, the children developed an appreciation for reading nonfiction. They had sorted through our nonfiction library many times and had made discoveries and organized books by topic, writing structure, and author. Although our nonfiction collection represented the work of many authors, our children came to notice that some authors, such as Jim Arnosky, Jonathan London, Joanne Ryder,

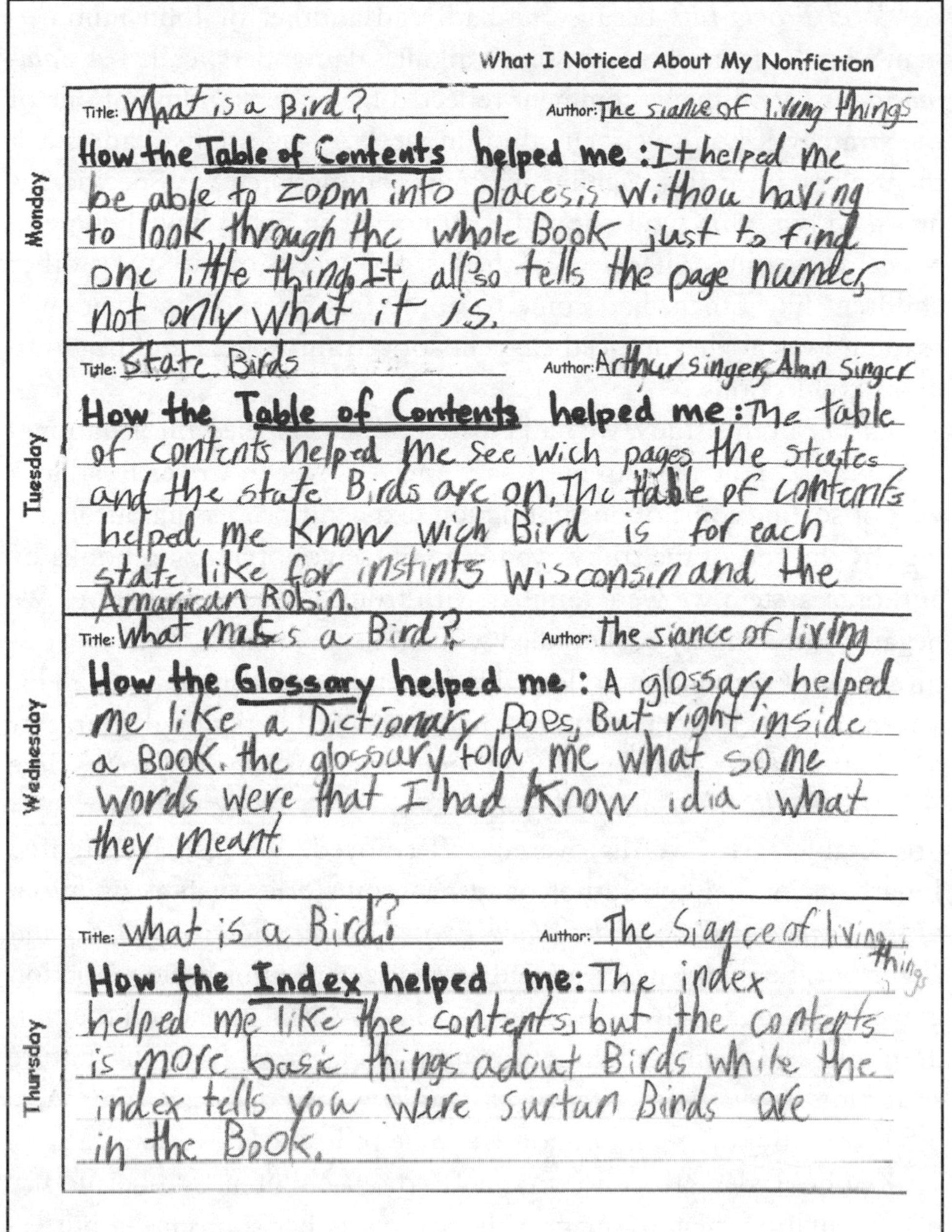
What I Noticed About My Nonfiction

Monday
Title: What is a Bird? Author: The siance of living things
How the Table of Contents helped me: It helped me be able to zoom into places, withou having to look through the whole Book just to find one little thing. It allso tells the page numbers not only what it is.

Tuesday
Title: State Birds Author: Arthur singer, Alan Singer
How the Table of Contents helped me: The table of contents helped me see wich pages the states and the state Birds are on. The table of contents helped me know wich Bird is for each state like for instints Wisconsin and the American Robin.

Wednesday
Title: What makes a Bird? Author: The siance of living
How the Glossary helped me: A glossary helped me like a Dictionary Does, But right inside a Book. the glossary told me what some words were that I had know idia what they meant.

Thursday
Title: what is a Bird? Author: The Siance of living things
How the Index helped me: The index helped me like the contents, but the contents is more basic things adout Birds while the index tells you were surtun Birds are in the Book.

Figure 3–16 *Stephen's nonfiction reading log*

and Gail Gibbons, had written several books. In many cases books by the same author, although about different topics, followed the same structure. These more prolific authors stood out, as they provided us with the same comforts and supports we felt when reading fiction books in series. The comfort of predictability was a concept Ethan spoke about when telling the class that he knew what to expect from

A Wood Frog's Life because he had read another of John Himmelman's books from the same series about salamanders, called *A Salamander's Life*. Ethan's comment reflected his understanding of one of the strategy lessons we focused on in week 4—questions readers ask themselves when approaching unfamiliar nonfiction texts. Specifically, he asked himself: "Do I know this author? If so, what have I come to expect from him or her?" Over the last few weeks of the study, other children, like Ethan, had come to apply this question to their own reading lives as they noticed elements of certain writers and began to make connections.

Earlier in this study, we had created baskets labeled Informational Fiction, A Dip in and Dip out Read, and A Cover-to-Cover Read as a way of sorting some of our nonfiction texts and processing our learning. By the end of the study, we found ourselves organizing books by author, a system we were familiar with from our work in fiction. We began a Jim Arnosky basket filled with books from his Crinkleroot nature series. Our children followed this friendly woodsman through his adventures in the same way they had the loveable fictional character Mr. Putter. In the same basket, we kept other Jim Arnosky books, like *All About Alligators* and *All About Deer*. These, too, were part of a predictable series we discovered and enjoyed. We also highlighted Jonathan London, the author of suspenseful stories such as *Phantom of the Prairie: A Year of the Black-Footed Ferret* and *Honey Paw and Lightfoot,* books we had read and categorized as informational fiction in week 2 of our study. These books had a powerful impact on the children and sent them searching for more books from London's nature collection. *Gone Again Ptarmigan* and *The Eyes of Great Wolf* were other titles by Jonathan London we came to love.

Joanne Ryder, an author that enticed our children into her nature world, inviting them to imagine themselves as her subjects—a butterfly, a snail, a lizard, and so on—and Gail Gibbons, author of more than one hundred informational books for children and perhaps the most prolific and recognizable author in the class, became the two authors on whom we would focus as we reinforced and practiced the lessons learned from this study. We wanted our children to distinguish with ease between different kinds of nonfiction, understanding the role and application of various features. We knew that the reinforcement work this week would provide our children opportunities to apply what they'd learned while exposing them to a more in-depth look at two nonfiction writers they had come to recognize.

As a way of planning for this week, we sat down with a stack of books by Gail Gibbons and Joanne Ryder. We looked through these stacks, knowing that this week we would ask our children to do the same. We examined them for voice, writing structure and style, illustrations, page layout, titles, and features, all elements we knew we wanted our children to discover and discuss. We designed the following sheet to support our own thinking and planning for week 6.

Planning for instruction: Looking closely at the work and supports of two nonfiction writers

	Gail Gibbons	*Joanne Ryder*
Voice	third person—reporting and informing on subject	second person—invitation to imagine oneself as subject
Writing Structure/ Style	• narrative • procedural, or how-to, writing • fact writing	• poetic • story-like
Illustration Style	• cartoonlike • distinctly separated, not blended	• soft, blended • habitat-rich
Page Layout	• text below illustrations • illustrations and text separate • boxed-in illustrations; left page different from right page	• text placement varied • illustrations and text blend together • mostly double-page illustrations—spread across two pages
Titles	straightforward—generally one word	poetic—phrase-like
Features	• diagrams • labeling • time lines • cycle maps • fun facts page • pronunciation keys • how-to instructions • maps • inserts • varied fonts	• close-up boxes • cycle maps

In week 5, we worked through a series of three ministudies about the specific features we thought were most useful in understanding the backbone of nonfiction. We began with big questions like What is a glossary? and What is an index? This week would begin similarly, only we would be asking our children what they knew about specific authors rather than specific features. We began the week prepared with two of our author baskets—one filled with books written by Gail Gibbons and the other filled with books written by Joanne Ryder. Before asking the children the question "What do you know about Gail Gibbons and her collection of books?" Karen told them that this week, they would be looking more closely at books written by both Gail Gibbons and Joanne Ryder. Jeannine was excited, stating that she loved Gail Gibbons books because she knew that if she went to the Gail Gibbons basket she could find a book on almost any topic. Others were equally excited as they began to answer the question at hand. "Well, Jeannine's right, Gail Gibbons has books on all kinds of subjects," Jenna said.

"Did you know that some of her books have keys that help you pronounce the hard words?" Diana asked. Some of the kids were unfamiliar with what she meant by "keys that help you pronounce the hard words." Knowing that the children had some exposure to whales, Karen selected a Gail Gibbons book on whales, appropriately titled *Whales,* to demonstrate what Diana meant. She opened the book to the page about echolocation and read how whales make clicking sounds that travel and bounce off objects, helping them guide their way.

"Bats do that same thing," said Nicholas. "I read about it in Gail Gibbons' other book on bats."

After reading about echolocation, Karen showed the class the special pronunciation key to which Diana was referring, which clearly showed how to pronounce *echolocation,* "ek-o-low-KAY-shun." Alexander said that he had seen pronunciation keys many times and that they really help when you get stuck on a tricky word. In response, Devin said, "I wish every hard word came with one of those pronunciation keys." The class agreed that the pronunciation guide was only one of the helpful features found in Gail Gibbons' books. Karen sent each partnership off with one Gail Gibbons book and a few Post-it Notes to mark their noticings about this author's choice of language, structure, and use of features.

As we conferred with the children, we looked for ways the children were applying what they had already learned in this study to their own reading work.

Did they know how to access information?
Could they name some of the features?
Could they speak about how the features helped them as readers?
Could they talk about the picture support?
Did they make comparisons to any other nonfiction texts?

The following day we reviewed the list of Gail Gibbons noticings we'd made when the children returned back to the rug. Here's a sampling from that list:

We noticed the pictures are illustrated. They look almost like a kid did them.
We noticed there were a few illustrations on a page and each one was in a box.
We noticed the fact page in the back of the book I was reading.
We noticed there were instructions on how to spin a web.
We noticed the title of my book was just *Bats,* and the one we read together was just *Whales*. Do all her books have just one-word titles?

After reviewing the list of noticings from the Gail Gibbons books, we thought about what we knew about Joanne Ryder. We took the children through the same process we had done the previous day:

ask the children what they know about her and her collection of books
make a list of what they know
read one book by author, demonstrating something distinctive
send the children off to do some of their own investigative work
call them back to the rug to process what they've discovered

It was through this repetition and practice that we reinforced the lessons the children had learned from this study. At the completion of this study, we were confident that our children would approach nonfiction books with the same level of enthusiasm as they had fiction books and would apply the nonfiction strategies they had learned to enable them to continue to grow as readers.

Through Melissa's Eyes A New Teacher's Voice

What I learned from this work

Being able to observe this work firsthand, I learned that using books to model the difference between fiction and nonfiction gave children a strong foundation to begin understanding nonfiction. Naturally, I wanted to buy every single book listed in this chapter because I did not believe I could do this kind of work without them all. I scoured my classroom library but found only a few of the books. With Mary Anne's and Karen's reassurance, I created my own text sets of fiction and nonfiction books, matching them toward the levels of readers in my room. I also learned how to use the distinction between genre to launch into more sophisticated conversations about fiction versus nonfiction versus informational fiction. I love using *The Whales* and *How the Whales Walked into the Sea* to engage children in understanding the gray area of informational fiction. Each year I look forward to the children's responses and welcome the challenge of how to lead them to discover the similarities and differences between fiction and nonfiction.

How I adapted this work to fit my classroom needs

This year the children in my class were different from those of previous years. They entered my room in September with a passion for nonfiction and were choosing nonfiction books as easily as they were fiction. I began to wonder: Should I focus only on strategies for reading fiction books without supporting those readers who loved choosing nonfiction books? Should I delve into nonfiction at this point in the year even though I have a nonfiction study saved for spring? I reminded myself that teachers need to be flexible and decided that my job was to support the readers in my room. By dipping into nonfiction in the fall, my students were better prepared to reexamine nonfiction in the spring. The text sets of fiction and nonfiction books served as reminders of the different features and clearly distinguished the two genres. Moreover, the work in the fall laid the groundwork for exploring challenging nonfiction books and tackling that gray area of categorizing nonfiction books in the spring.

CHAPTER 4

Getting Started in the Writing Workshop

Writing About Memories, Introducing Picture Books, and Experimenting with Forms and Techniques

Part 1 of this book illustrates how our children spent the year becoming active readers of text. Our children learned how to appreciate the roles of characters in books and understand the inner workings of fiction. Our children became thoughtful readers and were able to weave their understanding of story with their understanding of text complexities. In addition, they gained knowledge and exposure to the varieties and variables of nonfiction and learned how to enter nonfiction texts with a clear purpose, using their newfound knowledge of how features worked to help them navigate through nonfiction texts. While we taught our children to be active readers, we also taught them to look at books as writers. Part 2 of this book illustrates how as writers, they built a repertoire of techniques and became skillful in writing for various purposes for various forms. Just as we watched our children accumulate reading strategies, applying what they learned from one study to the next, our goal for our children was to have them accumulate writing techniques in the same methodical way.

During the course of a year, more than four hundred visitors from around the world visit the Manhattan New School. In most cases, visitors wander in and out of classrooms, watching instruction in action. Without fail, visitors comment on the high quality of student writing, and they often ask teachers: How do you get your kids to write like this? The simple answer to this question is *planning*. In many cases, visitors watch as we instruct our second graders in writing, perhaps to revise for voice or use simile. Asking second graders to look back at their writing to reflect on poetic qualities wouldn't elicit the same results if we hadn't been thoughtful in designing a road map to bring them there. Fortunately for us, we belong to a larger team, and our road map not only reflects the professional community in which we live daily but is one link connecting us to the curriculum chain that spreads across the grades.

Part 2 takes you through our road map, which was designed to support our children as they built a repertoire of techniques and became skillful in writing for various purposes and with various forms. As you watch the school year unfold, you'll learn that our writing plan is cumulative. The writing techniques our children learned in the fall through memory writing were not left by the wayside, but were applied to the work they did in creating setting (Chapter 5), where they accumulated additional techniques that would eventually support them in content area research and writing (Chapter 6).

Planning and Setting Goals for Writing Workshop

Our goals for the writing workshop reflected our belief that children needed texts as mentors, while teachers needed to understand how to use mentor texts to support children's writing growth. In this book, you'll notice that we use many mentor texts to understand the variety of ways in which writers craft. Figure 4–1 serves to illustrate the different ways we examined texts in preparation for planning and explicit teaching. Specifically, this planning served to support our fall work around memory writing.

Establishing Writing Habits

We began the year with the expectation that we were all writers. Questions and prompts such as Tell me about some of the writing work you did last year and Where is your favorite place to write? began to lay the foundation for the classroom community that we would build around our writing work.

Our second graders entered our classroom door in September with memories of summer imprinted in their minds. As we gathered on our rug during the first few days together, we shared our personal stories. Eli's excitement over his month spent in Maine was evident. "We went swimming every day and toasted marshmallows by the fire at night!"

Title	Type of Memory	Author's Craft/Writing Technique/Text Structure
When I Was Five by Arthur Howard	• collection of person reflections	• repetitive phrases, e.g., "When I was five . . ." "This was my favorite . . ." • lists—use of commas • seesaw—then/now • repetitive pattern with change • internal thought
The Best Town in the World by Byrd Baylor	• special place	• exaggeration—opinion • use of *and/or* to create lists or long sentences • text layout—poemlike • retelling of a memory heard, e.g., "My father said . . ."
Birthday Presents by Cynthia Rylant	• family memory • birthday memories	• "you" voice—narrator speaking directly to subject • intentional use of incomplete sentences • list like—use of commas • time line of one's life • repetitive pattern with change • snapshot illustrations
Hairs by Sandra Cisneros	• family memory • mother/child • sensory memory	• short introduction sentence • use of comma • simile • "obeys"—surprising language • echo
"That Was Summer" from *Sun Through the Window* by Marci Ridlon	• summer memory	• "you" voice • questions • repetitive phrases • the use of *and* to add details • vignettes—stand alone on one theme —summer • memories connected to smells of summer
When I Was Little by Jamie Lee Curtis	• childhood memory	• seesaw then/now • repetitive phrases • the use of *and* or *or* to add details • gives specific examples to validate memory
Letter to the Lake by Susan Marie Swanson	• summer memory • special place	• "you" voice • questions • repetitive phrases • flashback • past/present—shifts • illustration technique • black and white/color • use of metaphor

Figure 4–1 *Finding possibilities for explicit teaching in writing*

Teaching Possibilities	Ways to Use Book/Minilessons
• use of repetitive phrasing • use of comma • thinking about the comparisons between past and present • look at how endings vary from patterned text • the use of parenthesis	• highlight repetition on typed text—discuss purpose of technique • use T-chart to collect and compare past memories with present ones • highlight change in repetition • highlight use of commas—where would you pause?
• slowing down • exaggerate for effect to make your point • creating images • slowing down with *and/or* • writing from a different perspective	• pick line in writing to exaggerate • find place to add *and/or* to give more details • use line breaks to highlight *and/or* • sketch picture of one image to demonstrate power of language
• sequencing memories • tell story behind picture • saying more about birthday • use of commas to link details • use of varied sentence length • listen to stories about unremembered childhood events	• use a time line to sequence memories • bring in photographs to support memory • stretching out a memory through adding details • make a list of questions regarding unremembered childhood events
• finding a person/animal you feel bonded to • use of simile to be descriptive • use of words that would be considered surprising • the use of echoing	• plan with grid to include senses in writing • revise looking for a place to include a simile • revise—looking for a place to include surprising language
• voice—speaking directly to someone/something • creating images • repetitive language • using *and* to add details • using questions to connect to "you" • writing memories around a big idea question	• highlighted repetition and use of *and* on enlarged copy of poem—discuss effects of techniques • chart possible ideas for shared memories • preplan writing by role playing memory with partner • illustrate vignette(s) to support details
• generating lots of examples of change in life • adding details to support story behind change • using *and* and *or* to add details	• use T-chart to collect many ideas for writing seesaw memories • write stories with details to support seesaw idea
• voice—speaking directly to someone/something • creating images • artifact that inspires memories • repetitive language • use of questions to connect to "you"	• use a time line to show past/present/future • pull out lines to show images • change voice of piece about *place*

he told the class. Ethan shared the story of his summer kayaking excursions on Long Pond with his grandfather, and Emma told us of the long weekend her friend Graciela spent at her country house in New Jersey. Summer stories provided children with infectious inspiration during those first few days of school, as they began to record snippets of these stories with writing and pictures. We cherished our children's excitement as they told their personal stories. We began to see the writers behind the words.

As a way of supporting our children's excitement for writing, we designed a classroom that encouraged autonomy and created independence. Just as we had them choose reading spots (see Chapter 1), we wanted our children to find spaces in the class where they could feel most comfortable writing. We created predictability around storing writing supplies so that children could work efficiently and independently as writers. As another way of inspiring ideas for our young writers, we talked about scrapbooks and some of the things that writers keep inside for inspiration, such as ticket stubs, photographs, clippings, and notes. At this time we introduced our scrapbook equivalent—a memory collection notebook. The memory collection notebook served as a tool for children to collect ideas for writing. (See Figures 4–2 and 4–3.) It was in their writing folders, however, where children began to use those ideas to draft stories.

Figure 4–2 *Memory collection notebooks*

Figure 4–3 *Student writing folder*

A quick look at planning for a ministudy in establishing writing habits

Ministudy	*Time Frame*	*Goals*	*Possible Minilessons*
Establishing Writing Habits	2–3 weeks	• developing writer identity • establishing routines for independent writing • developing home-school rituals • developing good writing habits and behaviors	• discuss the essentials writers need in order to do their best work • model how to choose a writing space • talk about summer memories • record snippets through writing and pictures • introduce memory collection notebooks and begin collecting • introduce picture books that support memories

Ministudy	*Time Frame*	*Goals*	*Possible Minilessons*
			• conduct partner interviews • introduce various paper choices • discuss how to manage a writing folder

Adding Detail to Writing Using Illustration as a Preplanning Tool

After the first cycle and some quick publishing, we looked over our children's writing folders. Knowing they needed to focus on adding details to their writing, we designed a ministudy around this focus. Carmen Lomas Garza's *Family Pictures: Cuadros de Familia,* with its short photo album–like quality, detailed pictures, and short vignettes, provided a perfect model for us to conduct this work. This book supported the minilessons for helping our children add details to pictures as well as writing. In addition, this book contained many clear and varied beginnings that would support our young writers as they eventually attempted to revise their own short vignettes.

A quick look at planning for a ministudy in adding detail to writing using illustration as a preplanning tool

Ministudy	*Time Frame*	*Goals*	*Possible Minilessons*
Adding Detail to Writing Using Illustration as a Preplanning Tool	2–3 weeks	• to notice how writers use details to create images • to understand the impact of a strong beginning	• use models to highlight lines that create vivid images • model how to illustrate and gather ideas for writing around a picture (prewriting work) • use details to draft story • use picture book to examine the different ways writers begin a story

Changing Writing Form: Reshaping Memories into Letters

We had our students search through their folders and look for memories they could imagine shaped into a different form, such as a letter or a poem. This ministudy is an example of how memories can be shaped into letters. Being both a letter and a memory, *Letter to the Lake,* by Susan Marie Swanson, was a perfect mentor for this kind of writing. (See Figure 4–1.) Not only is this a letter written in memory form, but it also nicely illustrates writing techniques we had been trying out as writers—repetitive phrasing and questioning.

Shelley Harwayne, in *Writing Through Childhood* (2001), speaks to the uniqueness of *Letter to the Lake* when she writes:

> The notion of writing a letter to an inanimate object is surprising to most children, even when they realize that the letter is just in the child's mind. Children are quick to call out things they could write to in order to help recall their past experiences. Some of our students used the technique in their writer's notebook, addressing entries to their old apartments, their baby blanket, their bunk bed at camp, their grandmother's rocking chair, and even a bookmobile they visited when they lived in a rural section of our country. (119)

A quick look at planning for a ministudy in changing writing form: reshaping memories into letters

Ministudy	*Time Frame*	*Goals*	*Possible Minilessons*
Reshaping Memories into Letters	2–3 weeks	• to learn how to turn memories into letters • to use writing techniques in writing, such as repetitive phrasing and questioning • to understand the use of flashback	• examine the crafting technique: language, repetition, questioning to create images • use time line to model time frames • use a time line to show past, present, and future

CHAPTER 5

Creating Setting in Writing

Investigation Three

In *Writing Through Childhood*, Shelley Harwayne (2001) writes eloquently about the importance of looking within larger genre studies for smaller areas, such as place, that deserve greater instructional attention. By looking closely and designing a course of study around one small area within a genre, we give our children the opportunity to practice specific skills. It is these skills they carry with them and apply as writers to many genres. Shelley states,

> When teachers suggest ways to improve the quality of students' writing about a place, they usually tuck the information into a bigger course of study—perhaps one on writing picture books, short stories, or newspaper articles. They suggest ways for students to make the setting enhance the story, be the setting a town in Serbo-Croatia or grandmother's kitchen. Here, I am suggesting that learning to write about a place is a significant skill unto itself, and deserving of its own time in the sun. In other words, it need not be tucked into a more important genre study, but big blocks of time can and should be carved out to help young children write exceptionally well about places. (258)

During the fall months, our children spent a great deal of time writing personal stories. They recorded snippets of their lives through illustrations, artifacts, and writing in their memory collection notebooks. It was in these notebooks where children found the ideas they would eventually shape into forms, such as narrative, letter, and poetry. Our children wrote about special places where they spent their weekends and summers, they wrote about long days on the beach and kayaking at Grandpa's lake house. Place intrinsically played a role in their memory writing. And although we had already published a few pieces of writing in the fall under the umbrella of memory writing, we sensed that we needed to remain there for another cycle of writing. This time, within the comfort of memory writing, we would look to write well about the places that appeared several times in our children's memory notebooks, places that anchored those memories. This study began with Shelley's inspiration, as we watched her help children at Manhattan New School "understand how to notice the telling details of place, to capture its essence, to choose words and metaphors that help their readers imagine the place that is in their mind's eye" (Harwayne 2001).

Place plays an important role in our memories. Sights and smells from places we remember can conjure up details, bringing us back to special settings from our lives. The smells of coconut suntan lotion and hotdogs sizzling on a grill are redolent of times spent at the beach. Cracker Jack boxes and bundles of cotton candy bring to life long, sunny afternoons spent watching your first baseball game with Grandpa. For writers, anchoring a memory in a specific place can become a way to deepen writing about a memory. We found that for our young writers, it was a proven way to help them extend and deepen the quality of their writing.

For students, writing about themselves and their life stories comes naturally. In Jordana's writing folder, we found pages of snippets from times spent in the Poconos with her family. The pages in Grace's folder contained endless Fire Island memories, where she had spent several summers. Her pages treasured times spent at the beach, getting pizza at Mike's and ice cream at Scoops. They also spoke of greeting friends and family coming off the Fire Island ferry and nighttimes filled with stars and walks along sandy beaches. Whether it is a day spent on the sandy shore, a barbeque with relatives, or a fun-filled adventure at the amusement park, the memories our children cherish are easily transferred into written stories. Often, though, a young writer's preoccupation with methodically recording details of a particular event can overshadow the sense of place, leaving the reader on the outside of the memory.

We wanted our children to dig back into their memory collection notebooks and folders, looking for new ideas or already developed personal stories to rethink and craft with a different focus. In this writing study, we wanted our children to

- move beyond writing in a listlike fashion
- extend beyond a recollection of events
- create vivid images through use of various crafting techniques
- maintain focus around a particular place, considering time of day and/or time of year
- understand how to maneuver story through different time frames

To help our children advance through our place study, we focused on time—time of the day and time of the year—to help them come to understand the nuances of setting, or place, in a story. Understanding time and place would aid our children in personal and informational writing as well as assist them in slowing down and focusing on one aspect of writing. Rather than clumping the entire day around a particular place, we focused on writing about that place at a particular time of day.

As we approached this writing study, we knew that we needed to give our children mentors who would guide the work of layering their writing about memories. We looked first to what was familiar, for example, Cynthia Rylant, whose beautifully written books we had come to know and love in the fall in both reading and writing workshop. As readers, our children lived alongside her characters in series such as Mr. Putter and Tabby, Poppleton, and Cobble Street Cousins. As writers, they had learned lessons about memory writing from her picture books, namely, *Birthday Presents*, *When I Was Young in the Mountains*, and *The Relatives Came*. Cynthia Rylant's work would also serve as a bridge between our fall memory writing work and this study about setting and place. Now we would reread Cynthia Rylant's picture books with a new question in mind: How does Cynthia Rylant establish setting and show time passing in her work? Her book *Scarecrow* became a mentor text. In this book, not only does she show movement of time, but her repetitive phrases and use of personification allow children to feel an emotional attachment to the subject—a scarecrow.

Another mentor text we used was Brian J. Heinz's *Butternut Hollow Pond*. In this beautifully written book, the author uses the ecological setting of a pond and the interdependence of life around it to create suspense. We chose this book because we knew the children would appreciate its natural setting, the animals' struggles with life around the pond, and the scientific aspect to the book's writing and enjoy it because the writer described in detail life at the pond during different time frames.

At this point in the year, our students had developed a strong foundation as writers and were ready to layer their learning. They understood that successful writers are influenced by what they read, write best when they have a passion for their topic, learn lessons from other writers, and revise. Our students were experienced in writing personal stories, examining structures from other writers, and reshaping original pieces into different writing forms.

Week One: Making a Bridge

Goal: to deepen memory writing by focusing writing around a specific place

As adult readers, we have become fluent with place, or setting, in a story. For children, however, most of their noticings and writings have been focused on action (running, playing, kite flying, fishing). Most children never ponder the place where such activities occur (the field or playground, the park or the lake).

We began the inquiry in week 1 with the examination of *Scarecrow*. There was excitement in the room as Karen clipped an enlarged copy of *Scarecrow* to her easel. Our children had heard Karen read this book several times. They loved the language and the way Karen exaggerated the repetition as she read it aloud.

In *Scarecrow*, Cynthia Rylant brings an inanimate object to life through repetitive phrases such as "He doesn't mind" and "He doesn't care." We see her use repetition and personification again in her book *The Whales*, where she uses the phrase "The whales are thinking today." This repetition and bringing life to animals and/or objects inspired our children to try some of the same techniques in their own writing.

At first, when asked what they noticed in *Scarecrow* our children highlighted what they already knew from the read-aloud—repetition. Jenna said, "I love the way Cynthia Rylant repeats the phrase 'He doesn't mind'; it makes him seem like he's alive."

Other kids agreed and mimicked the phrase "He doesn't mind. . . . He doesn't mind. . . ." Karen underlined those phrases in the text on the enlarged copy.

Karen took the opportunity to point out the use of *he* in the text. She discussed the effects *he* had on the story—how it gave the scarecrow a more humanlike quality and made the reader feel more intimate with the scarecrow. Karen also pointed out that the writer was speaking as an observer from the perspective of a third person, something they were familiar with from our work with dialogue in the reading workshop.

Diana's hand quickly shot up as she began to announce that Cynthia Rylant also repeats the word *borrowed*. As a way of highlighting the repetition and personification within the text, Karen underlined the following listlike sentence and discussed its effects on the reader.

> His hat is *borrowed*, his suit is *borrowed*, his hands are *borrowed* . . .

- *author's message*—Repeating *borrowed* emphasized the point that nothing is his own. The message wouldn't have been the same if Cynthia Rylant had chosen not to repeat *borrowed*.
- *poetic quality in the form of a list*—The repetition of *borrowed* in a listlike form adds to the poetic quality of the text.
- *Personification*—The use of *he* and *his* allows the reader to identify with the subject; it brings the scarecrow to life and makes him humanlike.

Throughout the course of the week, we continued to examine *Scarecrow*. Children worked in partnerships with typed-text versions of the story to underline their noticings. Some discovered new surprises in the text, like how the birds say "lovely" while referring to the scarecrow. Others simply reinforced the class noticings, underlining the repetitive phrases and words. With this practice, children began to internalize the language and the craft of Cynthia Rylant's writing.

We asked kids to think about something they knew really well and could write about as if they were observing it closely. We knew from our study of her books and writing that Cynthia Rylant wrote from real-life experiences. We theorized with our children that she had probably spent time observing scarecrows. Thinking about Cynthia Rylant's book *The Whales*, Ethan made the following connection: "I bet she has spent a lot of time observing whales, too. If not, she wouldn't have been able to write *The Whales*." We then asked our children to think about the things in their lives that they knew well and had observed. For the most part, our children chose people and animals in their lives. Lauren flipped back through her memory collection notebook and found a piece written in the first person about her cat, Misty. With this familiar topic, Lauren applied what she learned from Cynthia Rylant about being a third-person observer, about repetition, and about personification to reshape her work into the following piece:

> Her eyes are green. Her whiskers are about an inch and a half. Her fur is very soft. But a cat picks what she does all day. So a cat doesn't mind that there is noise all around most of the time. Or that she has four feet. And a cat knows this. She is a cat, she is proud of having four legs. She is proud of having green eyes. But she loves her owners and that's what she cares about most of all.

Like Lauren, Caroline practiced writing techniques learned from Cynthia Rylant in her work about her dog, Coco.

> His bed was for sale, his leash was for sale, his collar was for sale, even he was for sale. When we come home it's nighttime so everybody has to go to sleep, even the new family member in the car. He doesn't care if he has to sleep outside in his little house. When the soft snow touches his little blue sweater, he runs all around as fast as a cheetah. When the grass turns bright green, he jumps up like a kangaroo. When the trees are bare, he sits on the ground and looks at the sky. When the flowers start to bloom, he skips all around. Then it's his special day. We give him his dog food cake. He crunches on every balloon except the red one with the blue string. He doesn't care if the dog food cake is a little stale. All he cares about is his family.

Examining the writing techniques in *Scarecrow* allowed for a natural shift into looking at how Cynthia Rylant described setting and time in her text. Caroline's writing, "When the soft snow touches his little blue sweater. . . . When the grass turns bright green. . . . When the trees are bare. . . . When the flowers start to bloom. . . ," demonstrates her attention not only to the way Cynthia Rylant uses repetition and personification but to the way she attends to the movement of time in her stories. This was the direction in which we would lead the class instruction. We revisited other Cynthia Rylant books, looking at the way she attends to the movement of time in stories. Figure 5–2 lists the books we used as mentors throughout the study.

Week Two: Immersion

Goal: to expose children to several texts that use time as a structure and to anchor their own writing in time

In week 1, our children observed how writers can use repetition to highlight a point and how writers can use time in a story. Our children came to understand how a writer could focus on a specific place and make it come alive by showing a particular time in the place being described by the writer. At this time, we also incorporated the knowledge we had gained and applied it to some of the nonfiction texts we were familiar with from our investigation of nonfiction.

In week 2, we wanted to immerse our children in the many ways writers describe time of day and time of year. We carefully chose narrative nonfiction texts that were rich with poetically written phrases that captured times of day and year. Figure 5–1 lists some of our favorites.

Mary Anne began the week reintroducing some of these nonfiction texts to the children. She chose to read *Box Turtle at Long Pond*, by William T. George, as a read-aloud. This book was different from the fiction books we had read by Cynthia Rylant in the way it was rooted in one place—Long Pond. She also loved the simplicity of the language and the visual images of setting created by both words and illustrations. Mary Anne challenged the children to listen for the phrases this writer used to show time and place, reminding our children of those phrases previously discussed from Cynthia Rylant's books.

The reading of the first page drew a lot of attention. Eli's hand popped up and he commented, "I know this is starting in the morning because it says, 'it is dawn at Long Pond,' and *dawn* means morning."

Jordana agreed, saying, "I'm sure it is morning because it says, 'a white mist covers the water,' and that happens in the morning."

Mary Anne acknowledged the noticings and reinforced how both phrases help to create a visual image of morning. She posted this page, knowing that it would be a useful model for our children. As Mary

	WEEK ONE	WEEK TWO	WEEK THREE	WEEK FOUR	WEEK FIVE	WEEK SIX
GOAL	to deepen memory writing by focusing writing around specific place	to expose children to several texts that use time as a structure and to anchor their own writing in time	to anchor memories in one specific place, zooming in on one particular time of the day	to follow place through several times frames	to use revision strategies to strengthen writing	to edit, illustrate, and celebrate
LITERATURE	MAKING A BRIDGE • *Scarecrow*, by Cynthia Rylant • *The Relatives Came*, by Cynthia Rylant • *Night in the Country*, by Cynthia Rylant • *Cookie Store Cat*, by Cynthia Rylant	IMMERSION • *In November*, by Cynthia Rylant *Water Voices*, by Toby Speed • *Box Turtle at Long Pond*, by William T. George • *Beaver at Long Pond*, by William T. George and Lindsay Barrett George	DRAFTING • *Butternut Hollow Pond*, by Brian J. Heinz • *Box Turtle at Long Pond*, by William T. George • *Beaver at Long Pond*, by William T. George and Lindsay Barrett George	WRITING AND REVISING • *Butternut Hollow Pond*, by Brian J. Heinz • *Box Turtle at Long Pond*, by William T. George • *Beaver at Long Pond*, by William T. George and Lindsay Barrett George	REVISING • *Butternut Hollow Pond*, by Brian J. Heinz • *Box Turtle at Long Pond*, by William T. George • *Beaver at Long Pond*, by William T. George and Lindsay Barrett George	EDITING, ILLUSTRATING, CELEBRATING • *Butternut Hollow Pond*, by Brian J. Heinz • *Box Turtle at Long Pond*, by William T. George • *Beaver at Long Pond*, by William T. George and Lindsay Barrett George • assorted titles from Vera B. Williams, Brian G. Caras, and Lindsay Barrett George
MINILESSONS	• examine *Scarecrow* for craft—what do we notice about Cynthia Rylant's work? • examine other Cynthia Rylant texts for ways she shows time in writing	• highlight phrases writers use to create image of time and place • sort the phrases children collect by time of day and time of year, creating a T-chart	• sort phrases into more specific time frames—add children's writing attempts to chart • read and highlight specific time frames crafted around a particular place	• revisit lines from Time of Day chart to help kids think about new ways of beginning new time frames • reread and highlight the ways Brian J. Heinz writes about different time frames at Butternut Hollow Pond • chart the ways Brian J. Heinz connects those time frames	• look at all the qualities of Brian J. Heinz's writing beyond time of day • create chart showing various crafting techniques, e.g., simile, metaphor, imagery	• demonstrate the use of spelling try sheet in editing process • use literature to discuss the use of space in illustrations as well as the choice of visual image to represent writing • review illustrations of Vera B. Williams, Brian G. Caras, and Lindsay Barrett George
STUDENT WORK	• examine typed text of *Scarecrow*, underlining noticings • draft new pieces, practicing techniques used by Cynthia Rylant	• sift through various texts, looking for phrases that create time • practice specific techniques discussed while reading *In November* • rework an old memory, attempting to anchor it in a specific time	• identify a place they know well enough to write about, anchoring that writing in one specific time of day • expand and revise their writing so that place and time of day are evident	• extend their writing to different times of the day • students apply lessons learned about connecting phrases to their own writing	examine their writing to revise, using techniques discussed in minilessons	• reread writing for punctuation and spelling • use spelling try sheet to work through spelling • sketch/draft illustrations that match writing • finalize illustrations, adding color and details

Figure 5–1 *Study at a glance: creating setting in writing*

THE COOKIE STORE CAT	SCARECROW	THE RELATIVES CAME	NIGHT IN THE COUNTRY
Winter passes, and spring, and summer, and fall and the Cookie Store Cat knows just where he belongs.	The earth has rained and snowed and blossomed and wilted and yellowed and greened and vined itself all around him.	It was in the summer of the year when the relatives came. . . . They left when their grapes were nearly purple enough to pick, but not quite.	And toward morning, one small bird will be the first to tell everyone that night in the country is nearly over.

Figure 5–2 *Cynthia Rylant mentor books that show time passing in different ways*

Anne continued reading the book, she posted other descriptive phrases that acknowledged time of day, including these:

- The sun is high overhead. The morning chill is gone.
- The sun is dropping in the sky. The air is getting cooler.
- The sun sets on the far side of Long Pond. The evening air grows colder.

Mary Anne then sent the children off in pairs to examine books we had collected with a strong sense of place and time. Mary Anne gave each of our children Post-its and asked them to note places in their books where phrases indicating time of day appeared, just as she had done during the minilesson when she examined *Box Turtle at Long Pond*. Following a successful work time, the children returned to the rug, excited to share their discoveries. Lindsay and Matthew noticed that in *Beaver at Long Pond*, William T. George and Lindsay Barrett George's companion text to *Box Turtle at Long Pond*, the writers used *dawn* and *dusk* to express time. They were quick to report to the class that *Beaver at Long Pond* begins at dusk while *Box Turtle at Long Pond* begins at dawn. Lindsay also informed us that although these two books are set in the same place—Long Pond—one spans a day while the other a nighttime. Over the next couple of days, our children collected several phrases from books with reference to time. Mary Anne knew it was time to make sense of these time phrases by sorting through them. Some described *time of day* while others described *time of year*. Mary Anne created a T-chart to help the class differentiate between the two.

Time of Day	*Time of Year*
The afternoon sun hangs low in the sky.—*Grand Canyon: A Trail Through Time*, by Linda Vieira	Deep snow covers the forest, in which wolves, moose and deer search busily for food.—*An Algonquin Year: The Year According to the Full Moon*, by Michael McCurdy
The sun inches higher in the sky and warms the desert.—*Desert Discoveries*, by Ginger Wadsworth	A robin gathers muddy twigs and grasses to build a nest in a nearby spruce.—*Disappearing Lake*, by Debbie S. Miller

Our children were beginning to notice the variety of ways writers anchor story in time of day or time of year. We knew that our children were ready to do the same. We asked our children to independently write "quick practices" that they would then share with the class. As the words connote, quick-practice exercises are short writings we periodically ask of our students in which they focus on a particular element of writing, in this case time and place. Although we value independence in extended writing time, we believe exercises serve to support young writers in practicing specific techniques—ones they may use later as independent writers. We also find the sharing of these exercises to be powerful, in that sharing widens the possibilities for all students. It provides confidence to those who found some success as well as support for those who struggled through the exercise. Our children keep their quick-practice writings in their writing folders.

As Mary Anne gathered the children on the rug the following day, she introduced *In November*, by Cynthia Rylant, a book filled with descriptive details that capture the essence of the fall. She wanted the children to notice the beautiful way Cynthia Rylant wrote about this particular time of the year. The following excerpt from *In November* is one of many in the text that provided inspiration for their quick practice.

> In November, some birds move away and some birds stay. The air is full of good-byes and well-wishes. The birds who are leaving look very serious. No silly spring chirping now.

Mary Anne sent the children off to write about a particular time of year. Hyunjoo and Dakota, in their quick-practice examples, were influenced by the writing in Cynthia Rylant's text. Each was able to tap into her experiences to capture a particular time of year. As a writer,

Hyunjoo called upon on the time she and her family spent in Buffalo, New York, during a snowstorm, while Dakota called upon her first-hand experience observing the birds of Fire Island.

> In December, the ground is covered with a white blanket of snow. The birds have gone south, water has frozen into ice, and pumpkins have rotted.
>
> In December, most of the animals take a winter nap, like bears, and other animals. When they awake, they know it is spring!—Hyunjoo Lee's quick practice, titled "December."

> In June, all the birds come back from their long, long trip and fly to their families. In June all the birds sing on the trees and the trees start to sprout and buds are coming out. In June a lot of people go to the beach and birds sing songs that people would love to hear.—Dakota Kornicker's quick practice, titled "June."

We used other books in this study to model similar techniques for establishing setting in writing. Later in week 2, in subsequent lessons, we used *Box Turtle at Long Pond* and *Beaver at Long Pond* to look at time of day, just as we had used *In November* to look at time of year. In addition, we used *Water Voices*, by Toby Speed, to look at both time of day and time of year and to teach the lesson of showing rather than telling. This riddlelike book, written in a kid-friendly way, contains lots of poetic techniques—simile, metaphor, and personification—that support the description of a time of year or a place. With descriptive lines such as "When the slide's so hot it burns your legs . . ." and "fans do a slow dance on tabletops," Toby Speed captures the essence of summer by showing us rather than telling us. Figure 5–3 provides a close-up look at the lesson plan we used to demonstrate this work.

Week Three: Drafting

Goal: to anchor memories in one specific place, zooming in on a particular time of day

By the beginning of week 3, we had collected several phrases that writers used to mark time in their writing, some from published texts and

Lesson Plan—Using *Water Voices* by Toby Speed

Prelesson Planning: Examine the text of Toby Speed in *Water Voices* and notice how the author creates time of year and time of day. Prepare chart tablet with two examples from *Water Voices*.

Goal: For students to learn how to show time of day and time of year in writing.

Lines from *Water Voices* that show TIME OF YEAR—SUMMERTIME	Lines from *Water Voices* that show TIME OF DAY—NIGHTTIME
When the slide's so hot it burns your legs and dogs pant and Popsicles drip, when carrots nap in the garden and kittens in the shade and fans do a slow dance on tabletops, I whirl like a string of pearls in the yard.	When your smile is dozy drowsy and your eyelids buttered with sleep, when the moon curls up like a cat in your quilt and all the shooing wind shivers away and the streetlamps wear halos and moths tap their secret codes on screens and stars wink and the curtains spread their wings and try to fly, I drift down from the sky and lick the grass

WRITING WORKSHOP (1 hour)

MINILESSON (20 minutes)

Students gather on the rug. Karen and Mary Anne introduce Toby Speed's book *Water Voice*. They read through the text engaging children in the clever ways in which the author writes about summertime and nighttime. Karen and Mary Anne refer to the two excerpts listed above, which were prepared on chart tablets. With the students, they examine the way Toby Speed creates time of year and time of day using the T-chart for support.

How does this writer show rather than tell? SHOW vs. TELL

How does this writer show us it is summertime?	How does this writer show us it is nighttime?
Summertime: • when the slide's so hot it burns your legs • fans do a slow dance on tabletops • when carrots nap in the garden	**Nighttime:** • when the moon curls up like a cat in your quilt • and moths tap their secret codes on screens • and your eyelids buttered with sleep

Before sending the children off to write, Mary Anne demonstrated how she used time of year to anchor a memory from her notebook about her mother making tomato sauce:

August:
- when the tomatoes come off their secure vines
- when the pavement is burning and those juicy tomatoes are turning their deepest shade of red
- when children are growing restless from whole days spent at the pool

STUDENT WRITING TIME (30 minutes)

Students are sent off to revisit their memory collection notebooks looking for places to use time to anchor a memory. They are asked to rewrite two or three lines like those demonstrated in the minilesson.

SHARE TIME (10 minutes)

Students come back to the rug to share their writing. Students are asked to show the lines they wrote as they attempt to structure an old memory around time of day or time of year.

Figure 5–3 *Lesson plan for* Water Voices

others written by our children. Our children's writing demonstrated the influence of the many texts we had read and examined at this point in the study. Our children had written several short phrases that wove time into place. Part of our plan for this week was to sort through these phrases and create charts for the class for time of day and time of year. We would then organize these charts into more specific time subcategories, such as midmorning and nighttime for the Time of Day chart and winter and spring for the Time of Year chart. The charts would support each child in his or her own writing and would also serve as a reference for the class. Figures 5–4 and 5–5 give a sampling of those two charts.

As part of our inquiry into time phrases, we introduced the eloquently written picture book *Butternut Hollow Pond*, by Brian J. Heinz. We had used this book earlier and would continue to use this book for the remainder of this study. Many of the writing qualities and techniques our children had practiced and learned to this point in the study are evidenced within the five time frames used to structure the writing in *Butternut Hollow Pond* (daybreak, midmorning, noon, end of day, and night). This text, with its easy-to-follow structure, would serve as a bridge between what our children already knew about good writing and our new focus of knowing how to establish setting in writing. Not only would our children be inspired by the beautifully written lines filled with writing techniques such as personification and simile, but they'd also get a sense of how setting and passage of time are established—our goal for the end of this study.

Our next big goal for our children was to have them look for and find a special place that would become the subject of their new writing pieces. We asked our children to revisit the writing in both their memory collection notebooks and their writing folders. Each child kept a memory collection notebook and a writing folder, which were filled with potential writing ideas and were similar to entries found in a writer's notebook. Our children's memory collection notebooks and writing folders were filled with ideas and inspirations for writing possibilities. On Monday, we wanted our children to revisit these treasures, thinking about the place behind one of their already existing writings. It would be this place they would focus on and use to learn how to write well about time and place.

At the start of this study, we knew that many children often write about events or activities, overlooking the importance of the place. That day, we asked them to look beyond the event or activity written

Time of Day

EARLY MORNING	MIDMORNING	NOON
In the early morning a pale twilight touches the edge of the sky. It's called dawn.—*Twilight Comes Twice,* by Ralph Fletcher	The sun inches higher in the sky and warms the desert. —*Desert Discoveries,* by Ginger Wadsworth	The sun is high overhead. The morning chill is gone. —*Box Turtle at Long Pond,* by William T. George
It's morning outside and the birds are chirping.—Eli Moskowitz, age 7	Five mallard ducklings take to the water, weaving behind their parents like floats in a parade. —*Butternut Hollow Pond,* by Brian J. Heinz	The air is filled with the songs of a hundred bees. —*Butternut Hollow Pond,* by Brian J. Heinz
In Florida when it's dawn there's a sunrise with lots of colors. The sun is not all the way up yet.—Karla Kirsch, age 7	God's painting is all blue with white balls on it, and he calls it mid-morning sky.—Caroline Frank, age 8	It's midday at the Great Lawn. People are riding their razors, bikes, and rollerblades.—Sarah Vaadia, age 8
Hampton, in Hampton at day break all the nocturnal animals sleep and the deer wake up and the sun is low. —Max Snyder, age 8	It's mid-morning on Fire Island and the beach is beginning to get crowded.—Dakota Kornicker, age 7	Now the sun is in the middle of the sky. The waves beat against the shore like a million hands clapping. —Alexandra Kessler, age 8
AFTERNOON	**EVENING**	**NIGHTTIME**
The afternoon sun hangs low in the sky.—*Grand Canyon: A Trail Through Time,* by Linda Vieira	The sun sets on Long Island, New York. The light gets turned off and all is dark. The crickets start to sing and their song is chirp, chirp. They would sing this song all night.—Rachel Kaplan, age 8	The moon inches above the mountains, casting a pale light on the sand.—*Desert Discoveries,* by Ginger Wadsworth
After lunch I get back in the pool. It feels hotter than ever.—Lauren Javaly, age 8	The sun is dropping in the sky and the air is getting cooler. —Karla Kirsch, age 7	The full moon is high above Florida. Everyone is home sleeping, reading or watching TV. It's very warm out, and the pool is still open.—Lauren Javaly, age 8
A car drives into the parking lot. People come out with suntan lotion and insect repellant. That's one thing to bring when you go to the Refuge in the afternoon. —Stephen Profeta, age 8	It is dusk at Long Pond. Most of the animals have settled down for the night—the birds in the trees, the wood ducks in the tall grasses and the painted turtles at the bottom of the pond. The beaver has opened his eyes. —*Beaver at Long Pond,* by William T George and Lindsay Barrett George	Now the sun is gone and the nocturnal animals come out. The misty wind freshens the air and the peaceful sound rustles through the trees.—Alexandra Kessler, age 8

Figure 5–4 *Lines from text that show time of day*

Winter	Spring
Deep snow covers the frozen forest, in which wolves, moose and deer search busily for food—*An Algonquian Year: The Year According to the Full Moon*, by Michael McCurdy	A robin gathers muddy twigs and grasses to build a nest in a nearby spruce—*Disappearing Lake*, by Debbie S. Miller
In December, the ground is covered with a white long, blanket of snow. The birds have gone south, water has frozen into ice and pumpkins have rotted.—Hyunjoo Lee, age 8	In June all the birds come back from their long trip and fly over to their families. —Dakota Kornicker, age 7
The snow falls covering the leftover leaves on the lawn like a protective blanket for my tulip bulbs that will eventually show themselves and welcome us into spring. —Karen Ruzzo	The days grow warmer. Butterflies bask in the sunshine, spreading their wings. Creeks dry up and no longer feed the lake. Inch by inch, foot by foot, the lake is disappearing. —*Disappearing Lake*, by Debbie S. Miller
Summer	**Fall**
When the slide's so hot it burns your legs, and dogs pant, and Popsicles drip, when carrots nap in the garden and kittens in the shade and fans do a slow dance on tabletops.—*Water Voices*, by Toby Speed	In November, some birds move away and some stay. The air is full of good-byes and well-wishes.—*In November*, by Cynthia Rylant
It's nearly summer here in the Sonoran Desert of Southern Arizona. Most animals are huddled in their nests, hiding from the restless sun. —*Cactus Café: A Story of the Sonoran Desert*, by Kathleen Weidner Zoehfeld	Then the first leaf falls and the sun shines bright and they swim in the lake until it's time to stay inside their little log cabin and sit in front of the fireplace, until the sun shines again.—Alexandra Kessler, age 8
I remember August, the end of summer, when tomatoes come off their secure vines. August, when children grow restless of whole days spent at the pool, when they look forward to buying their new school shoes.—Mary Anne Sacco	The first autumn snowstorm has dusted the tundra.—*Caribou Journey*, by Debbie S. Miller

Figure 5–5 *Lines from text that show time of year*

about in their notebooks and folders and focus on place. As children perused their writing folders and memory collection notebooks, many found a particular place behind their memory writing that reappeared, signifying importance. In Karen's conference with Ethan, she asked him to think about the kayaking memory he had written about in one of his published pieces from the fall. Although Ethan's writing was focused on the memory he and his grandfather shared while kayaking at Long Pond, Karen suspected the pond might have been a place Ethan had visited several times, a place he thought of as special. Ethan revealed that indeed he did hold a special place in his heart for the pond behind his grandpa's Massachusetts house in the Berkshires. During the conference, Ethan recalled several memories at Long Pond, where he had spent many summers. This was a natural place for Ethan to write about and use as an anchor for his memories. Figure 5–6 shows an example of Ethan's published memory narrative from the fall and Figure 5–7 shows his attempt at writing well about a place—Long Pond.

We wanted our children to understand the importance of being familiar with a place, to feel a part of it, so that their writings would reflect the same detail and excitement as *Butternut Hollow Pond*. We talked about how Brian J. Heinz, a veteran science teacher living in

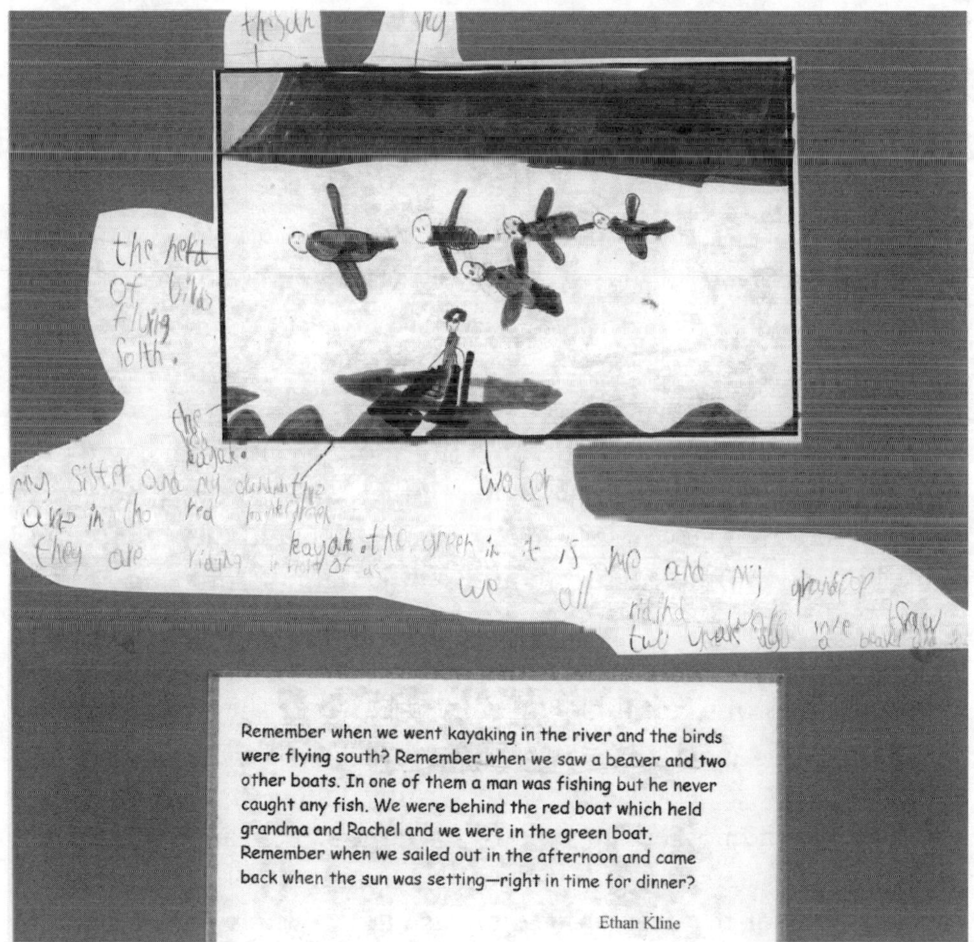

Remember when we went kayaking in the river and the birds were flying south? Remember when we saw a beaver and two other boats. In one of them a man was fishing but he never caught any fish. We were behind the red boat which held grandma and Rachel and we were in the green boat. Remember when we sailed out in the afternoon and came back when the sun was setting—right in time for dinner?
Ethan Kline

Figure 5–6 *Ethan's published memory narrative*

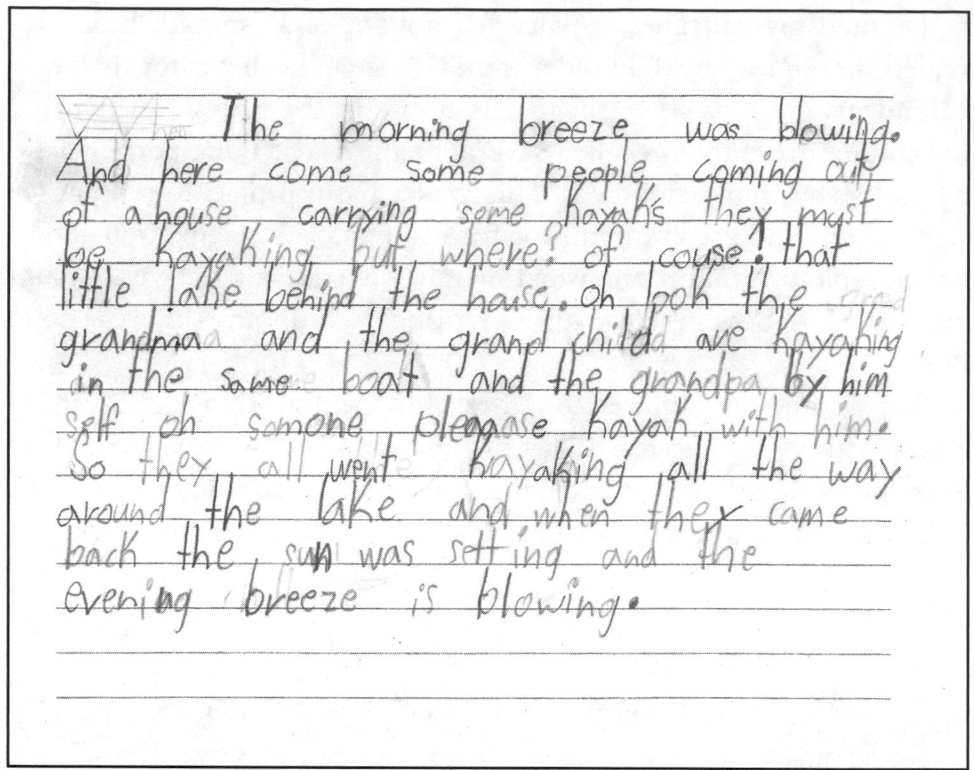
The morning breeze was blowing. And here come some people coming out of a house carrying some kayaks they must be kayaking but where? of couse! that little lake behind the house. oh look the grandma and the grand child are kayaking in the same boat and the grandpa by him self oh somone pleaase kayak with him. So they all went kayaking all the way around the lake and when they came back the sun was setting and the evening breeze is blowing.

Figure 5–7 *Ethan's writing about place: "Noon at the Lake"*

Wading River in Long Island, New York, had to have known and loved Butternut Hollow in order to write about it with such careful detail. Karen talked about how writers often write about places they know well or that leave a lasting impression. She told them that it was unlikely she would ever write about Brian J. Heinz's Butternut Hollow or the West Virginian mountains that anchor many of Cynthia Rylant's stories. She told them, however, that she had written about the mountains and lakes of Central New Hampshire, where she spent her summer and winter vacations as a child. Mary Anne also spoke to the important role experience plays in writing when she told the class about her grandmother's farmhouse in Italy, which she visited when she was seven years old. She could still recall the smell of the fireplace and the sight of the deep stone staircase leading up to the blue-and-white-tiled kitchen. Although Karen's special place was one she had visited many times, and Mary Anne's one she had been to just once, both places left a strong, lasting impression.

In addition to looking beyond events and activities pieces for special places to write about, we wanted our children to think both about places they had visited several times that may have appeared frequently in their writing as well as about places that may have appeared only once in their writing, those places that may have been less obvious choices for them as they reread their work.

Next, we asked our children to write about one particular time of day at their special places. We began by asking them to draft lists of what they observed around their special places. We provided some questions for direction and to help them recall the places by listening and looking carefully:

> What happens around this place at different times of the day?
> What are the sights, sounds, and smells around your place?
> What does the sky look like at a particular time of day?
> Do you see any animals? What are they doing?

After generating some general thinking around their places, we challenged our children to anchor their writing in a specific time of day. We put the "End of Day at Butternut Hollow Pond" time frame on an overhead, demonstrating how Brian J. Heinz writes about the end of the day at Butternut Hollow. We talked about how the line "The sky is blushed and, for a moment, all is still" helps us get a sense of *evening*. We then placed the first page from *Box Turtle at Long Pond* on an overhead, discussing how the lines "The sun is high overhead. The morning chill is gone" help us get a sense of *noontime*.

Before sending them off to write, we asked our children to select a particular time of day to use as a focus for writing about their places. Jordana, who had come to the rug knowing she would write about the Poconos, decided to zoom in and write about daybreak in the Poconos. Stephen, who was excited to write about the Refuge in Westhampton, decided to begin writing about dawn at the Refuge, and Ethan, as depicted in Figure 5–7, chose to zoom in on noon at Long Pond. Before leaving the rug, as we often do, we asked each child to articulate the time and place he or she would write about. We find asking kids to

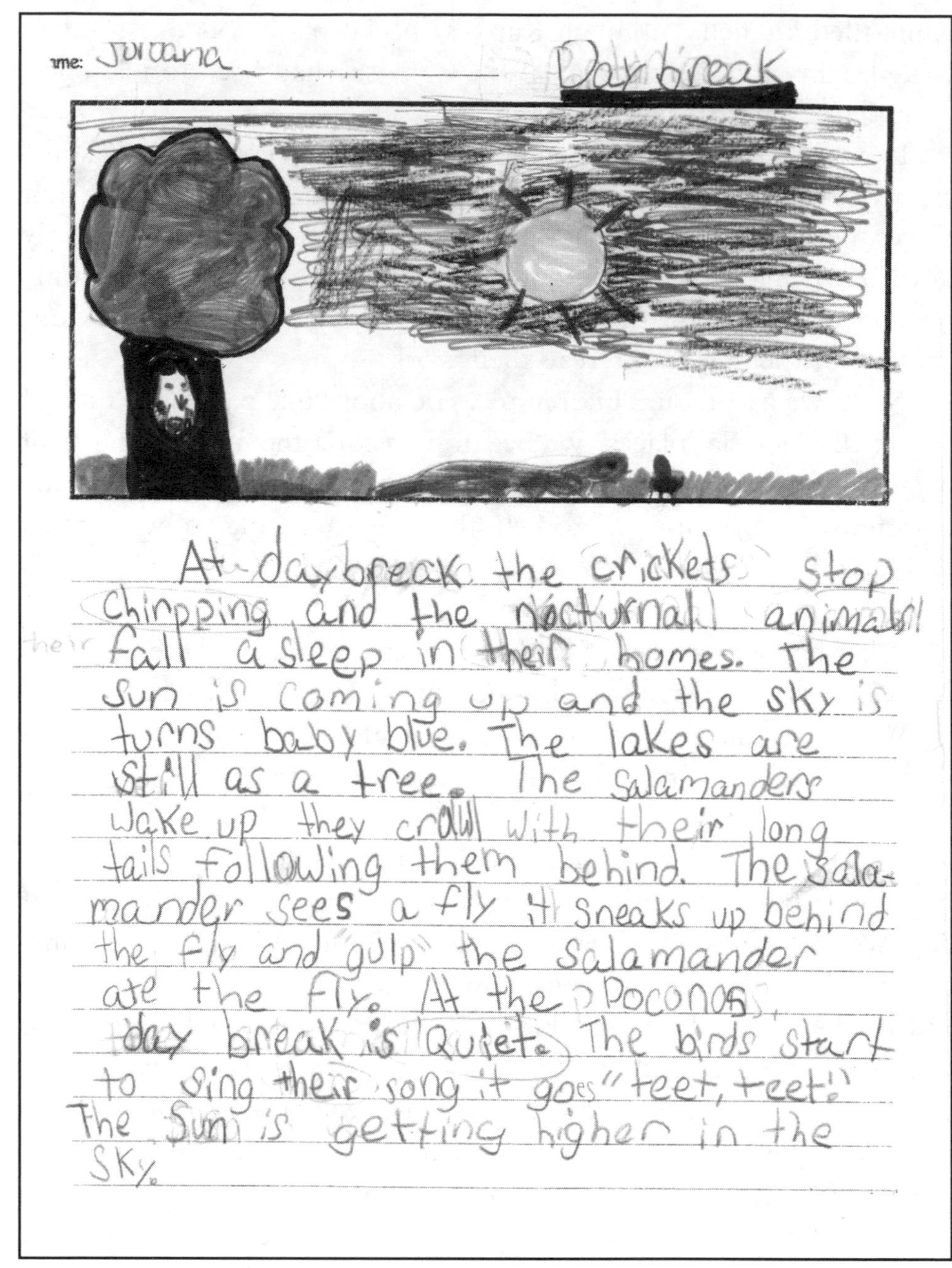
me: Jordana
Daybreak

At daybreak the crickets stop
Chirpping and the nocturnal animals
fall a sleep in their homes. The
sun is coming up and the sky is
turns baby blue. The lakes are
still as a tree. The salamanders
wake up they crawl with their long
tails following them behind. The salamander sees a fly it sneaks up behind
the fly and "gulp" the salamander
ate the fly. At the Poconos,
day break is Quiet. The birds start
to sing their song it goes "teet, teet!"
The sun is getting higher in the
sky.

Figure 5–8 *Jordana's draft on daybreak in the Poconos*

articulate their plans for writing workshop avoids unproductive writing time and allows children to get settled more quickly. We think of it as a rehearsal for our children. Figures 5–8 and 5–9 show what Jordana and Stephen produced from this minilesson when they zoomed in on time and place in writing.

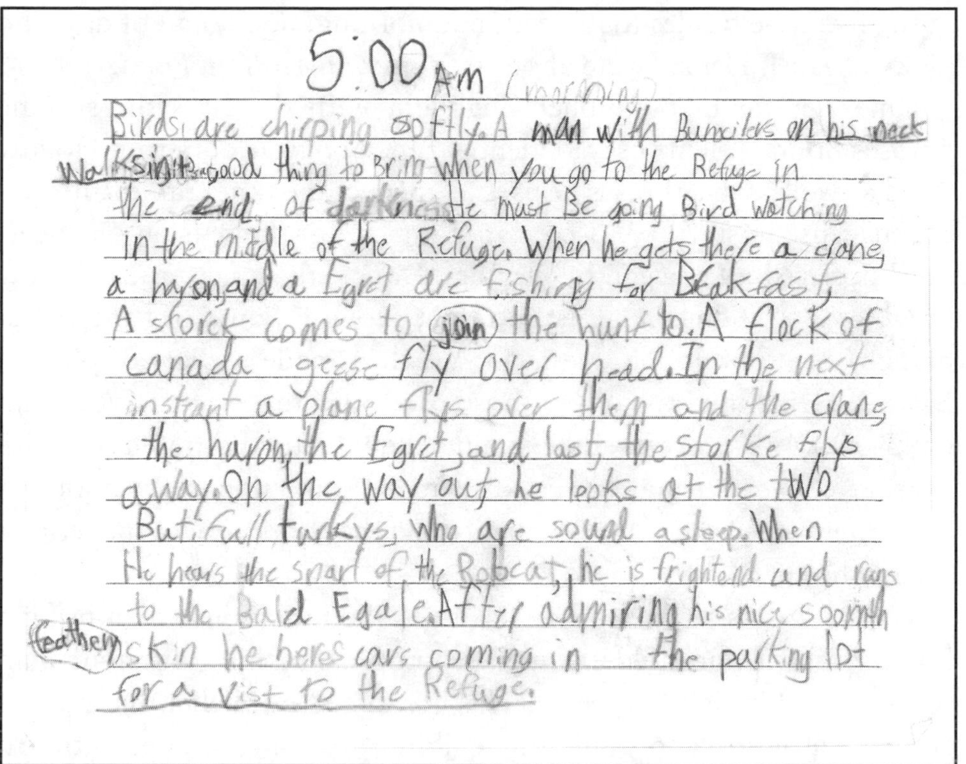

5:00 AM (morning)

Birds are chirping softly. A man with Bunocilers on his neck walks it's a good thing to Bring when you go to the Refuge in the end of darkness He must Be going Bird watching in the middle of the Refuge. When he gets there a crane, a hyron and a Egret are fishing for Breakfast. A storck comes to join the hunt to. A flock of canada geese fly over head. In the next instant a plane flys over them and the crane, the haron, the Egret, and last, the storke flys away. On the way out he looks at the two Butifull turkys, who are sound asleep. When He hears the snarl of the Bobcat, he is frighted and runs to the Bald Egale. After admiring his nice soomth (feathers) skin he heres cars coming in the parking lot for a vist to the Refuge.

Figure 5–9 *Stephen's draft on dawn at the Refuge*

Week Four: Writing and Revising

Goal: to follow place through several time frames

Our goal this week was twofold: we wanted our children to write about different times throughout the course of a day while also remaining genuine to their settings. Our children had already practiced writing with greater detail about one time of the day. Now, we challenged them to write about their special places at several different times of the day. In order for our children to write about their special places at different times of the day, they would have to focus on different techniques and clues writers used to show the passage of time.

To begin this week's work, we revisited the phrases from the Times of Day chart we had composed the previous week (Figure 5–4). These phrases were a reminder to the children about how they could begin their work. The one time frame they had just completed would serve as a springboard into several other time frames they would write this week around their special places. We also continued to look carefully at the five time frames (daybreak, midmorning, noon, end of day, and night) Brian J. Heinz wrote about in *Butternut Hollow Pond*.

In order for us to publicly highlight with the class the specific phrases Brian J. Heinz uses to identify time of day at Butternut Hollow Pond as well as the phrases he uses to connect the time frames and create suspense in story, we used transparencies of the text on our overhead projector. We began by writing "Daybreak at Butternut Hollow Pond" and "Midmorning at Butternut Hollow Pond" on the transparency being projected overhead. We then made a chart of phrases Brian J. Heinz used to convey those particular times of day. (See Figure 5–10.) As we reread and examined how he used different descriptions to convey setting, our children made some important noticings with reference to the storylike quality and the continuity of the writing across the entire day.

While we, as teachers, may have specific intentions when using a book, each of our children might capture something different than what we had initially expected. This reinforced our belief that finding good mentor texts to guide our children's writing was essential to

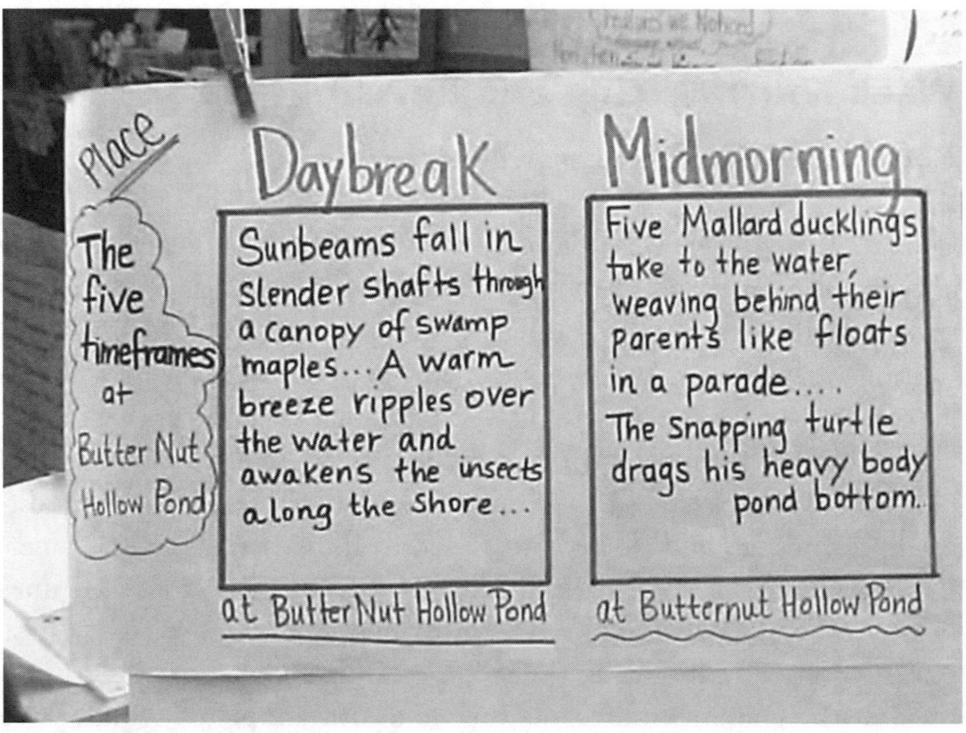

Place
The five timeframes at Butter Nut Hollow Pond
Daybreak
Sunbeams fall in slender shafts through a canopy of swamp maples... A warm breeze ripples over the water and awakens the insects along the shore...
at ButterNut Hollow Pond
Midmorning
Five Mallard ducklings take to the water, weaving behind their parents like floats in a parade....
The snapping turtle drags his heavy body pond bottom.
at Butternut Hollow Pond

Figure 5–10 *Our chart highlighting daybreak and midmorning phrases from* Butternut Hollow Pond

teaching writing. We looked at and studied all the time frames in *Butternut Hollow Pond*, and the children made relevant comments. The children began to notice how the food chain and interdependence of the animals around this pond serve as unifying features in the book. "The snapping turtle is after the ducklings," Emma commented. We pointed out how Brian J. Heinz connects his time frames to create continuity in his writing with the repetitive phrase "You need to be careful at Butternut Hollow Pond." We discussed the similarity to Cynthia Rylant's use of repetition in her writing and how she too uses this technique to engage the reader. Figure 5–11 highlights the storylike phrases and the time frames that are woven together in *Butternut Hollow Pond*. The children later used this knowledge to help them build continuity within their own pieces of writing.

In examining *Butternut Hollow Pond*, our children followed the animals' quest to eat while avoid being eaten. The drama that unfolded around life in the pond influenced some of the children's writing. While some of our children were determined to capture the same drama in their own writing using animals that live around their special places, others created more descriptive settings without using animals as subjects. For example, Stephen, in writing about the Refuge in Westhampton, New York, a place where he spends every summer, featured the animals that live at the Refuge and created a dramatic picture of this place as a bird-watching drama unfolds. Stephen writes, "In all the commotion the snapping turtle wakes up and starts chasing the man. You have to be careful when you go to The Refuge in the afternoon." Rachel, on the other hand, in writing about Long Island, New York, from where she had moved the previous year, focused her writing on the way that nature and human life intertwine, as she wrote: "The people working in the garden close the bird hotel doors . . . The crickets are slowing down their singing and the owls are getting tired. The moon has fallen and the sun has stepped onto Mother Nature's Elevator. . . ."

By the end of week 4, our children had written about several time frames in their special places. Jordana, who began with daybreak at the Poconos, had now written about midmorning, noon, end of day, and nighttime at the Poconos. Our children used their memories as well as their experience as readers and writers to create a sense of place. When Stephen read "A Day at the Refuge," we were able to get the sense of the softly chirping birds at dawn and the business of people applying suntan lotion to their skin in the afternoon.

What connects time frames to make writing more storylike?

	Daybreak at Butternut Hollow Pond	Midmorning at Butternut Hollow Pond	Noon at Butternut Hollow Pond	End of day at Butternut Hollow Pond	Night at Butternut Hollow Pond
Setting the Scene: Beginning Lines	Sunbeams fall in slender shafts through a canopy of swamp maples.	Five mallard ducklings take to the water, weaving behind their parents like floats in a parade.	On the hillside above the pond, wildflowers sway in a crazy quilt of colors.	The sky is blushed and, for a moment, all is still.	The water shimmers under moonglow, and wisps of fog dance over the pond like ghosts.
Creating Suspense with Interdependence of Pond Life	It's not safe here.	A monster lies in wait.	Something is not right in Butternut Hollow.	But sometimes there's just no escape in Butternut Hollow.	Butternut Hollow Pond, where the hunters and the hunt-ed are one in the same.

Figure 5–11 *Chart examining Brian J. Heinz's use of time frames and suspense*

Week Five: Revising

Goal: to use revision strategies to strengthen writing

Our job this week was to provide strategies needed for revision. Once again, we looked to the writing in *Butternut Hollow Pond* for support. In week 4, we examined it to see how Brian J. Heinz connected the time-frame vignettes to create story. This week we would study the craft of his writing. By *craft*, we are referring to the specific way words are put together and blended and how by changing the way in which words are put together, a writer can also change the meaning. We read *Butternut Hollow Pond* again, this time pulling out some of the crafting techniques Brian J. Heinz used. We spent the week discussing the craft and its effect on the writing and determined what we wanted to include in our own writing. Our children worked intensively this week with their writing partners, reading, rereading, and trying out crafting techniques. We created the chart in Figure 5–12 to organize the thinking that went on in the classroom during writing workshop and to visually support the lessons we were teaching.

Week Six: Editing, Illustrating, and Celebrating

Goal: to edit, illustrate, and celebrate

Although the revision process helped lift the quality of our children's writing, making it clearer, more organized, and more beautiful, our children still needed to edit their work. On Monday, the children came to the rug with their revised work on a clipboard, prepared to begin the editing process. Mary Anne asked them to reread their pieces three different times for three different purposes.

- Reread to see if your writing *makes sense*; make a note of any minor changes.
- Reread to listen for places where you, as a reader, naturally pause; mark those places with a period.
- Reread to look for words that don't look right; circle those words.

The editing process within the writing workshop is tailored to one piece of writing and is separate from our word study work, which is structured around inquiry and learning new words. It is during the editing process that we ask our children to attend to misspelled words in their writing work.

We use a spelling "try sheet" that we created during a whole-school study of Diane Snowball's *Spelling K–8*. The spelling try sheet is the place where the children work through the words that are misspelled in their revised pieces. This sheet allows children to go through the process of spelling, constructing their understanding of how words work while developing accuracy for the misspelled words in their

Crafting Techniques	Examples from Text	Effect of/ Comment on Craft	Examples from Children's Writing
strong verbs	• The woodchuck clambers along just ahead. • The cottontail explodes into motion.	• verbs used as descriptors • creates imagery	Baby birds nuzzle next to their mother. —Allie Kessler
similes	Five mallard ducklings take to the water, weaving behind their parents like floats in a parade.	• verb links two unrelated subjects: ducklings weave/ floats in a parade weave • creates imagery	It is very quiet at nighttime in Florida, like a lion trying to catch its prey.—Lauren Javaly
surprising language	The blacksnake slithers unseen, flicking his dainty tongue . . .	• *dainty*—unusual adjective used to make reference to the tongue of a blacksnake • creates element of surprise, striking—wows the reader	The black night fades into a candy-colored morning glow. —Allie Kessler
alliteration	The snake is a skillful and silent swimmer, scarcely disturbing the surface.	creates mood, voice, and fun	The waves sparkle suddenly in the sunlight.—Leah Solomon
repetition	He does not blink. He does not breathe. He does not dare.	creates rhythm	Hampton, at Hampton at daybreak. The nocturnal animals sleep. The deer wake up. The birds sing their song. —Max Snyder
onomatopoeia	• The frog takes aim. His sticky tongue flies out and . . . slurp! • As the bass circles back, kerploosh!	• adds sound • creates imagery	In Turkey, when the hot sun is already up, I'm at the beach getting thrown in the water. Splash! Splash! Splash! —Devin Keskinkaya
personification	• All are part of the nightshift at Butternut Hollow. • There's a raucous concert of frogs and toads . . .	• helps reader connect to subject created in these examples through noun choice	In Maine, there are lots of animals. It is daybreak. The old spider is just waking up. He is hungry. —Emma King

Figure 5–12 *Craft lessons learned from* Butternut Hollow Pond

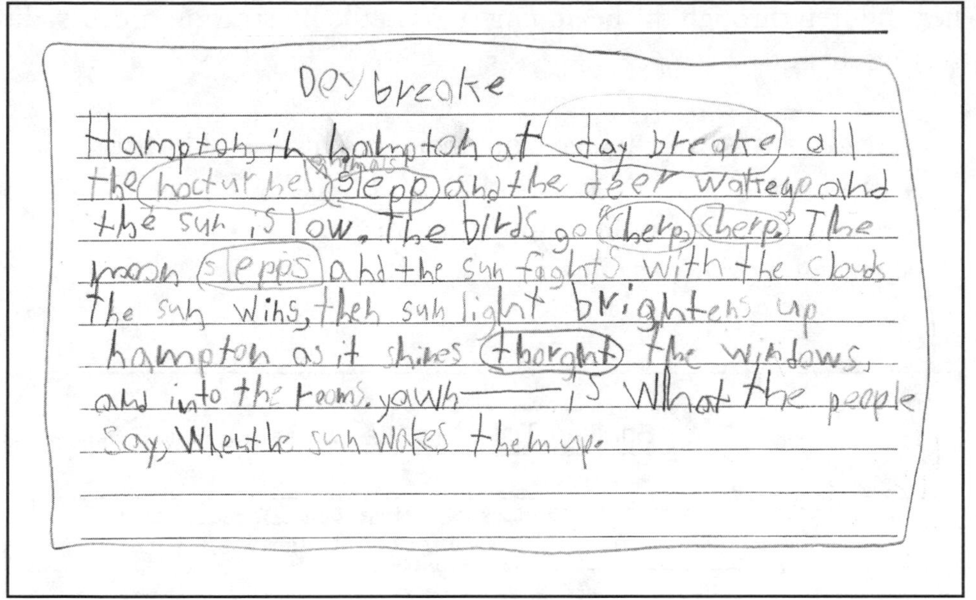

Dey breake

Hampton, in hampton at day breake all the hoctur hel slepp and the deer wateup and the sun is slow. The birds go cherp cherp. The moon slepps and the sun fights with the clouds the sun wins, then sun light brightens up hampton as it shines thorght the windows, and into the rooms. yawn — is What the people say, When the sun wakes them up.

Figure 5–13 *Max circled the words he was unsure of while editing*

writing. Figure 5–13 shows the words Max circled while editing and Figure 5–14 shows the words he practiced on his spelling try sheet.

Throughout the year, we asked our children to notice how writers present their work. While reading fiction and nonfiction picture books, we highlighted illustrations in the texts we read. We marveled over Brian G. Caras' bold, childlike illustrations in the High Rise Private Eyes series, by Cynthia Rylant, and *Puddles*, by Jonathan London. We were also fans of Vera B. Williams' border illustrations in *A Chair for My Mother* and *Cherries and Cherry Pits* and the realistic naturalist paintings of Lindsay Barrett George in *Box Turtle at Long Pond*. These illustrators, along with the many others we admired, draw us in and make the words on the page come alive. As we admired and highlighted both published and classroom illustrations, we tried to convey to our children the integral part pictures play in their writing work. Just as we spend several days writing for clarity and precision, our illustrations demand the same time.

In the final days of this writing study, Karen asked our children to come to the rug with their finished writing pieces. Her goal was for them to reread their writing, thinking like an illustrator. Karen took her children through the beginning steps in the illustration process, directing them to

reread to decide the image from their writing they'd like to capture
decide how they would capture that image
sketch and draft their image

Spelling Try Sheet For **Copied Spelling**, use this strategy:

Name: Max

Date:

Look, Say, Name, Cover, Write, Check
Look at the word so that you have a picture of it in your head.
Say the word.
Name the letters.
Cover the word.
Write the word.
Check the word, letter by letter

First Try	Second Try	Correct Spelling	Copied Spelling
day breake	day braeke	daybreak	day break
hocturhel	hoctrnle	nocturnal	hocturhal
slepp	sleepp	Sleep	sleep
Cherp	churp	Chirp	chirp
thorght	thought ✓	thought	thought

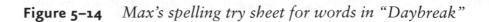

Figure 5–14 *Max's spelling try sheet for words in "Daybreak"*

The following day, she took her children through the final steps in the illustration process, directing the children to

select the image they liked the most
choose and add color
think about background and foreground
complete the final illustration

Jordana decided to divide her illustrations into sections, a technique she learned from the nonfiction writer and illustrator Gail Gibbons (see Figure 5–15). Stephen chose to depict one scene from his setting with animals around that place in the way Brian J. Heinz does in *Butternut Hollow Pond* (see Figure 5–16).

By the end of the week we were ready to celebrate our writing with others. This is a time for the children to present their final work to the school community and reflect on the lessons learned in the study. We invite family members and school administrators into our classroom to

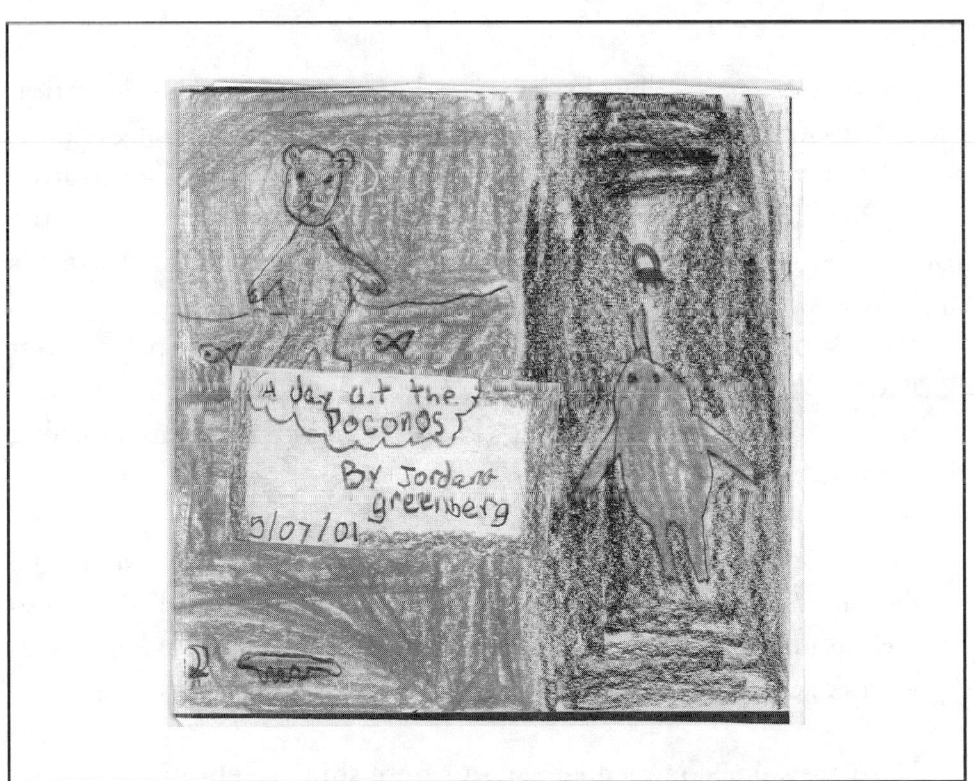

Figure 5–15 *Cover of Jordana's final piece, "A Day at the Poconos"*

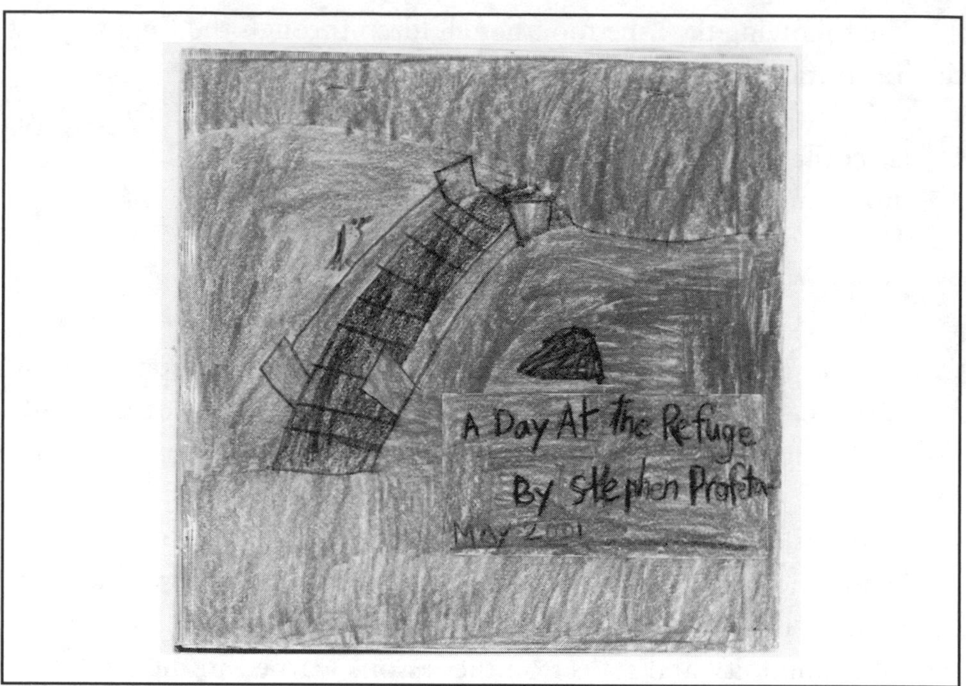

Figure 5–16 *Cover of Stephen's final piece, "A Day at the Refuge"*

read and celebrate our hard work. In addition, we use the celebration time to invite the people we admire and love into our learning experience. We ask kids to share what they learned as writers and illustrators as they proudly present their writing work. It becomes clear from the comments visitors make on premade comment sheets that the work is impressive and appreciated.

During our publishing celebration, Alexander's setting piece about Port McDonald, a beach he visited often in his native home of Australia, elicited responses to the following excerpt from his morning time frame:

> At Port McDonald in the morning the sun is touching the waves before they hit the dry sand. Before people come, the shells get washed away so their feet don't hurt. The waves fly and crash against the rocks and other waves . . .

Here are some comments from our publishing celebration:

Reader: Sara Scungio (Alexander's mom)

Comment: Alexander, the way you described Port McDonald made me feel like I was there and I remembered all the times we went there together.

Reader: Rob Snyder (Max's dad)
Comment: I've never been to Port McDonald but now I know what it looks like. Thanks! Great description of surfing.

Reader: Bruce Lieber (Lindsay's dad)
Comment: I really want to go to Port McDonald after reading this piece. I especially like how you described the surf crashing against the rocks.

Reader: Caroline (classmate)
Comment: I love your book. It gives me such a good picture in my mind of Port McDonald! I wish I was there.

The invitation in Figure 5–17 is a glimpse into the behind-the-scenes work that led to the final celebration of this study.

The setting study proved an invaluable experience for our young writers. The development of this important skill, anchoring their personal memories in one place, led them to apply these lessons toward future writing.

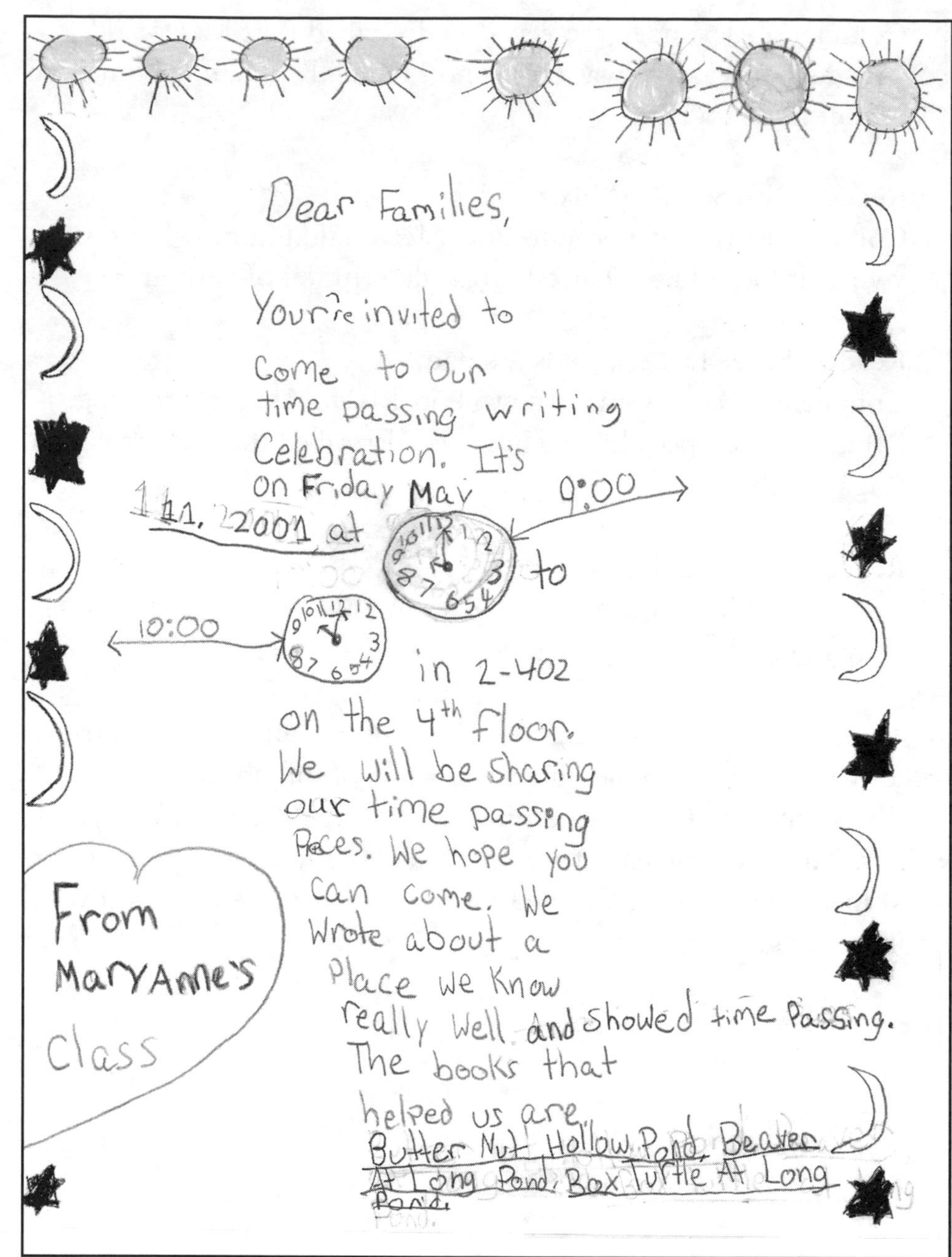

Dear Families,

You're invited to
Come to our
time passing writing
Celebration. It's
on Friday May
11, 2001 at
9:00
to
10:00
in 2-402
on the 4th floor.
We will be sharing
our time passing
Pieces. We hope you
can come. We
wrote about a
place we know
really well and showed time passing.
The books that
helped us are
Butter Nut Hollow Pond, Beaver
At Long Pond, Box Turtle At Long
Pond.

From
MaryAnne's
Class

Figure 5–17 *Invitation to publishing celebration*

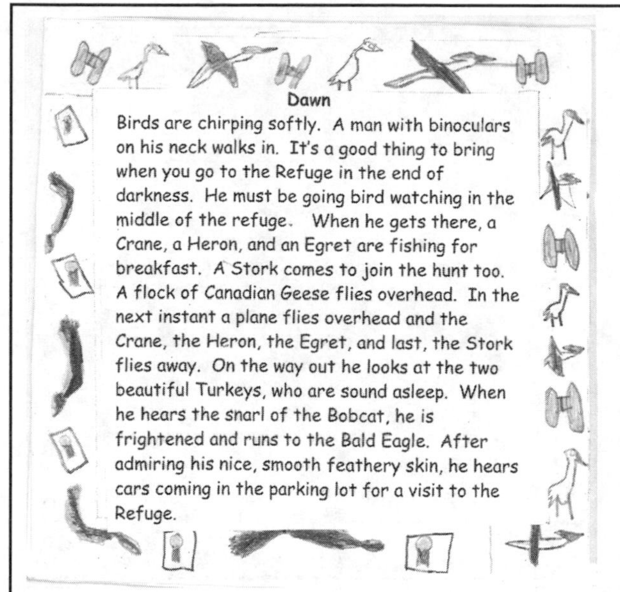

Dawn

Birds are chirping softly. A man with binoculars on his neck walks in. It's a good thing to bring when you go to the Refuge in the end of darkness. He must be going bird watching in the middle of the refuge. When he gets there, a Crane, a Heron, and an Egret are fishing for breakfast. A Stork comes to join the hunt too. A flock of Canadian Geese flies overhead. In the next instant a plane flies overhead and the Crane, the Heron, the Egret, and last, the Stork flies away. On the way out he looks at the two beautiful Turkeys, who are sound asleep. When he hears the snarl of the Bobcat, he is frightened and runs to the Bald Eagle. After admiring his nice, smooth feathery skin, he hears cars coming in the parking lot for a visit to the Refuge.

Midmorning

A man walks into the parking lot, with a sketchpad and a pair of sunglasses, a strange thing to bring when you arrive to the Refuge at midmorning. He must be going to sketch the eels in the pond. When he gets there, the eels are hitting themselves with their long skinny bodies. He quickly starts sketching, for it is very rare to see animals fight. They only do it to settle arguments. After a few sketches, he starts the walk home.

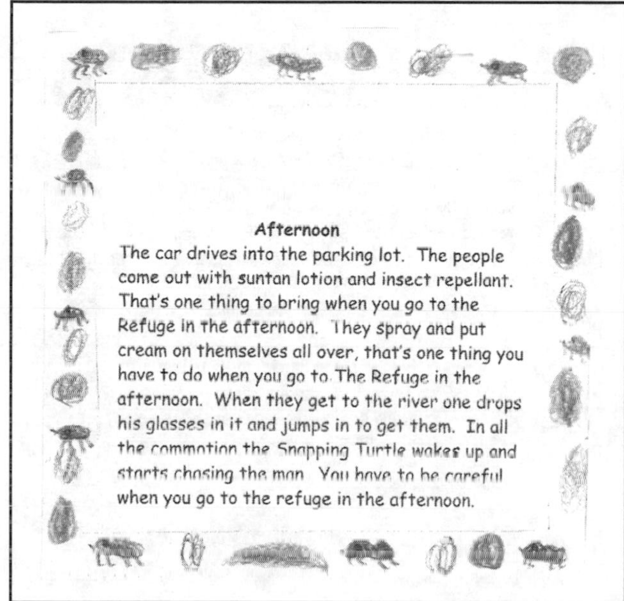

Afternoon

The car drives into the parking lot. The people come out with suntan lotion and insect repellant. That's one thing to bring when you go to the Refuge in the afternoon. They spray and put cream on themselves all over, that's one thing you have to do when you go to The Refuge in the afternoon. When they get to the river one drops his glasses in it and jumps in to get them. In all the commotion the Snapping Turtle wakes up and starts chasing the man. You have to be careful when you go to the refuge in the afternoon.

Dusk

Canadian Geese are walking around a patch of grass. A car does a right turn into the parking lot. The geese fly away into the trees. The people have two containers of bug spray so they don't get covered. That's a smart thing to bring when you go to the Refuge at the beginning of darkness. They must be on their way to Dear Pond to look for toads. When they get there, they slip and slide in the mud. You need to wear boots when you go to the Refuge in the beginning of darkness. One sees a toad and jumps for it and misses. You need a raincoat when you go to the Refuge in the beginning of Darkness.

Figure 5–18 *Stephen's final work*

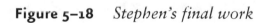

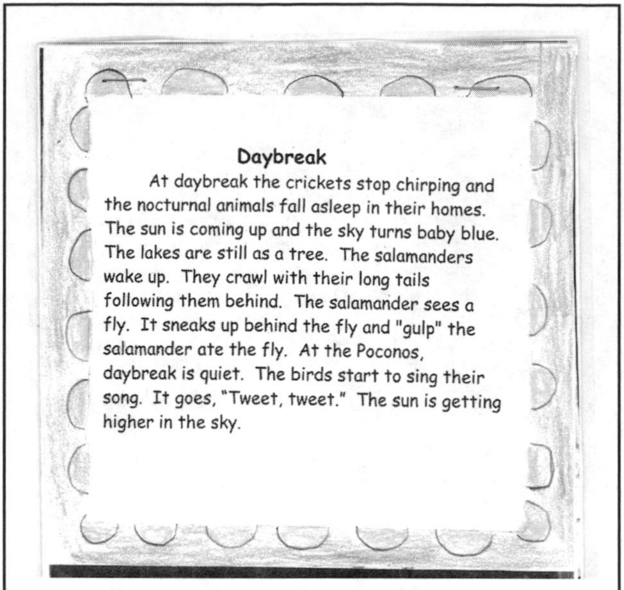
Daybreak

At daybreak the crickets stop chirping and the nocturnal animals fall asleep in their homes. The sun is coming up and the sky turns baby blue. The lakes are still as a tree. The salamanders wake up. They crawl with their long tails following them behind. The salamander sees a fly. It sneaks up behind the fly and "gulp" the salamander ate the fly. At the Poconos, daybreak is quiet. The birds start to sing their song. It goes, "Tweet, tweet." The sun is getting higher in the sky.

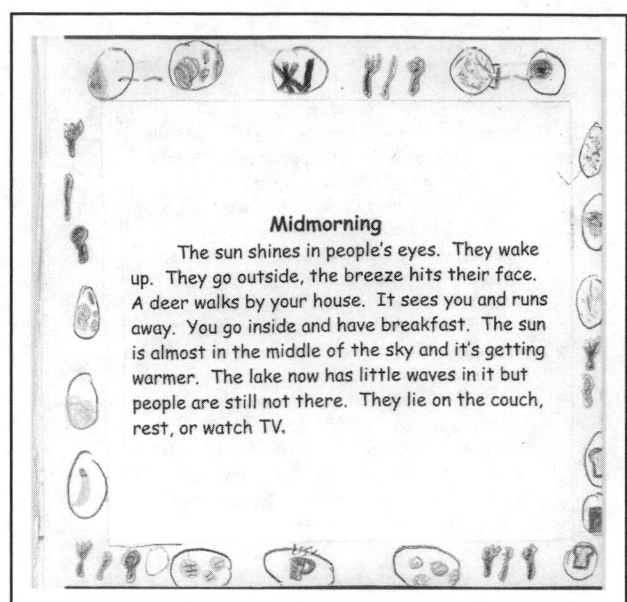
Midmorning

The sun shines in people's eyes. They wake up. They go outside, the breeze hits their face. A deer walks by your house. It sees you and runs away. You go inside and have breakfast. The sun is almost in the middle of the sky and it's getting warmer. The lake now has little waves in it but people are still not there. They lie on the couch, rest, or watch TV.

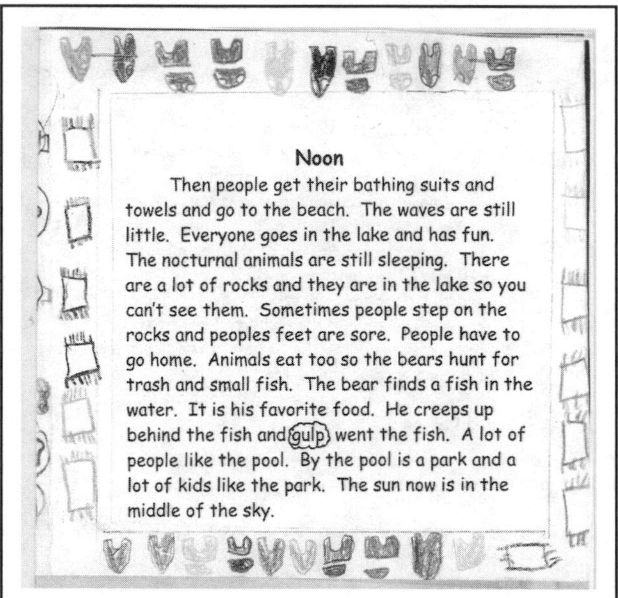
Noon

Then people get their bathing suits and towels and go to the beach. The waves are still little. Everyone goes in the lake and has fun. The nocturnal animals are still sleeping. There are a lot of rocks and they are in the lake so you can't see them. Sometimes people step on the rocks and peoples feet are sore. People have to go home. Animals eat too so the bears hunt for trash and small fish. The bear finds a fish in the water. It is his favorite food. He creeps up behind the fish and gulp went the fish. A lot of people like the pool. By the pool is a park and a lot of kids like the park. The sun now is in the middle of the sky.

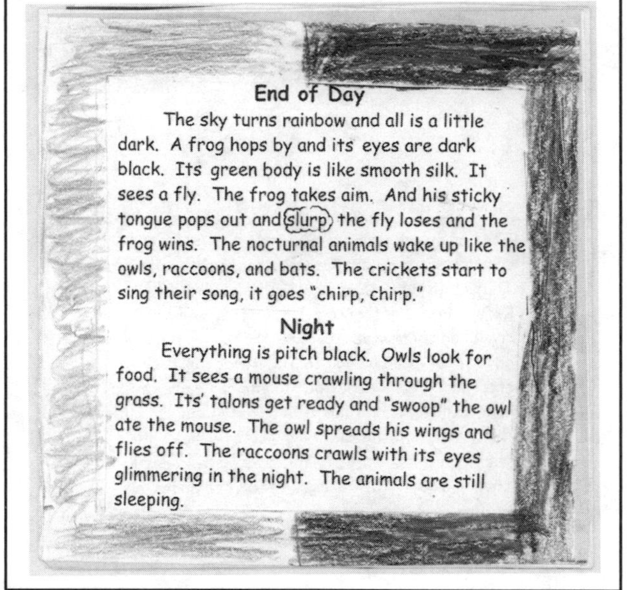
End of Day

The sky turns rainbow and all is a little dark. A frog hops by and its eyes are dark black. Its green body is like smooth silk. It sees a fly. The frog takes aim. And his sticky tongue pops out and slurp the fly loses and the frog wins. The nocturnal animals wake up like the owls, raccoons, and bats. The crickets start to sing their song, it goes "chirp, chirp."

Night

Everything is pitch black. Owls look for food. It sees a mouse crawling through the grass. Its' talons get ready and "swoop" the owl ate the mouse. The owl spreads his wings and flies off. The raccoons crawls with its eyes glimmering in the night. The animals are still sleeping.

Figure 5–19 *Jordana's final work*

Through Melissa's Eyes: A New Teacher's Voice

What I learned from this work

I saw with my own eyes the passion that Mary Anne and Karen have for authors, engaging their children, in turn, to possess the same passion as writers. I learned that beautifully written picture books provided a model that pushed my students as writers. Using *Butternut Hollow Pond* exposed children to the possibilities of writing—writing like an observer, grounding your story in one place over time. Using this mentor text, I learned how to deepen my students' writing, focusing the children on the craft of using language to add details and provide a picture in the minds of the audience. Through the language, the children were engaged in this powerful story.

How I adapted this study to fit my classroom needs

I found other mentor texts to elevate the children's writing. *When Morning Comes* and *When Night Comes*, by Ron Hirschi, and *Grand Canyon: A Trail Through Time*, by Linda Vieira, helped give my students more examples of writing as an observer about a special place. I noticed that the children needed to know a place really well in order to write about it at different times of the day. Therefore, I decided to use our school, MNS, as an example to demonstrate how to write a time-passing story. This was a place that the children all shared an experience with and a high level of interest in. Scaffolding the work in this way helped the children choose language, link the different times of day with transitional phrases to create cohesive pieces that depicted a whole day, and apply the lessons learned to their independent writing. Take a look at what we wrote:

> ***Night at MNS***
>
> The moon shines softly, casting a slender beam of light across the empty classroom. No one is around. It is silent, strangely quiet. Books sit still on the shelves, waiting to be read the next morning by children.

CHAPTER 6

Content Area Research and Writing

Investigation Four

Russell Freeman, a Newbery Award–winning nonfiction writer, in talking about his craft, suggests,

> Certainly the basic purpose of nonfiction is to inform, to instruct, hopefully to enlighten. But that's not enough. An effective nonfiction book must animate its subject, infuse it with life. It must create a vivid and believable world that the reader will enter willingly and leave only with reluctance. A good nonfiction book should be a pleasure to read. It should be just as compelling as a good story.

Luckily for us, writers like Jonathan London, Debbie S. Miller, and Brian J. Heinz understood the essence of Russell Freeman's words as they created such books as *The Eyes of Gray Wolf*, *Disappearing Lake*, and *Butternut Hollow Pond*. The intention of these books is to instruct and inform, but it is the artful presentation of the language that allows us, as readers, to enter willingly and leave only with reluctance.

Karen thought back a few years to when she and her second graders studied biographies. Around this time, she had come to love the work of African American painter William H. Johnson. While reading Steph Harvey's *Nonfiction Matters* (1998), this stuck with her: "Passion is contagious. Teachers who share their passions develop learners who want to explore theirs." She decided to use William H. Johnson and the picture book biography of his life and work by Gwen Everett, *Li'L Sis and Uncle Willie: A Story Based on the Life and Paintings of William H. Johnson*, to begin examining the components of biographies. The study went well. The children came to understand that biographies tell the story of someone's life and that dates and locations of major events are usually included in a biography. Passion proved contagious. Not only did the kids grow to love William H. Johnson, mimicking his primitive style with bold colors and lines in their own pictures, but they became learners ready to explore their own interests and questions. Following some exploration into our nonfiction library, the children chose to learn about writers, artists, athletes, politicians, and pioneering women. They paid close attention to the facts and events that shaped the lives of those they studied and they represented their understandings on presentation boards. Each of the six sections on the presentation board demonstrated something of importance in the life being represented. The presentation boards were lovely and the celebration was a smashing success.

In retrospect, however, we realized the study was flawed. The children walked away knowing a lot about the people they studied, with some understanding of the components of biography and with little understanding about the qualities of good writing. The writing seemed dull and regurgitated. We hadn't shown the children how to write biographies with the same enthusiasm and voice they had demonstrated at other points in the year during writing workshop. We hadn't shown them good examples of writers who weave factual information into narrative so that a reader might enter willingly and leave only with reluctance. In retrospect, we decided their learning, although exciting for the moment, was more about acquiring content information than about growing as readers and writers.

This year, however, we approached the research and writing of nonfiction from a different perspective. Since we had already investigated the various forms of nonfiction in the reading workshop, and written setting pieces with the support of a variety of narrative nonfiction books in the writing workshop, we knew our children were far more prepared for the research and writing of nonfiction than those in years past. As Ralph Fletcher tells us in his introduction to *Nonfiction Craft Lessons* (Portalupi and Fletcher 2001), "Too often we see the same tired encyclopedia-inspired writing that is so hard to read." We knew, this year, our children were armed with skills they would need to produce writing that would not only inform and instruct but be a pleasure to read—writing in which an understanding of structure, voice, and craft would be evident.

	WEEK 1	WEEK 2	WEEK 3	WEEK 4
GOAL	to gain a general understanding of birds by developing and exploring own questions	to gain a general understanding of one particular bird	to research, collect, and process information about one bird	to draft writing with attention to voice
	IMMERSION	IMMERSION/RESEARCH	RESEARCH/ PROCESSING	DRAFTING
LITERATURE	• *Peterson Field Guides for Young Naturalists: Backyard Birds* • *Birds, Nests, and Eggs*, by Mel Boring • *A Hummingbird's Life*, by John Himmelman • *What Makes a Bird a Bird?* by May Garelick	• *Urban Roosts:Where Birds Nest in the City*, by Barbara Bash • *Peterson Field Guides for Young Naturalists: Backyard Birds*	variety of texts from birding library, including field guides	• *Whose Tracks Are These?* by Jim Nail • Joanne Ryder books, including *Where Butterflies Grow* • *Are You a Butterfly?* by Judy Allen and Tudor Humphries
MINI LESSONS	• from known to unknown: What do we know about birds? What do we want to know about birds? • demonstrate how nonfiction features and structures help you locate specific information • Further explore one specific question: What makes a bird a bird?	• make list of all New York City birds • chart what we know about the American robin and some wonderings • model how to read for, highlight, and extract information pertaining to physical descriptions	• demonstrate how to use the research sheets to collect and record information about physical attributes • demonstrate how to process facts by showing learning in narrative form • demonstrate process of collecting, recording, and processing for remaining categories	• demonstrate how to make list of facts, then weave into narrative • underline facts, naming them into categories • model how to shift writing from "I" voice to "you" voice using a collection of Joanne Ryder books
STUDENT WORK	• write down questions and wonderings about birds • look for specific information to answer class-generated questions • locate information about feathers	• select top three bird choices on an index card • compose T-chart, noting what they know and want to know about the bird they are studying • read for information specific to physical description illustrations of final book	• extract information pertaining to the physical attributes of their bird • process facts collected into narrative form • collect, record, and process for remaining categories	• list facts and weave them into first-person narrative • second-person narrative pieces using "you" voice

Figure 6–1 *Study at a glance: content area research and writing*

WEEK 5	WEEK 6	WEEK 7
to weave facts from each research area into different drafts and begin revision process	to revise with focus of instructing and entertaining while cohesively weaving drafts together with attention to setting	to edit final draft and illustrate each section of writing
Drafting/Revising	**Revising/Editing**	**Editing/Illustrating/ Publishing**
• *It's a Frog's Life*, by Steve Parker	• *River of Life*, by Debbie S. Miller • *It's a Frog's Life*, by Steve Parker • *Condor's Egg*, by Jonathan London • *Birds, Nests and Eggs*, by Mel Boring • *Butternut Hollow Pond*, by Brian J. Heinz	• *Flute's Journey*, by Lynne Cherry • *Butternut Hollow Pond*, by Brian J. Heinz
• read food section of *It's a Frog's Life* to demonstrate how to weave facts into narrative with voice • demonstrate how to draft in each research area	• use *River of Life* to demonstrate weaving facts and narrative • use *It's a Frog's Life* to demonstrate voice • use *Condor's Egg* and *Butternut Hollow Pond* to craft with attention to setting • use *Birds, Nests and Eggs* to demonstrate how to compare an unknown quantity to a known quantity	• use enlarged copy of spelling try sheet to model editing for spelling • model rereading drafts for punctuation and capitalization • examine favorite texts for illustrations, noting page layout, color, and style
• weave facts from each research area into a different narrative	• reread writing, checking for factual accuracy • students try infusing voice into listlike pieces • write lead sentences that establish setting • examine places in their writing to try out a comparison	• spelling try sheets to edit final draft • students reread drafts with attention to punctuation and capitalization • cover illustrations and inside

While investigating nonfiction in the reading workshop, we considered various possibilities for a content area research and writing study. We thought about woodland animals, butterflies, and even minerals as a way of framing our study. We knew we wanted to conduct a whole-class inquiry study, one that would provide a common classroom experience while leaving room for our children to explore their unique interests. Around this time, Ben Berkowitz, a second grader in our class, came across the book *Urban Roosts: Where Birds Nest in the City*, by Barbara Bash. He was fascinated by how many birds actually roost in our common city fixtures—in the warmth of the streetlights, under elevated subway platforms, and in the crevices of city museum gargoyles. This was so much a part of our everyday world—we were all fascinated!

In our preliminary research around this topic, we came to learn that every year, birders, both novice and seasoned, from all over the country flock to New York's Central Park for a prime view of more than two hundred species of birds. Hailed by many as one of the best spots for birding, this 843-acre gem of a park, containing habitats ranging from freshwater to woodland to meadows and streams, is only steps away from the Manhattan New School. Our students, mostly native New Yorkers, would learn to see their own city park in a whole new way. Central Park would become a beloved place for us to visit for firsthand knowledge about birds and their varied dwellings and behaviors. The children would learn that their city is more than an urban center for business; they would learn about its natural role as vital home, or stopping ground, to many of the world's feathered creatures. We would learn that the Ramble, a 37-acre section of Central Park, is famously known as a haven for warblers during the month of May, and that a certain red-tailed hawk and its babies have attracted the attention of many New Yorkers, creating a following of watchers and a story made popular in the best-selling book *Red-Tails in Love*, by Marie Winn. We would also learn that the Harlem Meer, situated at the north end of the park and known to us as a place for ice-skating, was a prime location to spot the waterbirds we'd read about in guides: Canada geese, red-winged blackbirds, black-crowned night herons, great egrets, swans, and more.

We knew we had found a topic that would engage the children while meeting our criteria for designing a whole-class study.

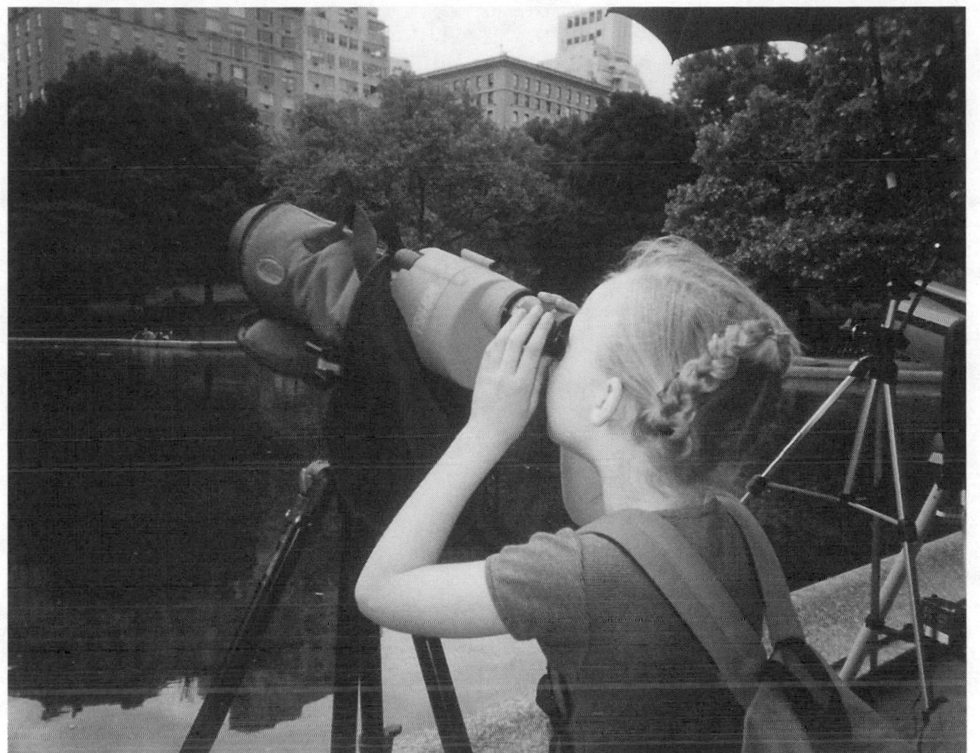

Figure 6–2 *Our children birding in Central Park*

Reasons for Whole-Class Content Study	*How This Supported Our Bird Study*
managed resources	Finding resources on one topic helped make our study manageable. The local library, as well as parents and colleagues, helped us collect books on birds. Our computer teacher helped children gather information on the Internet, while our art teacher planned projects that contributed to the synthesis of their learning. We looked to local birders to help us with our fieldwork.
focused planning	One topic helped us focus our planning. We designed cumulative minilessons to meet the needs of our students.

Reasons for Whole-Class Content Study	*How This Supported Our Bird Study*
shared community	Studying one topic allowed us to collect, sort, and classify information, filling the room with attribute charts that supported research and writing. One topic also allowed for a shared experience that became contagious beyond the walls of our classroom.

Week One: Immersion

Goal: to gain a general understanding of birds by developing and exploring own questions

We used the nonfiction investigation time in reading workshop to sort through many books. We started by looking at the entire class library, fiction and nonfiction. We then put aside the fiction books and looked more deeply at our nonfiction collection, sorting by author, structure, topic, and so on, until we had a host of nonfiction subcategories. Once we decided, as a class, to frame our research and writing study around birds, we sifted once again, scouring the class and local library for bird books. By the time we were ready to begin week 1 of Learning the Content Area Research and Writing study, we had a well-established birding library filled with field guides, picture books, and various research texts we would use to dip in and out of as we gathered information. We found beautiful baskets to house our books and placed them in what we call the "prime real estate" of our classroom—essentially meaning the shelves and countertops most accessible to children. In addition, we found chapter book read-alouds with birds as a central theme. These books would serve to provide a shared classroom experience while supporting our content study and building upon the foundation in fiction laid out in the first half of the year. Here's a list of some of the chapter books we considered for class read-alouds:

There's an Owl in the Shower, by Jean Craighead George
My Side of the Mountain, by Jean Craighead George

On the Far Side of the Mountain, by Jean Craighead George
Frightful's Mountain, by Jean Craighead George
Trumpet of the Swan, by E. B. White
The Fledgling, by Jane Langton

Our second graders are fortunate to receive swimming lessons once per week at Asphalt Green, a local community pool. For some of our children, this program is their first attempt at swimming. Before becoming skillful swimmers with refined stroke and proper breathing techniques, it is necessary for our children to feel comfortable in the water. That is the first step. With each week, we watch how the instructors supportively challenge our children to move slightly beyond their comfort level, helping them make gradual gains as swimmers. By the end of the swimming course, our children have gained comfort, acquired skills, and developed techniques to refine those skills.

Like with swimming, when we learn something new, we must jump in, navigate our way by first acquiring the essentials, and then fine-tune these essentials through strategy and technique to achieve proficiency. We view our inquiry studies through a similar lens, jumping in, finding our way to the essentials, and beginning the refining work necessary to develop proficient learners. The initial questions in the study about what makes a bird a bird led to more refined questions about bird anatomy and habitats. These questions fueled our research on birds and led us to our writing work.

The minilessons at the beginning of week 1 consisted of determining what our children knew about birds and what they wanted to know. We began with a two-column T-chart; one side read, "What do we think we know?" and the other side read, "What do we want to know?" After listing what we knew about birds, the children went off in partnerships to discuss and write down some of their wonderings. Emma and Graciela questioned where birds live. "Do they live in our city?" Emma wondered, "I know they live in gardens because I saw some in my cousin's backyard in Queens," replied Graciela. When the children reported back, we listed their wonderings on the T-chart. These questions provided the framework for our research. (See Figure 6–3.)

In looking over the questions from the T-chart, we saw that they naturally fit into categories, such as habitat, migration, food, reproduction, and physical attributes. Emma and Graciela's wondering, for example, was one of many that led us to discuss and investigate the habitat of birds. Other questions, such as "Where do birds go?" led us

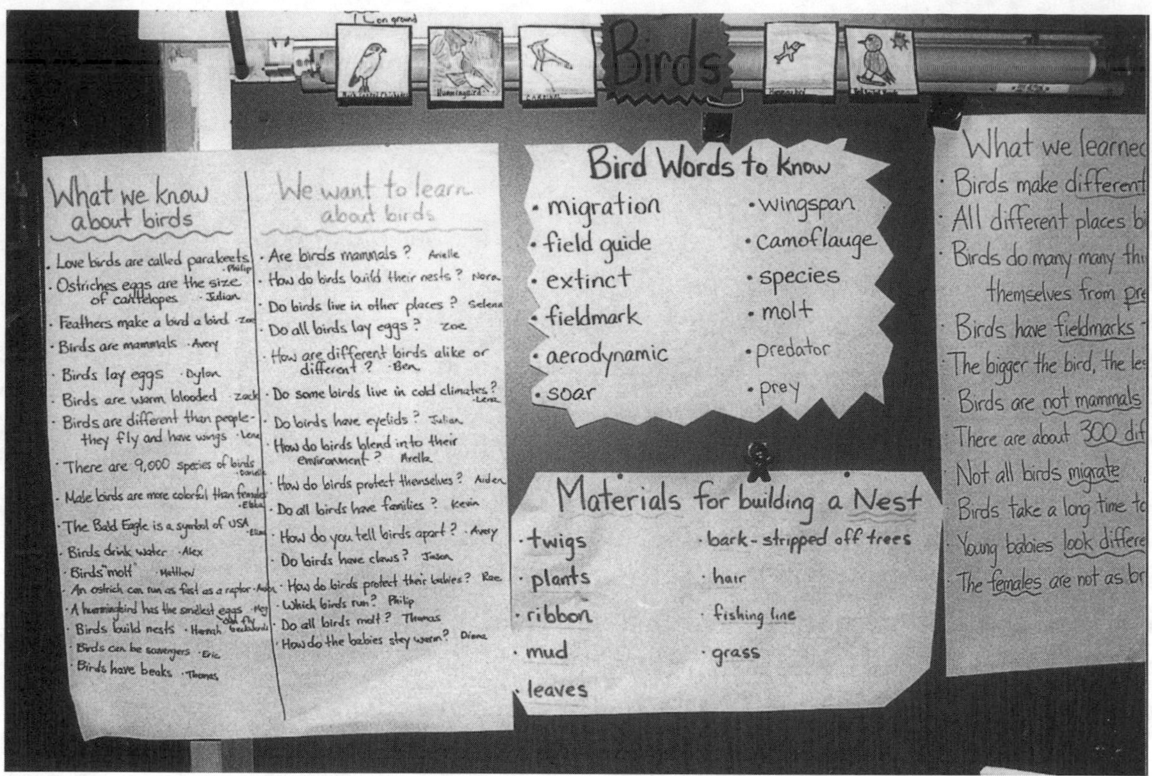

Figure 6–3 *T-chart and other information about birds*

to explore how birds migrate. These varied categories helped us scaffold and organize learning into more manageable pieces. Before going off to find answers to the charted questions, we revisited some of the nonfiction reading strategies we learned while investigating nonfiction in our reading workshop. We had learned how text features help us navigate through nonfiction and how a table of contents and an index help us locate specific information. We wanted our children to be aware of their purpose as nonfiction readers and to know which books to look to when investigating specific questions. Our minilessons shifted to reviewing nonfiction features and structures. We made overhead samplings of three nonfiction structures: a field guide, a narrative text, and a nonnarrative text. We used *Peterson Field Guides for Young Naturalists: Backyard Birds* to examine the layout of a field guide, *A Hummingbird's Life*, by John Himmelman, to examine a narrative text, and *Birds, Nests and Eggs* by Mel Boring, to examine an example of a nonnarrative text. Once we were familiar with the layout and content of each of these books, Karen reread the questions posted on the chart tablet and asked, "Would any of these books be helpful in answering our questions?"

Amanda, who was interested in blue jays, answered, "I can find out how big a blue jay is by reading *Backyard Birds*, I think I can also find out what blue jays like to eat." Amanda was right! The field guide was a place she could go to learn about the physical characteristics as well as the food preferences of individual birds. The children were excited to answer the questions they had previously written. They had an understanding of where to go and how to search for information, and they had questions they wanted answered—enough to keep them researching and engaged for quite a while. We sent the children off with Post-It Notes to locate and extract information relevant to their questions. (See Figures 6–4 and 6–5)

Figure 6–4
Using Post-it Notes to locate and extract information

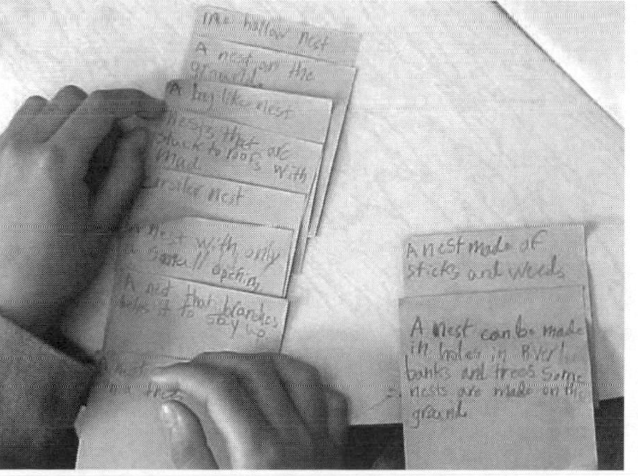

Figure 6–5
Organizing Post-its in preparation for class discussion

We spent the next couple of days immersed in books, finding answers to our questions and forming new questions. Gathering information seemed to mushroom, as learning led to new questions. Our children took ownership of their learning, inquiring about birds beyond writing workshop time. They looked to our birding library during reading time and brought books home to further their exploration of birds with their families. They researched birds in computer class and used their knowledge of computer research to locate information from their home computers.

Some of the questions were specific to particular bird species, while others were broad, such as What makes a bird a bird?, helping us understand birds in general. Developing an understanding of this question was central to our work in researching birds. We decided to spend some time focused on this, asking the children what they knew about the difference between birds and other animals. "A bird flies and other animals don't," Liam said.

"Birds have beaks that they use to eat with," said Rebecca.

We acknowledged all their responses, knowing that the defining factor is simply *feathers*. We used the appropriately titled book *What Makes a Bird a Bird?* published by Mondo, to dispel some of the inaccuracies. The children were intrigued that it's simply *feathers* that make a bird a bird. Their fascination sent them off looking for more information about feathers. They returned to the rug that day with Post-it Notes marking all the new information they'd gathered about feathers. Here's what they found:

Feathers help a bird fly.

Feathers are controlled by tiny muscles.

Feathers keep rain and snow away from a bird's skin.

Down feathers provide insulation while contour feathers support flight.

Most birds replace their feathers every year—a process called molting.

Ducks and geese lose their wing feathers, grounding them for a few weeks in summer.

Birds cannot live without feathers.

Feathers help camouflage.

Feathers contain veins.

A hummingbird has a thousand feathers.

Week Two: Immersion/Research

Goal: to gain a general understanding of one particular bird

In all of this research, some children developed an interest in particular birds. Diana seemed intrigued with the great egret, while Alexander and Nicholas were fascinated by all birds of prey and particularly the great horned owl. Dakota focused on the songbirds she saw while visiting her grandmother in the country, while Ethan, after a sighting in Central Park the previous weekend, was captivated by the red-tailed hawks nesting on Fifth Avenue. The children now had a general understanding about birds. They had spent week 1 following their own questions as well as supporting each other as they made discoveries. It was time to dig deeper in our study. We asked the children to think about the birds they found most fascinating, birds that would become the focus of their research, varieties that we would eventually compare and contrast to deepen the study. We encouraged children to think about the many varieties of birds found in New York City. Here are some of the birds included in our class list:

Some birds of particular interest to our children

common loon
European starling
mourning dove
indigo bunting
white-throated sparrow
gray catbird
American redstart
black-capped chickadee
American goldfinch
northern mocking-bird
rock dove (pigeon)
red-winged black-bird
house sparrow
downy woodpecker
red-tailed hawk
great egret
cedar waxwing
belted kingfisher
Baltimore oriole
mallard
ruby throated hummingbird
yellow warbler
red-breasted nuthatch
American robin

While we wanted our study to include a fair representation of New York City birds, including birds of prey, woodpeckers, waterbirds, and songbirds, we also wanted our children to have choice over the birds they would study. We asked the children to each write down the three birds they found most fascinating. We then developed partnerships based on interest and personal work habits. Although each child was paired off with a classmate to investigate one particular bird, they would each eventually produce their own writing and develop their own projects. The partnership, however, supported the management of research and resources and made learning easier to scaffold. Rather than studying twenty-six birds, one for each child, we, as a class, studied just thirteen, one for each partnership.

At this point, the study shifted from gathering general information about birds to gathering information about a particular bird. We used the American robin as a model for all the research work going forward in the study. As a minilesson, we charted what we already knew about the American robin and then charted some wonderings. This T-chart was similar to the one we used at the beginning of the study that served as a model for their research and thinking. After modeling, we sent the children off with blank T-charts to do the same work. Here's what Emma and Lindsay said about the subject of their study: the ruby-throated hummingbird.

Emma and Lindsay's recordings of facts and questions

What Do You Know?	*What Do You Want to Know?*
• The ruby-throated hummingbird is a small bird. • The ruby-throated hummingbird flaps its wings very fast. • The ruby-throated hummingbird has a long beak. • The ruby-throated hummingbird flies fast. • The ruby-throated hummingbird likes flowers.	• Is the ruby-throated hummingbird the smallest bird in the world? • Why is it called a hummingbird? • Does the ruby-throated hummingbird stay in New York during the winter? • Does the ruby-throated hummingbird eat flowers? • How do ruby-throated hummingbirds build nests?

We wanted them to use what they already knew about birds and researching to locate, collect, and synthesize information pertinent to their individual research and writing. Questions such as What does my bird look like? Where does it live? and Does it go away for the winter? assisted in our planning and helped us scaffold their learning as we subdivided their questions into the following categories:

physical description
habitat and migration

nesting, eggs, and young
food and beak

Since the children were so interested in the shape, size, and color of their birds, physical description seemed like a natural place to begin. Mary Anne chose an excerpt from *Backyard Birds* to demonstrate how nonfiction writers read for information. Beginning with a short excerpt, she modeled the process with this first research category—physical description—in mind. This excerpt on nuthatches, filled with information about the way nuthatches look, supported our goal of reading for information:

> Most birds climb up trees, but nuthatches are different. Nuthatches go down tree trunks first. That is why they are sometimes called "upside down birds." This behavior helps them find insects in the bark of trees that birds climbing up may have missed. These small birds have blue-gray backs with lighter-colored breasts. They have large heads, strong bills like a woodpecker, and short, square-cut tails. Nuthatches often show up together with chickadees and woodpeckers at feeders. . . . The White-breasted Nuthatch has a white face and breast. The Red-breasted Nuthatch has a rusty red breast and is smaller than the White-breasted.

Mary Anne read this excerpt from the overhead aloud twice, the second time directing the children to look for all aspects of the bird's physical appearance. She introduced what *physical* meant and made the term specific to birds by highlighting color, shape, and size. She told them that physical description refers to the way something *looks*, not the way it acts. At this point, Matthew suggested our class create a diagram of bird features like the ones he had examined in *Backyard Birds* and other field guides. It was a brilliant idea. This would help our children develop the language necessary to examine the specific birds they were to focus on this week. (See Figure 6–6.) In doing this, we were able to introduce specific vocabulary such as *talons*, *crest*, and *bills* to identify features and words such as *rusty red*, *cone-like*, *plump*, and *pointy* to describe those features. (See Figure 6–7.)

Embedded in the nuthatch excerpt was information about its behavior as well as its physical attributes. We anticipated some confusion in distinguishing between general information and information pertaining solely to physical attributes. That day, the focus of the minilesson was to read and extract information simply about the way the

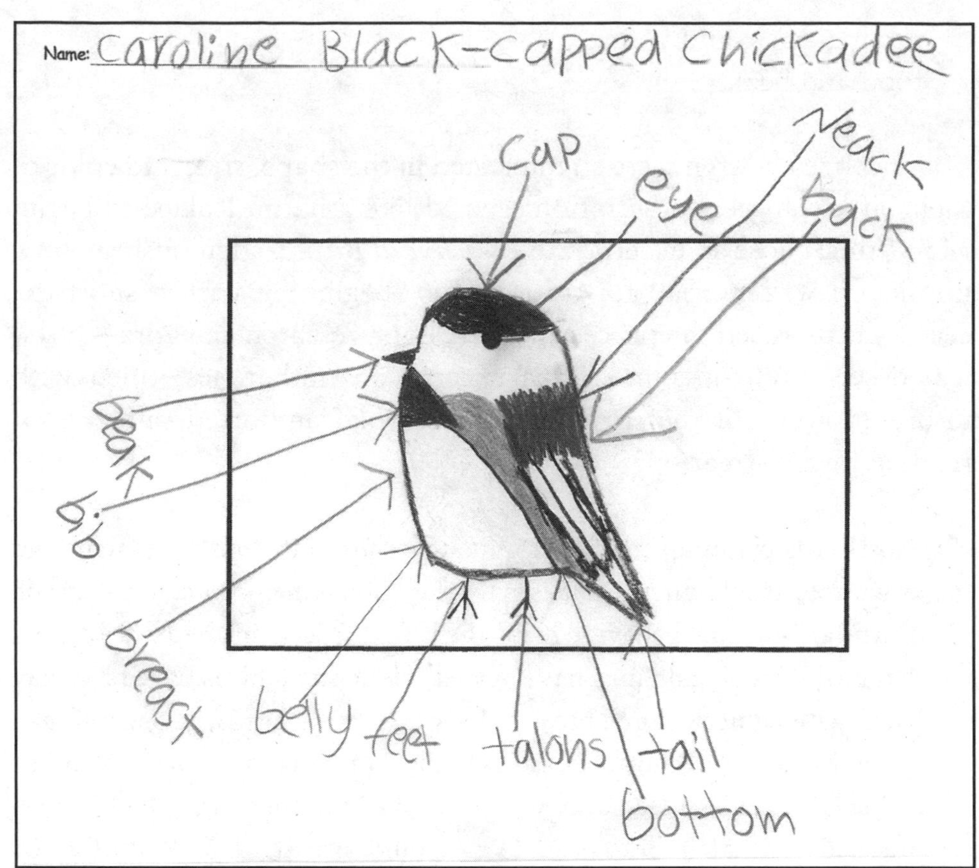

Figure 6–6 *Caroline's bird diagram*

nuthatch looks. Since physical description was the first category our children would be researching, we wanted them to be clear about how to read and locate specific information, tuning out extraneous facts and resisting the temptation to pay more attention to interesting information. . . . at least for now! Before reading this excerpt, Mary Anne alerted the children to listen and look for information regarding physical features of the nuthatch. As expected, there was some confusion following the read. When asked to name the physical characteristics of the nuthatch, Dan answered, "Nuthatches go down tree trunks head first."

"Going down head first is what the bird is doing," Jordana replied. The discussion that evolved from this confusion allowed us to clarify our focus—to locate and extract information pertaining to physical attributes. We sent the children off to practice this same exercise using an excerpt from *Backyard Birds* about the cardinal. (See Figure 6–8.)

Bird vocabulary

body	beak	feet	tail feathers
big	curved	talon	broadwinged
Short	lage		long
plamp	Straiaht		rounded
Slender	cone or conical		Short-square
bulky	flat		Short-broad
stoky	stubby		triangular
dainty	short		
sturdy	thick		
round	stardy		

Figure 6–7 *Karla's vocabulary list*

Week Three: Research/Processing

Goal: to research, collect, and process information about one bird

The children were becoming more and more enthusiastic about their research and future writing. Birds flew into our lives and took hold of our attention. Our classrooms now had full shelves and baskets devoted to the bird books we had collected and would continue to collect. (See Figure 6–9.) In addition, we made research and writing folders exclusively for this study to help the children organize their research and writing. (See Figure 6–10.) The children returned from the

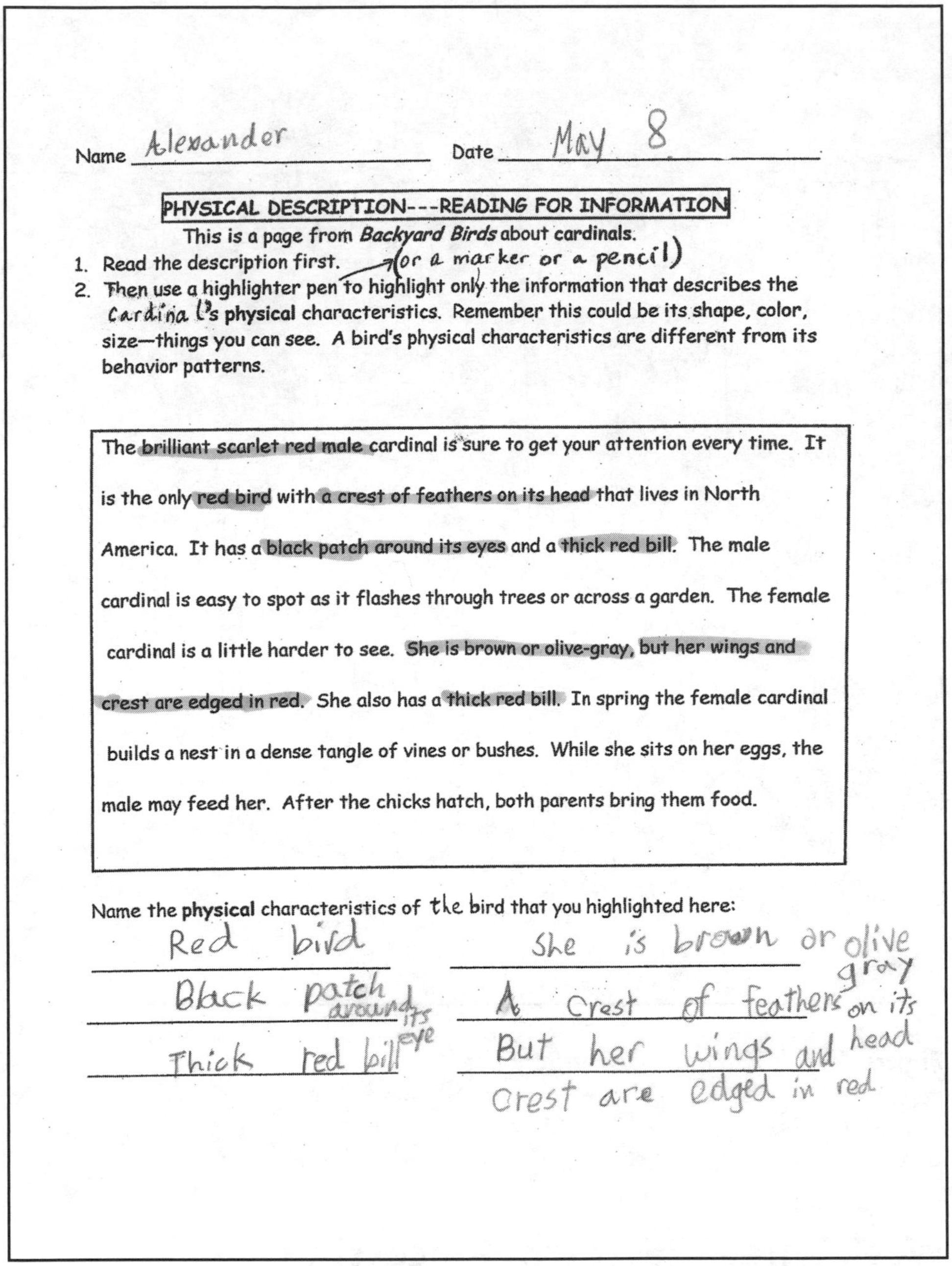

Name Alexander Date May 8

PHYSICAL DESCRIPTION---READING FOR INFORMATION

This is a page from *Backyard Birds* about cardinals.

1. Read the description first.
2. Then use a highlighter pen (or a marker or a pencil) to highlight only the information that describes the Cardinal's **physical** characteristics. Remember this could be its shape, color, size—things you can see. A bird's physical characteristics are different from its behavior patterns.

The brilliant scarlet red male cardinal is sure to get your attention every time. It is the only red bird with a crest of feathers on its head that lives in North America. It has a black patch around its eyes and a thick red bill. The male cardinal is easy to spot as it flashes through trees or across a garden. The female cardinal is a little harder to see. She is brown or olive-gray, but her wings and crest are edged in red. She also has a thick red bill. In spring the female cardinal builds a nest in a dense tangle of vines or bushes. While she sits on her eggs, the male may feed her. After the chicks hatch, both parents bring them food.

Name the **physical** characteristics of the bird that you highlighted here:

Red bird | She is brown or olive gray
Black patch around its eye | A Crest of feathers on its head
Thick red bill | But her wings and Crest are edged in red

Figure 6–8 *Alexander's attempt at reading for information*

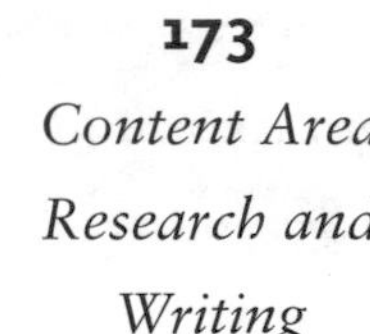

Figure 6–9 *Bird library*

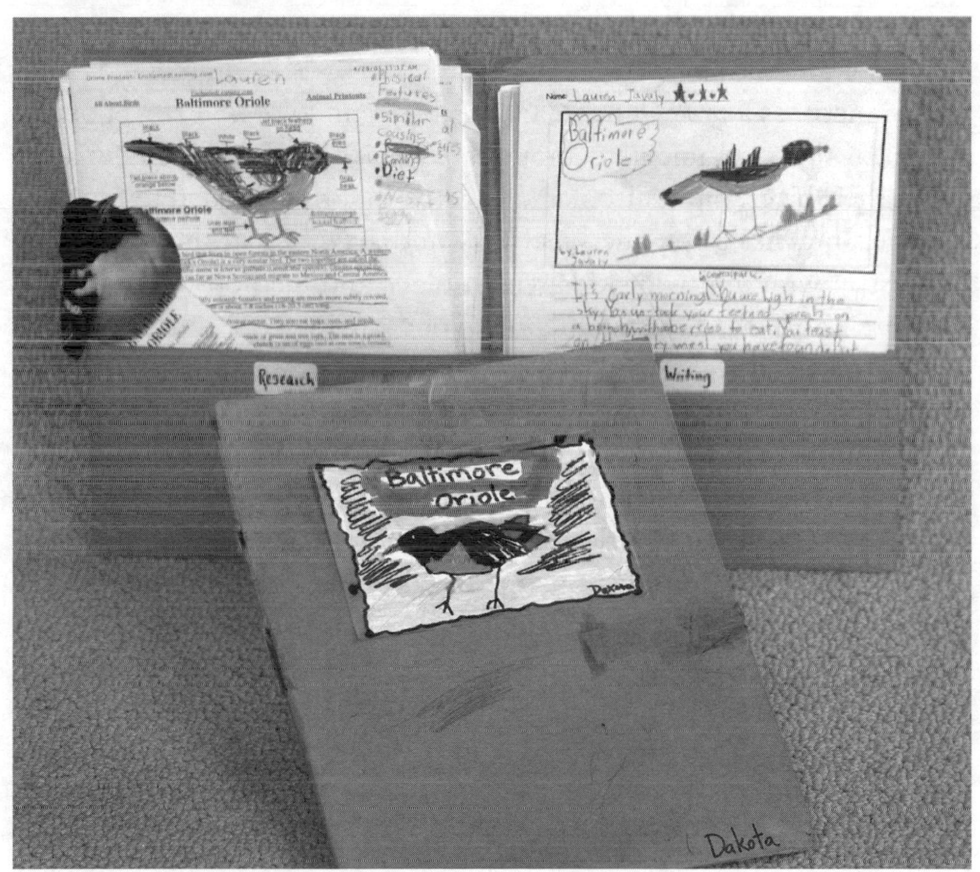

Figure 6–10 *Lauren's and Dakota's bird folders*

weekend excited to learn more about birds, particularly about the individual ones they were studying. They entered the room on Monday with notes from parents offering support. Some wanted to tell us about their own birding expertise and gather resources, while others offered to organize trips and connect with local birding organizations. This newfound learning was clearly infectious!

In preparation for their individual research, we designed research sheets based on the children's questions from week 2. Our first task was to look again at physical description but this time with attention to the specific birds they were researching. The research sheet contained several questions that would support the children in locating information specific to physical description and specific to the birds they were studying. In addition, the research sheet left room for processing that information by turning facts into narrative.

Mary Anne demonstrated how to use the research sheet. As she put a transparency of the physical description research sheet on the overhead, the children recognized the questions from their work in week 2. "I know what color my bird is; it's black and white," Graciela cried.

"But it might have other colors under its wing," Katie interrupted.

"Or it could change colors in different seasons," commented Allie.

"Sometimes a male and female are different colors," Eric reported.

All of these comments demonstrated that the children knew a lot about their birds, but it also demonstrated that they needed to be more specific. In order to pursue specificity and accuracy in their research, this lesson would provide kids with a place and method for collecting accurate information. After all, one of our writing goals was to inform and instruct and we needed to be accurate in our reporting to readers.

Mary Anne prompted the children to think more about researching skills than content when she asked, "How will we find the information we need to answer these important questions?" They thought back to when they studied nonfiction in reading and began to comment on how the features of nonfiction, specifically the table of contents and the index, would help them locate the information needed for their research. Before the children went off in their partnerships to collect and record information about their birds, Mary Anne used the American robin to demonstrate how they would fill in the sheet.

Once the children had collected and recorded information, Mary Anne demonstrated how to process their recordings. In this minilesson, Mary Anne took the information about the American robin, reflected on what she had learned, and demonstrated how to process it by weaving it into narrative form. She also showed the children how to record the internal thoughts floating in her head as she processed the information. The children went off to process their own findings, thinking about turning facts into narrative and adding internal thoughts. (See Figure 6–11.)

Week 3 continued with students completing similar research and processing sheets for the other three categories:

habitat and migration (see Figure 6–12)
nesting, eggs, and young (see Figure 6–13)
food and beak (see Figure 6–14)

Name: Class Model
What is the name of your bird? The American Robin

MINILESSON ONE: COLLECTING AND RECORDING
MINILESSON TWO: PROCESSING

Physical Description

Things I need to know

1. Describe your bird. What does it look like?
The American Robin has a rusty-orange chest. It has a yellow bill. The male has a black head and tail. The female's head and back are brown. It has lines on the throat and white underfeathers.

2. What is the **wing span** of your bird? 17 inches

3. What is the **weight** of your bird?

4. What is the **length** of your bird? 9–11 inches

5. What is the **length** of your bird's beak?

6. What does your bird's beak look like?
The beak is yellow and pointy

7. Describe the **shape** of your bird?
The American Robin is a plump bird. It has a small but round-shaped body.

8. What **special features** does your bird have?
The Robin has a rusty orange or reddish breast that people notice. It has a white ring around its eye.

What did I learn?

I learned that an American Robin is not hard to spot because of its rusty red-orange chest. The males have a black head and back while the female's have a brown head. The American Robin is between 9 and 11 inches long. That is longer than I thought! When it's wings are spread open, it's winspan measures about 17 inches. The American Robin's body shape is a little plump. It's a little bit round too. The American Robin's beak is yellow. It stands out because of it's color. The Robin has white lines on its throat and white underfeathers.

Figure 6–11 *Demonstration research sheet*

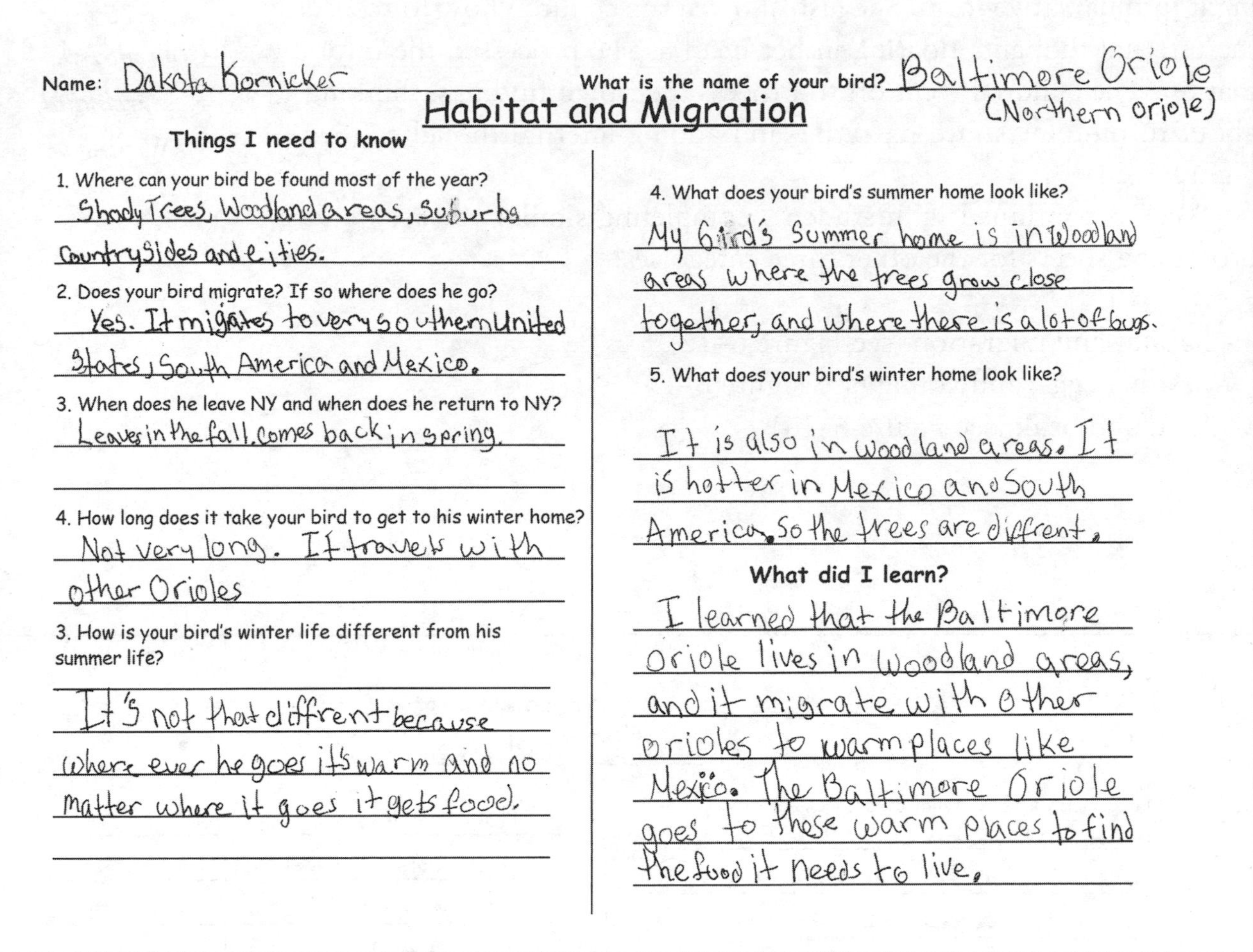

Name: Dakota Kornicker What is the name of your bird? Baltimore Oriole (Northern oriole)

Habitat and Migration

Things I need to know

1. Where can your bird be found most of the year?
Shady Trees, Woodland areas, Suburbs countrysides and cities.

2. Does your bird migrate? If so where does he go?
Yes. It migates to very southern United States, South America and Mexico.

3. When does he leave NY and when does he return to NY?
Leaves in the fall, comes back in spring.

4. How long does it take your bird to get to his winter home?
Not very long. It travels with other Orioles

3. How is your bird's winter life different from his summer life?
It's not that diffrent because where ever he goes it's warm and no matter where it goes it gets food.

4. What does your bird's summer home look like?
My Bird's Summer home is in Woodland areas where the trees grow close together, and where there is a lot of bugs.

5. What does your bird's winter home look like?
It is also in wood land areas. It is hotter in Mexico and South America. So the trees are diffrent.

What did I learn?

I learned that the Baltimore Oriole lives in woodland areas, and it migrate with other orioles to warm places like Mexico. The Baltimore Oriole goes to these warm places to find the food it needs to live.

Figure 6–12 *Dakota's research on habitat and migration*

For each of these categories, the children researched, recorded, and began to formulate sentences about what they'd learned. All of this collected research would provide a factual basis for the narrative nonfiction work they would do later in this study.

Name: Karla Kirsch

What is the name of your bird? American Redstart

Nesting - Eggs - Young

Things I need to know

1. How does the male attract a female? It sings a song.

2. Who builds the nest and where is it made? The nest is made in a large tree

3. What is the nest made of? grass, bark shreds, plant fibers and spider silk.

4. How many eggs are laid? a clutch of 4 eggs

5. What color are the eggs? white speckled with brown

6. What time of year are the eggs laid? May, June, July

7. How many times of year does your bird nest? once

8. How long do the eggs take to hatch? 12 days

9. What do the babies eat? insects

10. How long do the babies stay in the nest? 30 days

11. After hatching, how long is it before the young leave home?

Notes: The American Redstarts learn to fly when they are 9 days old.
Also the mate helps incubate the eggs.

words that may help you understand your research:

embryo- an animal at its earliest stages of growth, before birth or hatching

brooding- sitting on eggs to keep them warm so they can hatch

preen- to trim and clean feathers with the beak

clutch- a group of eggs laid at one time

down- the bird's soft baby feathers

molt- to replace feathers

fledgling- a young bird reared, feathered and able to fly

incubation- the development time in the egg before hatching

egg tooth- the bump on the top of a baby's beak that the baby uses to break out of its shell during hatching

nestling- a bird too young to leave the nest

Figure 6–13 *Karla's research on nesting, eggs, and young*

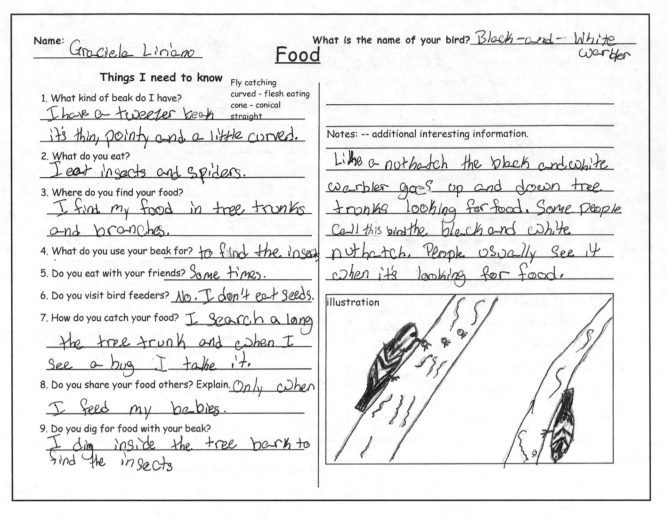

Name: Graciela Liriano

Food

What is the name of your bird? Black-and-White Warbler

Things I need to know

1. What kind of beak do I have?
   Fly catching
   curved - flesh eating
   cone - conical
   straight
   I have a tweezer beak it's thin, pointy and a little curved.
2. What do you eat? I eat insects and spiders.
3. Where do you find your food? I find my food in tree trunks and branches.
4. What do you use your beak for? to find the insects
5. Do you eat with your friends? Some times.
6. Do you visit bird feeders? No. I don't eat seeds.
7. How do you catch your food? I search a long the tree trunk and when I see a bug I take it.
8. Do you share your food others? Explain. Only when I feed my babies.
9. Do you dig for food with your beak? I dig inside the tree bark to find the insects

Notes: -- additional interesting information.

Like a nuthatch the black and white warbler goes up and down tree trunks looking for food. Some people call this bird the black and white nuthatch. People usually see it when it's looking for food.

illustration

Figure 6–14 *Graciela's research on food and beak*

Week Four: Drafting

Goal: to draft writing with attention to voice

Now, in week 4, our children had taken hold of their learning. In addition to class birding trips in Central Park with New York City's renowned birder Starr Saphir and local trips to the Queens Aviary and Inwood Hill Park, the children planned weekend excursions to Central Park and Jamaica Bay National Wildlife Refuge, looking for birds they had come to know and love. They did additional research at home and visited our local libraries for resources. Although our children cherished all the books in our birding library, they had a special attachment to *The Sibley Guide to Birds*, written and illustrated by David Allen Sibley. The children used this book, which includes more than six thousand detailed illustrations of birds, as a constant reference, weaving new learning about bird species into what they knew from their prior research. Our students shared their newfound knowledge with all those who would listen. Parents, neighbors, and relatives learned about birds, becoming interested in our work and reporting back on how the bird study had influenced their own lives. (See Figure 6–15.)

June 27

Dear MaryAnne,

You know how much you've taught Max. Do you know how much you've taught me as well?

Before the children were born, Rob & I went to the Amazon to a rain forest and an Indian village. We learned to see things we'd never seen before — vines & hanging plants and epiphytes and tropical fish and birds. When we came back, we suddenly saw things in Central Park we'd never seen before and the world has never been the same for us.

The trips to Central Park with Starr were like that for us. Now, when we go canoeing in the woods of Connecticut or even walking on 82nd Street we see things we had never seen before, not just the birds themselves but also the relationship between humans and the world of wildlife. And it's all so close to home! Thank you for a wonderful year.

You'll be missed

Love,

Clara Hemphill Snyder

Figure 6–15
Parent letter written by Clara Hemphill Snyder

Our students' knowledge of birds was impressive and noticeable. They owned it. And as though our students lived a bird's life themselves, they began to speak about their birds in the first person. "I eat you!" Alexander snickered to Diana upon discovering that the bird he was studying, the great horned owl, sometimes ate the great egret, the subject of Diana's work. Tension between predator and prey grew as others scanned the room looking to see if they, too, were in danger.

We chose Jim Nail's book *Whose Tracks Are These? A Clue Book of Familiar Forest Animals* as a way of capitalizing on the enthusiasm that had developed around talking about birds in the first person. The children loved using the clues to figure out which animal was being written about. One of the pages in the book gives the following clue:

> Look closely as these tracks. Do they look like they were made by a dog? If you get just a quick look at me you might mistake *me* for a dog, too. I hunt small animals such as mice for my food. Can you tell from these tracks what happened here? I caught a mouse to take back to my babies, called kits. . . . . When you're in the forest, especially at the edge of the forest, look carefully. You might catch a glimpse of my reddish-brown fur—or just my white-tipped bushy tail as I run into the woods to hide.

With each clue page came a buzz. Our students listened attentively to the details so that they would be able to make smart guesses about to which animal the author was referring. After reading the previous excerpt, the children were happy to report that they were sure it was a fox. Stephanie said it was the reddish-brown fur that gave it away, and Devin said that he knew that foxes were like dogs. Other kids were confused. Diana mentioned that she thought it was a fox, but not knowing that foxes call their young "kits" confused her. She was thinking back to when we read Jonathan London's book *Phantom of the Prairie: Year of the Black-Footed Ferret* and learned that prairie dog babies are called kits. The specificity that Jim Nail used in his writing supported the students' sophisticated dialogue. Karen referred back to Jim Nail's choice of words: *reddish-brown fur* and *white-tipped bushy tail*. They talked about how these descriptive details help the reader create a mental picture.

We knew that with all the information we had gathered about the birds we were studying, we too could write a Jim Nail–inspired clue book that would engage and inform our readers. Karen used the American robin to model exactly what we wanted the children to do that day. Placing the worksheet they would soon use on the overhead, she modeled how to use it by making a list of what she knew about the American robin and then weaving those facts into narrative. (See Figure 6–16.)

The following day, Karen referred back to her American robin piece, marking the categories of facts woven into her writing. Together, on the overhead, the class investigated what she did as a writer. The kids noticed that she not only included facts about the American robin's color, behavior, and food preference but had chosen to include both a physical comparison and a behavioral comparison, which added to the depth of the writing. (See Figure 6–17.)

Together, the children thought about the facts they might mention in their own pieces. They came up with a chart (see page 182) to support their own writing as they continued to craft their Jim Nail-inspired pieces.

Name: Class Model

Topic: The American Robin

Facts I Know	Use your facts to craft a piece using what you learned from other writers	Name the technique or style you tried. What writer taught you this technique/style?
• Robins lay pale blue eggs — about 3 or 4 per clutch • Robins are the first bird we see in the Spring • Robins use twigs, leaves and mud to build their nests • Robins eat worms and insects • Robins can be found in parks and backyards • The Robin has a rusty-red breast	If you look closely you might catch a glimpse of my rusty red breast. Don't mistake me for a red-breasted nuthatch. I don't walk down trees looking for food. I hop along the ground searching for worms and insects. I am larger in size and plumper than the Red-breasted nuthatch. It's springtime and I'm out looking for twigs, leaves and mud to build my nest. I want my nest to be secure. Soon I will lay 4 or so pale blue speckled eggs that I will keep warm for 12 days before they hatch. I am a very common bird. I can be seen in backyards. Some even think I'm the first sign of Spring. Who am I? I am the American Robin. Keep an eye out for me come April.	1. Voice – using "first person" or "I" voice 2. Clue-like styled writing I learned this technique from Jim Nail's book, Whose Tracks are These?

Figure 6–16 *Class demonstration of weaving facts into narrative*

PHYSICAL COMPARISON

BEHAVIOR

COLOR

BEHAVIORAL COMPARISON

FOOD PREFERENCE

NESTING MATERIALS

CLUTCH NUMBER/EGG COLOR

INCUBATION PERIOD

HABITAT

CONNECTION TO HUMAN LIFE/STORY

If you look closely, you might catch a glimpse of my **rusty red breast.** **Don't mistake me for a red-breasted nuthatch, I don't walk down trees looking for food. I hop along the ground** searching for **worms and insects.** **I am larger in size and plumper** than the red-breasted nuthatch. It's springtime and I'm out looking for twigs, **leaves and mud** to build my nest. I want my nest to be secure. Soon I will lay **4 or so pale blue speckled eggs** that I will keep warm for **12 days before they hatch.** I am a very common bird. **I can be seen in backyards. Some even think I'm the first sign of spring.** Who am I?

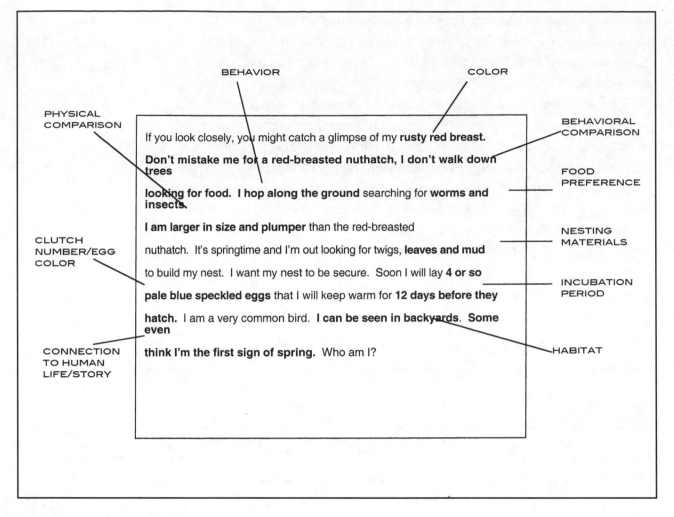

Figure 6–17 *Marked-up American robin piece*

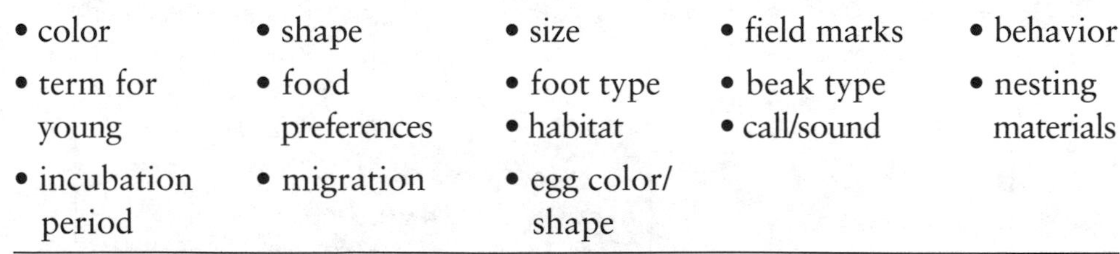

Facts to include in clue book narratives

• color	• shape	• size	• field marks	• behavior
• term for young	• food preferences	• foot type • habitat	• beak type • call/sound	• nesting materials
• incubation period	• migration	• egg color/ shape		

After writing time that day, the children were excited to share their work. While some decided to add mystery by holding facts back, most knew to provide important details without actually revealing a bird's identity. This practice helped them help play with language while synthesizing their content knowledge. They shared their writing with others in the class to get a sense for how successful they were at modeling their writing after Jim Nail. Caroline's piece is shown in Figure 6–18.

We used our category chart to think through Caroline's work. We discovered that she included the following categories from our chart in her writing:

physical comparison
shape
behavior
food preference
call/sound
color
field marks

The children had great fun drafting in the first person, in which they, as writers, spoke in the voice of the subject—their birds. As an alternative to first-person writing, we revisited the Joanne Ryder books that we'd studied while investigating nonfiction in the reading workshop. We reread several titles from her collection, including *Where Butterflies Grow, The Snail's Spell,* and *Lizard in the Sun.* On an overhead, we projected the following excerpt of *The Snail's Spell*, asking the children about the content information in the piece as well as what they noticed about the voice of the writing.

You are two inches long,
lying on the brown ground
all soft and grey.
Imagine you have no arms
and legs now.
Imagine you
cannot walk or run.

Instead you glide
and make your own
smooth sticky path
to ride on.

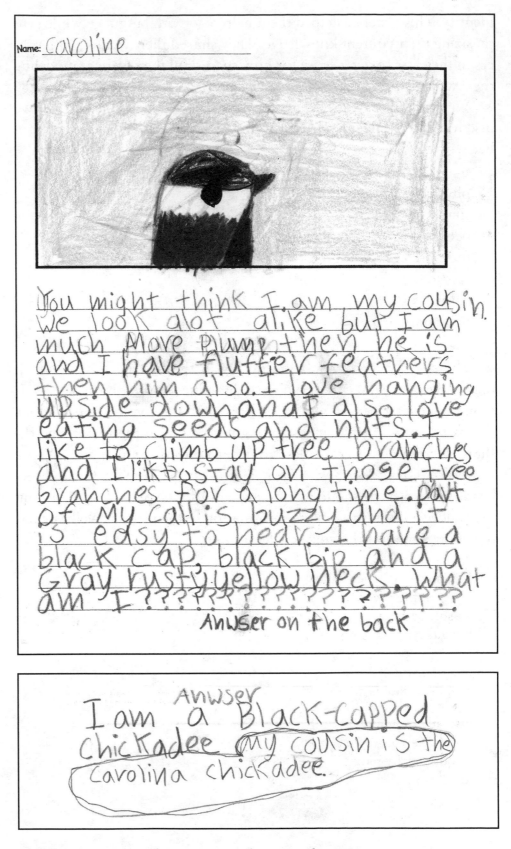

Name: Caroline

You might think I am my cousin. We look alot alike but I am much More plump then he is and I have fluffier feathers then him also. I love hanging upside down and I also love eating seeds and nuts. I like to climb up tree branches and I lik to stay on those tree branches for a long time. part of my call is buzzy and it is easy to hear. I have a black cap, black bip and a Gray rusty yellow neck. What am I ??????????????????????

Anwser on the back

Anwser
I am a Black-capped Chickadee my cousin is the Carolina chickadee.

Figure 6–18 *Caroline's Jim Nail–inspired writing*

Alexander referred back to our category chart, noting that Joanne Ryder made reference to the size, color, behavior, and body shape of the snail. He came up to point to where he found this information and Karen underlined it with an overhead marker for all to see. Leah noticed that rather than *I*, the writer used *you*, as though she were talking directly to the snail. The children remembered how at the beginning of this book, Joanne Ryder asks the reader to imagine himself as the snail. Sara, who often looked at text through the eyes of a writer, noticed the poetic language in the excerpt. She commented on the repetition of the phrase "Imagine you. . . ." She also noticed the rhyming of *brown ground* and the alliteration of *smooth silky path*. Before going off to write that day, Karen introduced *Are You a Butterfly?* by Judy Allen and Tudor Humphries. As Karen read this book, the children noticed that, like Joanne Ryder, the writers of this book spoke directly to the subject—the butterfly. The difference in this text, however, was that the voice of these writers not only described the subject, as in *The Snail's Spell*, but instructed the subject on what to do to make it through its life cycle, changing from egg to chrysalis to butterfly. The following lines from *Are You a Butterfly?* clued us in to this disguised procedural text:

> Grip the leaf with your legs to hold it steady. Then eat it.
> Now eat the next leaf
> Eat every leaf you can reach.
> Then move to another bunch of leaves and eat them too.

Using the information they had gathered on their subjects, the children went off to a very successful writing time. Here's what Jenna wrote that day about the bird she was studying—the magnolia warbler:

> It's midmorning in the forest and you fly across the sky in midair. The morning chill is gone, but it turns gray as clouds spread across the sky. It starts to pour rain. You hop up the tree to your nest with your perching feet. The storm passes and you start chirping. What a lucky bird you are. You attracted a mate. After three days, you lay four pale blue eggs with brown spots, another twelve days pass. Your little ones have hatched and they are very hungry. Your male mate takes the look out. Time for you to get insects and spiders. Gulp, gulp, gulp. Your young ones have gulped down every piece of food you brought them.

Nine days have passed and it's time for your young ones to fly from the nest. Time to fly south for the winter . . . Goodbye, goodbye magnolia warbler.

We spent the remainder of the week drafting with particular attention to voice. "Here are some of the additional texts we used to support this work:

First Person—"I" Voice	*Second Person—"You" Voice*
• *It's a Frog's Life*, by Steve Parker • *It's an Ant's Life*, by Steve Parker	• *Cow*, by Malachy Doyle • *Are You a Ladybug?* by Judy Allen and Tudor Humphries
• *Atlantic*, by G. Brian Karas	• *Are You a Spider?* by Judy Allen and Tudor Humphries
• *The Tree*, by Dana Lyons	• *Lizard in the Sun*, by Joanne Ryder

Week Five: Drafting/Revising

Goal: to weave facts from each research area into different drafts and begin revision process

Week 4's success of developing two drafts—one written in the first-person "I" voice and the other written in the second-person "you" voice—allowed the children to practice processing the information they had collected in an entertaining way. At this point the class had completed research sheets on all four of the information categories. We also created attribute charts on bulletin board space, measuring and comparing such things as wingspan and bird length. (See Figure 6–19.) These charts, along with *The Sibley Guide to Birds* and other assorted field guides and nonfiction books, gave the children easy access to information on all the birds we were studying as well as many more. Internalizing the writing in Jim Nail's *Whose Tracks Are These?* provided a reliable structure that they tested over and over at home and in school, writing about not only the birds they were studying but the many others they had come to know. They also enjoyed writing in the second-person narrative style inspired by Joanne Ryder books. And they naturally flip-flopped between first and second person. We found,

Figure 6–19 *Bird attribute chart*

however, that they gravitated toward writing in the first person. They loved putting themselves into the position of the birds. The childlike style and playful quality of first-person narrative was clear and accessible to all the children in the class.

This week we would capitalize on their confidence in writing in the first person as we revisited the research sheets from week 3 and drafted narratives specific to each of the categories they had researched: physical description, habitat, food and beak, and nesting, eggs, and young. It was our intention to eventually weave these pieces together into final narrative books about their birds. We began by revisiting the first-person narrative book *It's a Frog's Life*, by Steve Parker, as a model for this work. In addition to it being in the first person, we also chose this book because it was subdivided in a similar way with categories such as food, habitat, and reproduction *and* for its humor and engaging quality. The section of the book about food, named "Hungry All the Time," was plump with factual information and seemed a perfect first example of how a writer using the first-person narrative can instruct as well as entertain.

As Mary Anne began to read *It's a Frog's Life,* Max remembered this book as the one written *by* Frog. "This is the one where the frog is speaking to us," he noted.

"It's funny—especially the beginning of the book where it says, 'If found, return to Frog, at the pond,' " remembered Rebecca.

"It's like the frog is talking to us, telling us what it's thinking in its mind," Stephen added.

Mary Anne planned to read a couple of pages, knowing her focus was to show how Steve Parker wove facts into narrative, using the "I" voice and infusing humor. She prefaced the reading by acknowledging the practice they had done in week 4 with voice, knowing they would again be weaving facts into narrative with attention to voice this week. The difference this week was that the children would need to produce drafts on each of the individual categories they had researched, whereas the previous week they had blended all the subtopics into one piece. "Now," she started, "I want us to relook at the way Steve Parker (or Frog!) tells us a lot about what Frog eats while entertaining us with voice and humor." The children prepared to listen for this combination in writing differently than when looking at the book as readers. They were now writers of nonfiction, attempting to teach their readers. Mary Anne read aloud the excerpt that she had placed on the overhead for all to follow.

> Whrrrr. A big—and I mean BIG—dragonfly whizzed past me today and landed on a leaf. I was hungry, and dragonflies are very tasty. Some are so big that if I catch them, I don't have to eat again for days! But they're strong, too. They can give you nasty jabs with the sharp claws on their feet.
>
> I catch small flies by flicking out my tongue and SNAP—they're stuck on its sticky tip. This monster looked too big for that, so I went for the bold approach. I leaped up and grabbed it in my fabulously wide mouth. Let me tell you—that leap was INCREDIBLE!
>
> It was kind of a struggle to swallow the dragonfly, but I got it down in the end. It was the best meal I've had in a long time.

After reading the excerpt, Mary Anne led the children in a discussion on how the writing informs and instructs as well as entertains. Together the class composed a chart to record some of this thinking. A T-chart seemed to work best for this type of recording. It looked as follows:

What I Learned About What Frogs Eat	*How Steve Parker Weaves These Facts into Narrative with Attention to Voice and Humor*
Frogs like to eat dragonflies.	Whrrr . . . A big—and I mean BIG—dragonfly whizzed past me today. . . . I was hungry, and dragonflies are very tasty.
Frogs catch smaller insects with their tongues.	I catch small flies by flicking out my tongue and SNAP—they're stuck on its sticky tip.
Larger insects such as dragonflies need to be caught by leaping first.	This monster looked too big for that, so I went for the bold approach. I leaped up and grabbed it in my fabulously wide mouth. Let me tell you—that leap was INCREDIBLE.
Frogs have large mouths.	. . . in my fabulously wide mouth.

Since food was the focus of that day's minilesson, many of the children went off to attempt their narratives about their birds' food preferences. Others chose to begin with physical description because they felt it was a natural place to begin. Regardless of which subtopic they chose to focus on first, their job this week was to write drafts for each of the categories they had researched: physical description, habitat, food and beak, and nesting, eggs, and young. They reflected back on their research sheets and processing sentences as they began to draft. Figure 6–20 shows Alexander's research sheet and Figure 6–21 shows his first draft. He chose to save the food section for later, zooming in on physical description for now.

Over the course of the week, all the children composed narratives about the physical descriptions of their birds. Here are some great lines from their writing:

> Hello. Hello . . . I chirp as I pass by . . . I am so cheerful if my tweezer beak got glued together with peanut butter I would still be very cheerful.—James
>
> My rusty red breast ought to catch your eye.—Rachel
>
> You might catch a glimpse of my long, pointy tapered tail as I walk by. Don't confuse me with a Rock Dove . . . I'm much more slender.—Eli

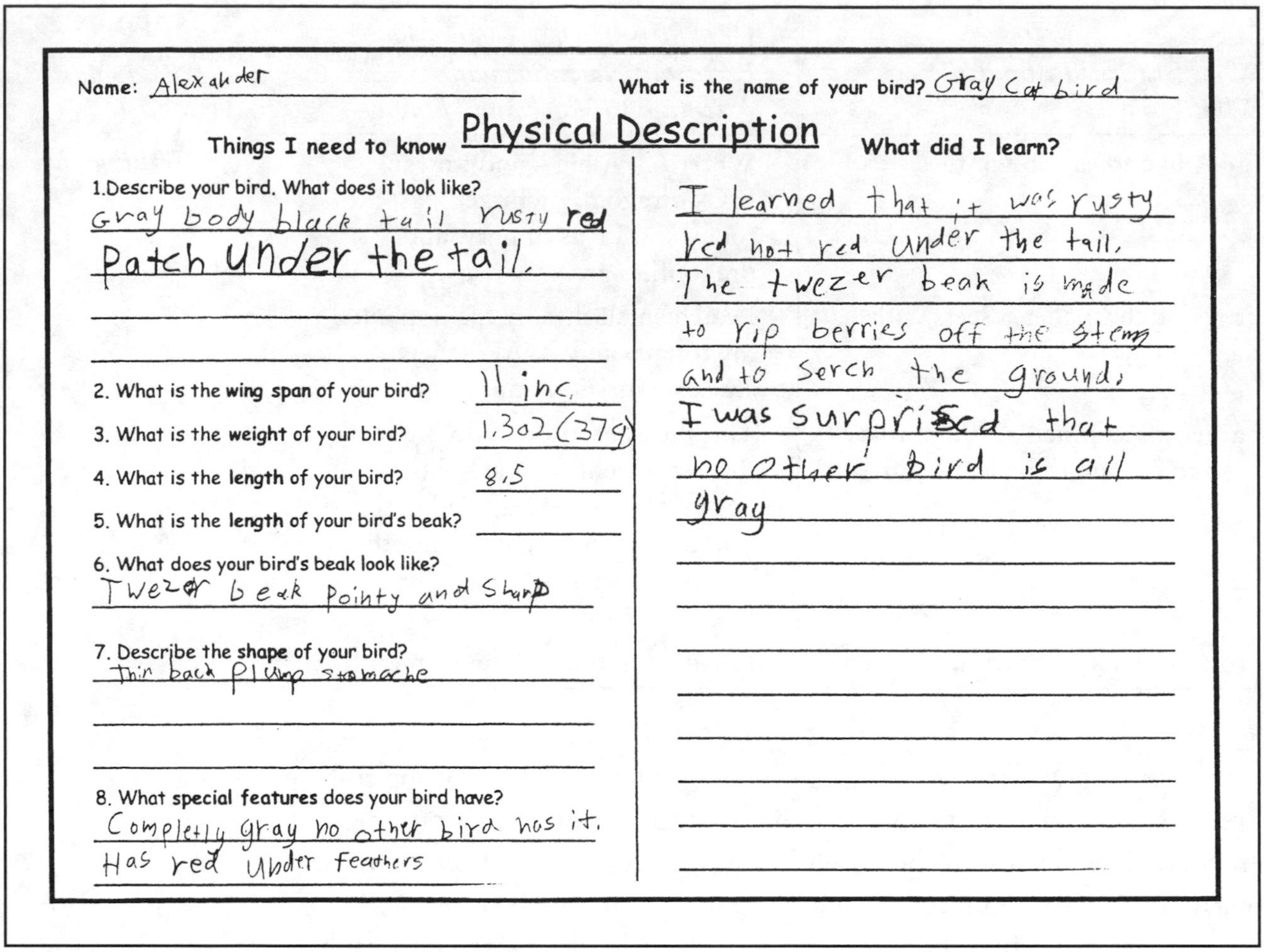

Name: Alexander

What is the name of your bird? Gray Cat bird

Things I need to know **Physical Description** What did I learn?

1.Describe your bird. What does it look like?
Gray body black tail rusty red Patch under the tail.

2. What is the wing span of your bird? 11 inc.

3. What is the weight of your bird? 1.3oz (37g)

4. What is the length of your bird? 8.5

5. What is the length of your bird's beak?

6. What does your bird's beak look like?
Twezer beak Pointy and Sharp

7. Describe the shape of your bird?
Thin back Plump stomache

8. What special features does your bird have?
Completly gray no other bird has it. Has red under feathers

I learned that it was rusty red not red under the tail. The twezer beak is made to rip berries off the stems and to serch the ground. I was surprised that no other bird is all gray

Figure 6–20 *Alexander's research sheet*

Well, I would love some nuts and seeds to eat from you . . . I have a tweezer beak—it means I'm an insect and seed eater.—Alexander

Oh, did I tell you that I am a little bit plump and my beak is like a tweezer? I want to tell you something else. The female's throat is white and mine is black.—Graciela

You might spot my square-cut tail if I am flying. If I am perched on a tree in courtship you will easily spot my rusty red breast. If you blink an eye I will be gone.—Matthew

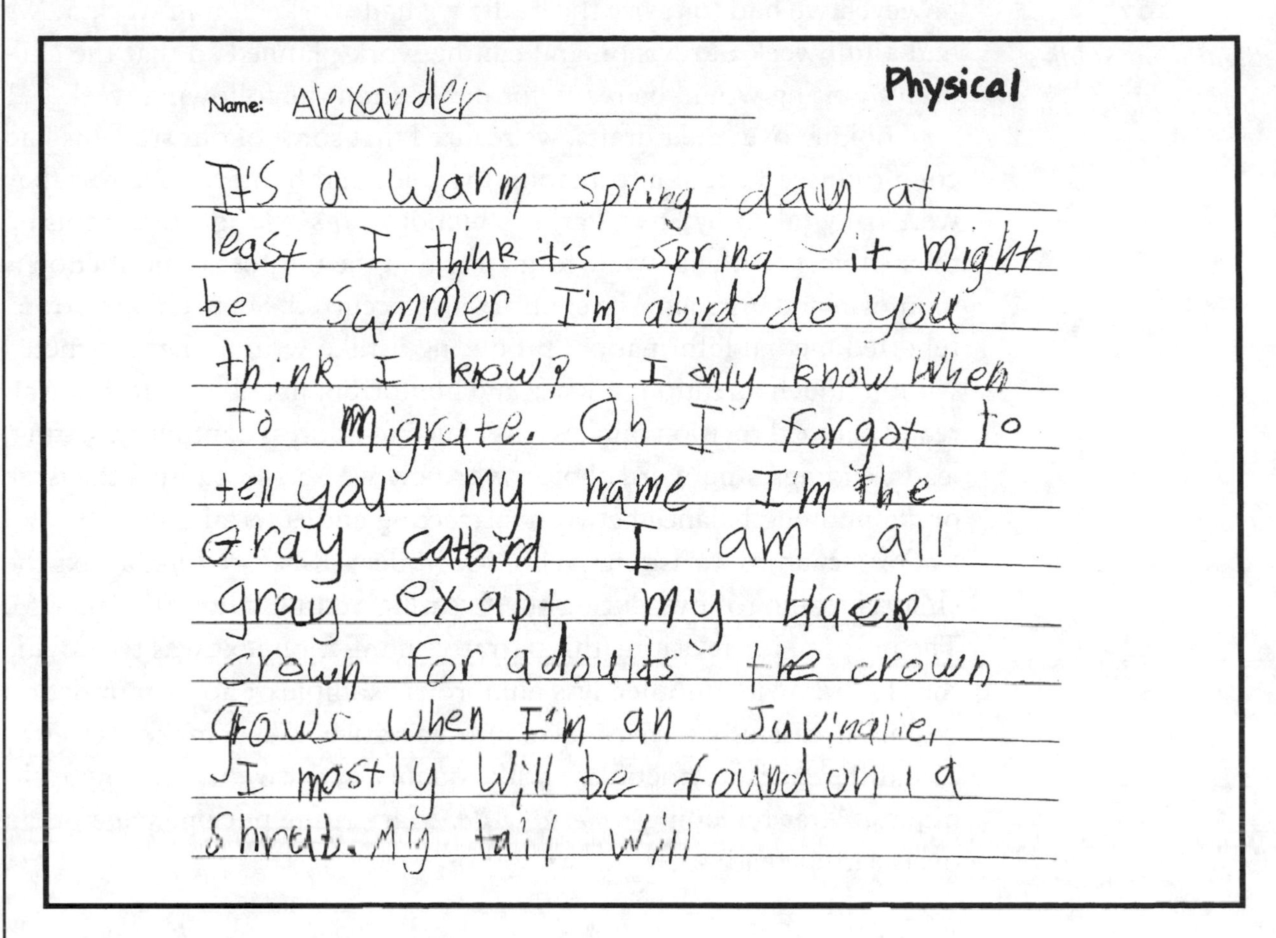
Physical

Name: Alexander

It's a warm spring day at least I think it's spring it might be summer I'm abird do you think I know? I only know when to migrate. Oh I forgat to tell you my name I'm the Gray catbird I am all gray exapt my black crown for adoults the crown grows when I'm an Juvinalie, I mostly will be found on a shrub. My tail will

Figure 6–21 *Alexander's rough draft*

Week Six: Revising/Editing

Goal: to revise with focus of instructing and entertaining while cohesively weaving drafts together with attention to setting

With the completed drafts in hand, we began to envision the end product. We knew we were going to produce narrative books that would instruct as well as entertain. We started to plan for the layout as well as for the illustration work that would take place in week 7 of the study. Parents coordinated art materials and supplies that we needed to complete the books. In addition, we began to think about the author's page and the dedication. Before any of that work would take place, however, we had to revise the drafts we had worked on in week 5. We had a full week of revision and editing work planned so that the children's writing would be ready for publication the following week.

Looking over their drafts, we realized that some of our students had compromised factual information for voice and humor. It seemed they were truly taken by Steve Parker's humor in *It's a Frog's Life*, infusing their subjects with life while forgetting that the purpose of nonfiction is to inform and instruct. The contrary also occurred. Some children over-reported factual information, producing listlike writing that instructed without much attention to voice and humor. So, in addition to some already planned revision minilessons aimed to address continuity, setting, leads, endings, and word choice, we knew we had to address the issue of maintaining balance between instructing and entertaining.

We began by revisiting Debbie S. Miller's *River of Life*, a text the children came to love during the Creating Setting study (Chapter 5). The purpose for revisiting this narrative nonfiction text was to provide the children with another, less humorous example of how a nonfiction writer successfully weaves facts into narrative. What makes *River of Life* different is its poetic, storylike quality and various crafting techniques. After rereading *River of Life*, Mary Anne put one page on an overhead. It read:

> A kingfisher sends its loud rattling call above the river. He wears a bluish-gray feathered crest. He catches wiggly salmon with a beak that looks too long for his head. Beneath the surface, a rainbow trout chases salmon fry. The trout catches a glimpse of something shiny. Will it take a bite?

Mary Anne asked the children, "What factual information did the author include in this writing?" The children reread the excerpt, extracting information as they did in week 2 of this study when they read excerpts from *Peterson's Field Guide* looking for information pertaining to physical description. Now, however, our students were reading for information wearing the hat of a writer. We wanted our students to see how Debbie S. Miller crafted without compromising factual information. The children extracted the facts they learned from this excerpt while Mary Anne underlined them with an overhead marker and listed them on chart paper:

Kingfishers have a loud, rattling call.
Kingfishers have a bluish-gray feathered crest.

Kingfishers have a long beak.
Kingfishers eat salmon.
Kingfishers fly near rivers.

As Mary Anne listed the facts on a chart, she directed the class to think about the way Debbie S. Miller was able to weave facts into narrative without compromising accuracy. Mary Anne wanted the children to do the same work with their own writing drafts. Before sending the kids off to write, Mary Anne instructed them to underline the facts in their drafts as she had done in this minilesson. She also told them to check the facts for accuracy, making any necessary changes. As the children went off to write, she pulled together the small group of children whose writing was still very listlike. Here's an example of a listlike piece, written about the eastern screech owl. Although factual, it is not elaborate or entertaining and does not distinguish the eastern screech owl from other birds of prey.

> My beak is curved. My beak is pointy. I eat insects, reptiles, amphibians, small mammals, birds, fish, and mice.

What these children needed was quite different from the content of the minilesson demonstration that day. These children were overfocused on facts, sacrificing voice and humor to report their learning. With this group, Mary Anne revisited one of the minilessons from week 5, using *It's a Frog's Life* to demonstrate weaving facts with voice and humor. This time she contrasted the *It's a Frog's Life* excerpt with an encyclopedia-style excerpt on frogs. She knew the difference would be enough to help them understand how to find a balance between instructing and entertaining. (See Figure 6–22.)

Now that the children had found balance between instructing and entertaining, it seemed time to consider setting as a way of anchoring their writing. Although it had been only weeks since our study of setting had ended, the children needed to be reminded of the lessons learned during that study. It seemed while some children had internalized and used the lessons from the setting work illustrated in Chapter 5, others hadn't. With this in mind, we turned to Brian J. Heinz's *Butternut Hollow Pond* and Jonathan London's *Condor's Egg*. Each of these nonfiction narrative texts establishes a strong, visual setting while teaching its readers about a subject—ponds or birds. In Jonathan London's *Condor's Egg*, the author tracks the lives of two California

WHAT DO FROGS EAT?

Frogs eat living animals. They eat insects, worms, spiders, and centipedes. Large frogs may eat mice or small snakes. A frog's tongue is very long; it can reach out quickly to catch its prey. Frogs don't drink. They absorb water from their surroundings through their skin. Frogs swallow their food whole. When they swallow they often retract their eyes. This helps force their food down.

encyclopedia-like excerpt

HUNGRY ALL THE TIME

Whrrr. A big—and I mean BIG—dragonfly whizzed past me today and landed on a leaf. I was hungry, and dragonflies are very tasty. Some are so big that if I catch them, I don't have to eat again for days! But they're strong, too. They can give you nasty jabs with the sharp claws on their feet.

I catch small flies by flicking out my tongue and SNAP—they're stuck on its sticky tip. This monster looked too big for that, so I went for the bold approach. I leaped up and grabbed it in my fabulously wide mouth. Let me tell you—that leap was INCREDIBLE!

It was kind of a struggle to swallow the dragonfly, but I got it down in the end. It was the best meal I've had in a long time.

Fast Food . . .

I only eat living animals. Nothing dead—UGH! Butterflies are pretty—and pretty tasty.

Flies are yummy, too. So are bees. Bees get so busy collecting pollen from flowers that they don't notice me creeping up!

. . . and slow food!

Snails are terrific! So slow and easy to catch! I scrunch them up and spit out the pieces of shell.

Frogs have no teeth so we slurp up worms whole. They wriggle all the way down. Dee-licious!

Excerpt from *It's a Frog's Life,* by Steve Parker

Figure 6–22 *Two excerpts with contrasting writing styles*

condors. As in many of the texts used in the setting study, the lead sentence in *Condor's Egg* establishes setting by bringing the reader "among the rugged slopes of inland cliffs." We wanted our students to also bring their readers into their subjects' homes by writing leads that established setting.

After reading *Condor's Egg* and revisiting lines from *Butternut Hollow Pond* that supported setting, the children went off to their drafts to write leads that would establish setting. As Mary Anne conferred with Eli, she asked him to think about how he could transfer what he learned from *Condor's Egg* to his own writing about the mourning dove. He was effective in reworking a lead phrase that established setting. It read: "Among the tall trees sits a Mourning Dove resting on the bottom branch." This line allowed the reader to see the mourning dove in its specific habitat among the trees, sitting on a branch. Other children thought to provide a wider sense of place as they wrote about their birds in Central Park. Jenna, in writing about the magnolia warbler, initially wrote, "I've just arrived from the south and now I'm back in Central Park." The minilesson helped her think back to lessons learned from *Butternut Hollow Pond*, and she revised by adding the line "It's midmorning and I'm returning to my Pin Oak Tree." Other children were equally successful in writing leads that established setting.

> It's a spring afternoon in Central Park. People are lifting up their binoculars to spot me, but they can't because my colors are dull, not bright like my mates.—Karla, writing about the American redstart
>
> Welcome to my nest. You may have noticed that I live in a hole in this birch tree.—James, writing about the black-capped chickadee
>
> My friends live in every single state in the US except Hawaii. I live in a pine tree in Central Park on the Great Lawn. But I'm warning you, if you go near my territory, I will attack you.—Alexander, writing about the great horned owl
>
> It's early morning at the Ramble in Central Park. I'm singing my sweet song, tee-tew, tee-tew. It's spring and I just came back from Florida, my winter home.—Lauren, writing about the Baltimore oriole

By the end of week 6, we felt good about our work. We had reread our drafts several times, making sure we had maintained balance between instructing and entertaining, and we had rewritten our leads to establish setting. In the last days of the revision process, we wanted to clarify meaning by adding details and comparisons and paying attention to word choice.

Karen revisited *Birds, Nests and Eggs*, by Mel Boring, one of the books the children relied on during their research process. In this book, the author uses coins to compare such things as the egg size of birds. This technique of comparison helped the children visualize and understand the exact size of the eggs. We knew that many of the children reported weight in ounces and size in centimeters—concepts difficult for them to grasp. Karen spoke to the children about how comparing something fuzzy with something well known helps the reader gain a complete and thorough understanding. Here are some lines from *Birds, Nests and Eggs* that helped us gain an understanding of the hummingbird's size, nest, and eggs:

> The hummingbird weighs no more than a penny.
> A hummingbird nest is the size of half a golf ball.
> Hummingbird eggs are white and smaller than a dime.

The children were in disbelief over the comparisons. Karen used a dime to show the children exactly what the egg comparison meant. This form of nonstandard measurement allowed the children to truly comprehend some of the facts they had read. They were eager to find places where they could try this in their own writing. After writing time, they shared some of the comparisons they made. Here's how this lesson changed their writing:

Lindsay located the following line in her writing about the ruby-throated hummingbird: "My weight is 0.11 ounces." After learning that a hummingbird weighs less than a penny, she compared the weight of a penny with that of a paper clip. Her revised line read: "My weight is 0.11 ounces. I weigh about as much as three paper clips. Boy, is that light for a bird!" Not only did Lindsay add a comparison to clarify this fact, but she remembered the strategy of adding internal voice, like many writers we looked at did in their own work.

Liam also made a comparison to help the reader gain a better image. Knowing a standard ruler is 12 inches long, he compared the length of the blue jay to a ruler. He wrote: "My body is 11–12.5 inches long and that is about the size of one ruler."

In our final revision minilesson, we asked the children to reread, making sure their details provided a clear and accurate picture for the reader. Had everyone included enough details to create a precise and visual description of his or her bird? Karen used James' piece of writing below in her minilesson to illustrate how his detail added clarity and created a visual image for the reader. She read his work, underlining his revision work. The children talked about how each addition supported clarity. The children then went off in their bird partnerships to check over their writing for places where they might need to add more details.

Nesting, Eggs, and Young (Revisions)

Hello again! Welcome to my nest. You may have noticed that I live in a hole in this birch tree. I add stuff inside to make it soft. I use rabbit fur, down, hair, feathers and spider webs. My eggs are white with brown speckles. I nest once a year. I feed my babies caterpillars, snails, spiders, insect eggs, beetles, ants, and aphids. My mate and I build our nest together and it takes about two weeks to build. My mate and I also stay together for several years and she tries to attract me. She does the wing-quiver and the tee-ship call. It goes like this. Ah-hem . . . Tee-ship. Tee-ship. Tee-ship. Bye!

—from "The Black-Capped Chickadee," by James Zebooker

Week Seven: Editing/Illustrating/Publishing

Goal: to edit final draft and illustrate each section of writing

By the end of this study the children's writing contained all the ingredients for a narrative that informs, instructs, and entertains. The writing was impressive and near publication. Because we had drafted and revised with careful attention to detail and accuracy, the kids were not overcome by enormous editing challenges. Also, the method of checking for spelling inaccuracies mentioned in the previous chapters was almost second nature at this point (see Figure 5–14). Repeatedly using this sheet (adapted from Diane Snowball's work) helped children internalize strategies for spelling while fostering the development of good spelling habits. With the editing work done, we put aside writing to focus on illustration. Figures 6–23 through 6–25 shows three of our students' completed writing.

By the end of this week, we would be ready to share our writing in the form of narrative books with our families and school community. This week's work was to create high-caliber illustrations and final products that would match the serious writing work we had done thus far in the study. Because of the scientific angle of the bird study and the specificity of our research and writing, we needed our artwork to adhere to the same standards. Illustrations done for the nonfiction books, as well as for our field guide project (described later in the chapter), all portrayed birds in their true and magnificent colors. Their physical

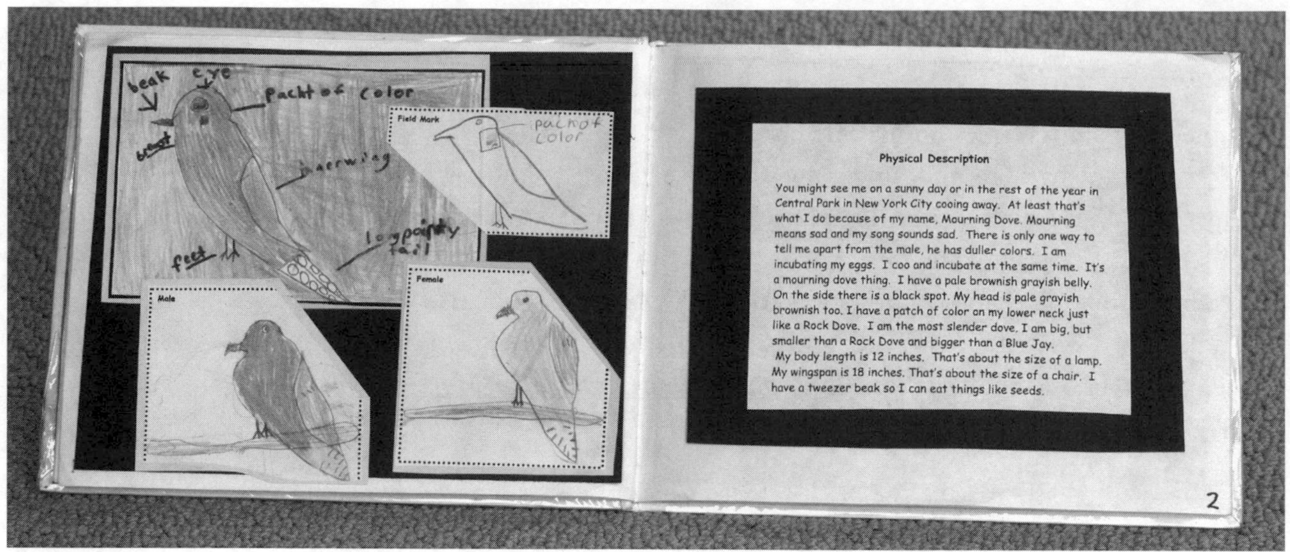

Figure 6–23 *Grace's final physical description page*

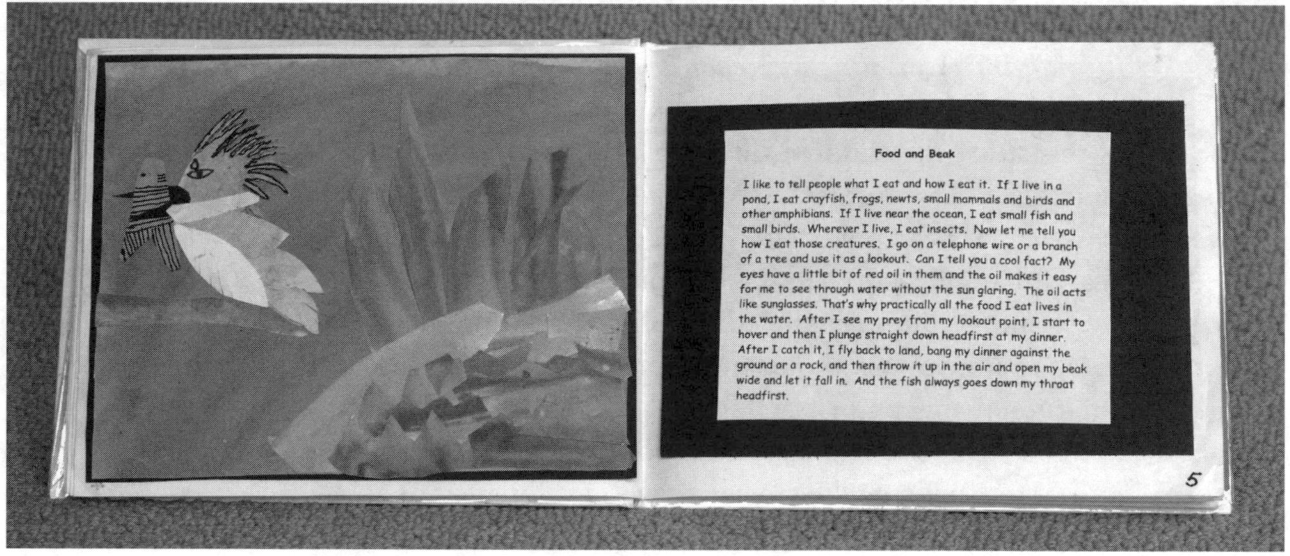

Figure 6–24 *Stephen's final food page*

features were detailed and exact, as were their eggs and nests. Our children had already spent a great amount of time looking at pictures of their birds, as well as sketching and drawing. With this experience, we knew, the children would not be overwhelmed by enormous illustration challenges. In addition to the art that supported the writing, children created color bird portraits that we mounted alongside their self-portraits. Actual-size papier-mâché bird creations made in art class

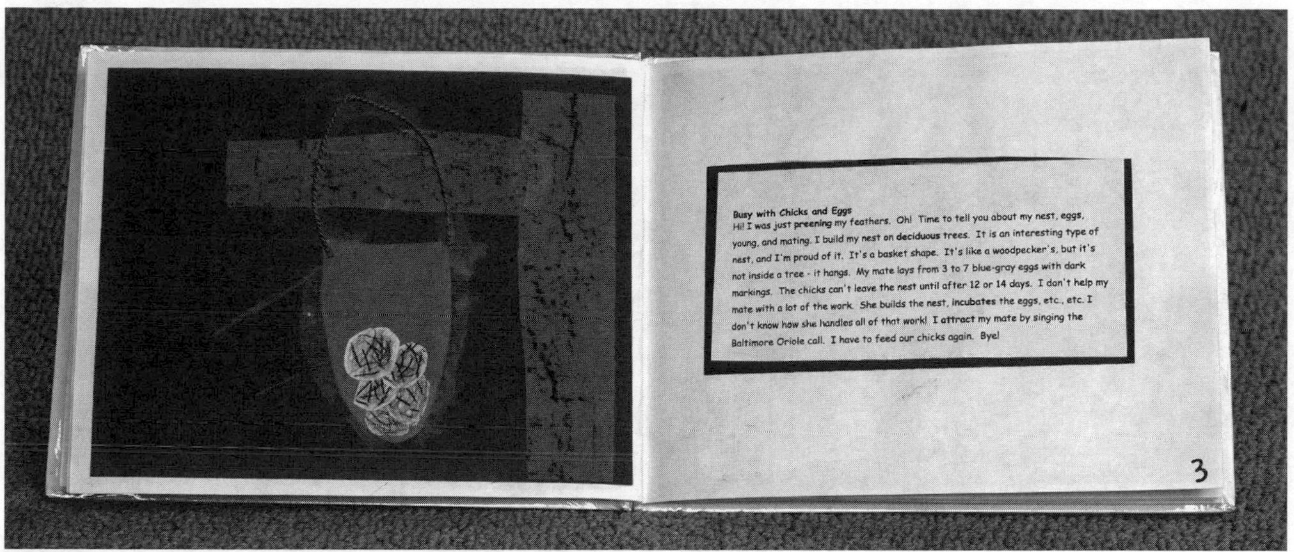

Figure 6–25 *Lauren's final nesting, eggs, and young page*

hung from our ceiling, allowing us to imagine our classroom as an aviary. With all this appreciation for art right in our classroom, inspiration for children's book illustrations was abundant.

In these final days of work, we chose some covers of nonfiction picture books to give the children a variety of exciting choices for their own illustrating. The artwork of Lynne Cherry stood out and several children modeled their covers after the border illustrations she had drawn in *Flute's Journey.* The bold action-style illustrations drawn by Bob Marstall in *Butternut Hollow Pond* were also a favorite, along with his wraparound cover illustration (illustration moving from front to back cover). The children looked to certain illustrators as art mentors, just as they had looked to certain writers as writing mentors. (See Figures 6–26 and 6–27.)

Other Writing Forms That Emerged from the Content Area Research and Writing Study

By the end of the Content Area Research and Writing study, the children had produced beautifully written nonfiction narratives about their birds. These artfully designed books contained writing that

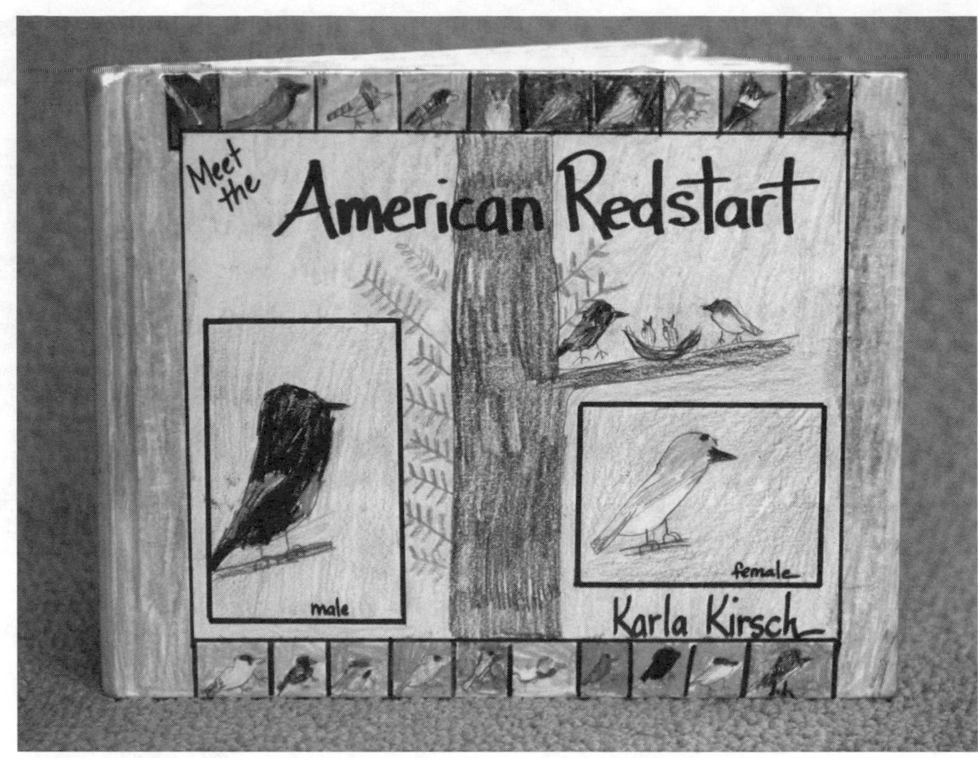

Figure 6–26 *Karla's front cover, inspired by the work of Lynne Cherry*

Figure 6–27 *Grace's wraparound cover, inspired by the work of Bob Marstall*

captured the heart and mind of everyone who read them. These picture book productions were clear demonstrations of our primary writing goal—to inform, instruct, and entertain our nonfiction readers.

In addition to our primary writing goal, we met several others that were imbedded in the study. We worked on a *field guide* that included all the birds studied across the second grade at Manhattan New School. With this project, the intent of the writing was to inform but not to entertain. It was our intention that the children would be able to use this guide in the field as they located birds. We wrote the book for a particular audience—birders—and the children wrote to their readers on the back blurb, informing them on what they would find in the volume: "This field guide will tell you how to look for a bird. There are color pictures so you can identify them. The birds are most likely to be seen in Central Park. This book will also tell you how they look, what they eat, their size, some facts and tips. Happy Birding!" (See Figures 6–28 and 6–29.)

We also worked on *songs* written to familiar tunes such as "Mary Had a Little Lamb," "Row, Row, Row Your Boat," and "Take Me Out to the Ball Game." The children were very excited to write these songs. Several children wrote a collection of songs about the birds they had studied; others enjoyed sticking with the same tune and writing songs about different birds. Here's an example of one of our favorites:

THE HUNTING SONG (TO THE TUNE OF "TAKE ME OUT TO THE BALLGAME")
By Alexander Familant

Take me out to go hunting.
Take me to Central Park.
Get me some insects, some rats and mice.
I don't care if the weather's not nice.
For it's swoop, peck, peck, and devour.
Soon night will turn into dawn.'
'Cause it's one, two, three rabbits gone,
At the old Great Lawn.

Aside from songs, our children chose to write *letters* and *dedications* to those who helped us make our content area writing study so successful. Some children thanked parents for taking them birding on the weekends, some wrote to us for inspiring them to learn about birds, and others wrote to birding experts that had come to speak to us or had taken us out into the field. Petrit's letter thanks Starr for the

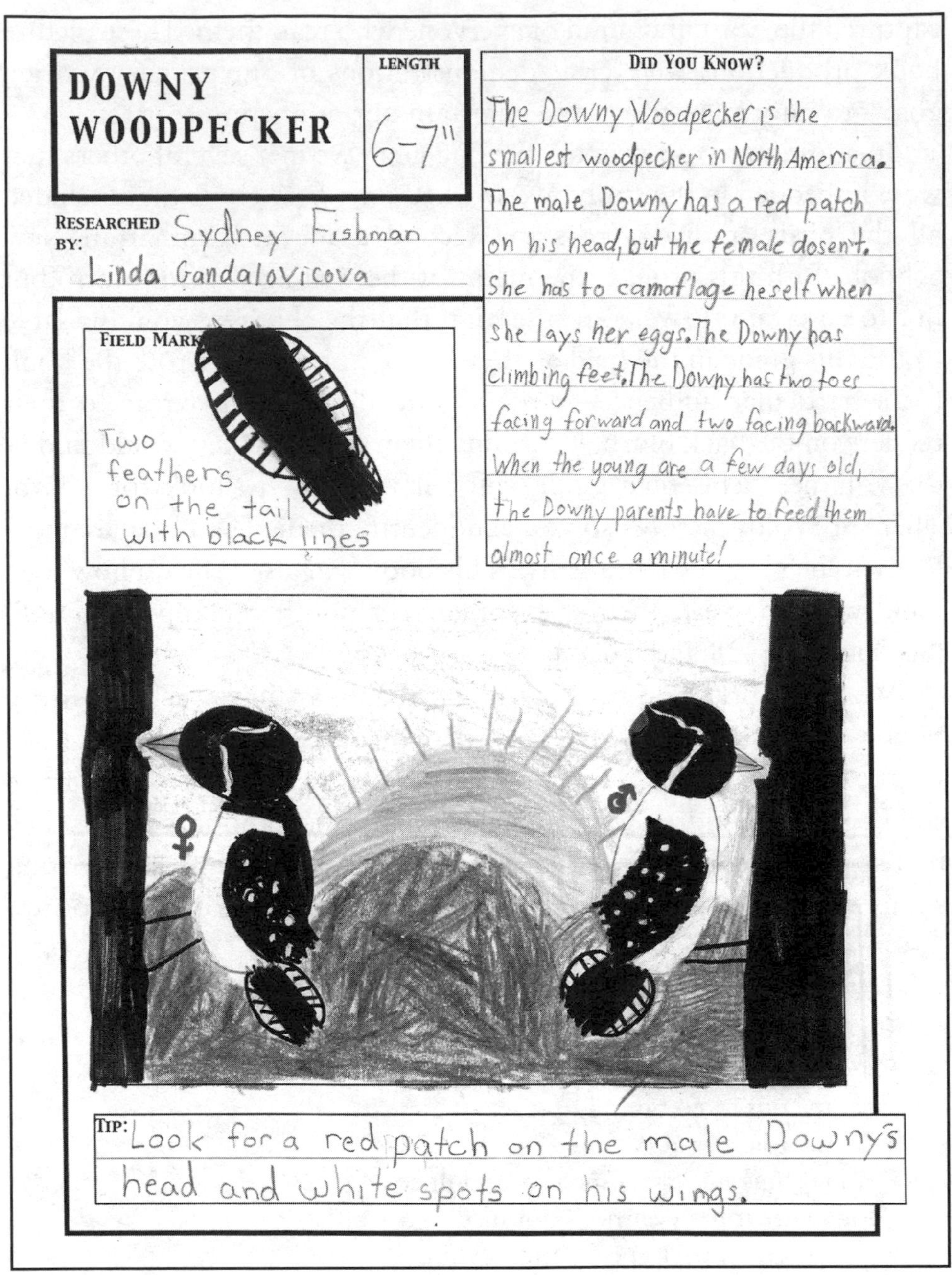

DOWNY WOODPECKER
LENGTH
6-7"
DID YOU KNOW?
The Downy Woodpecker is the smallest woodpecker in North America. The male Downy has a red patch on his head, but the female dosen't. She has to camaflage heself when she lays her eggs. The Downy has climbing feet. The Downy has two toes facing forward and two facing backward. When the young are a few days old, the Downy parents have to feed them almost once a minute!
RESEARCHED BY: Sydney Fishman
Linda Gandalovicova
FIELD MARK
Two feathers on the tail with black lines
TIP: Look for a red patch on the male Downy's head and white spots on his wings.

Figures 6–28 *Part one of downy woodpecker field guide page*

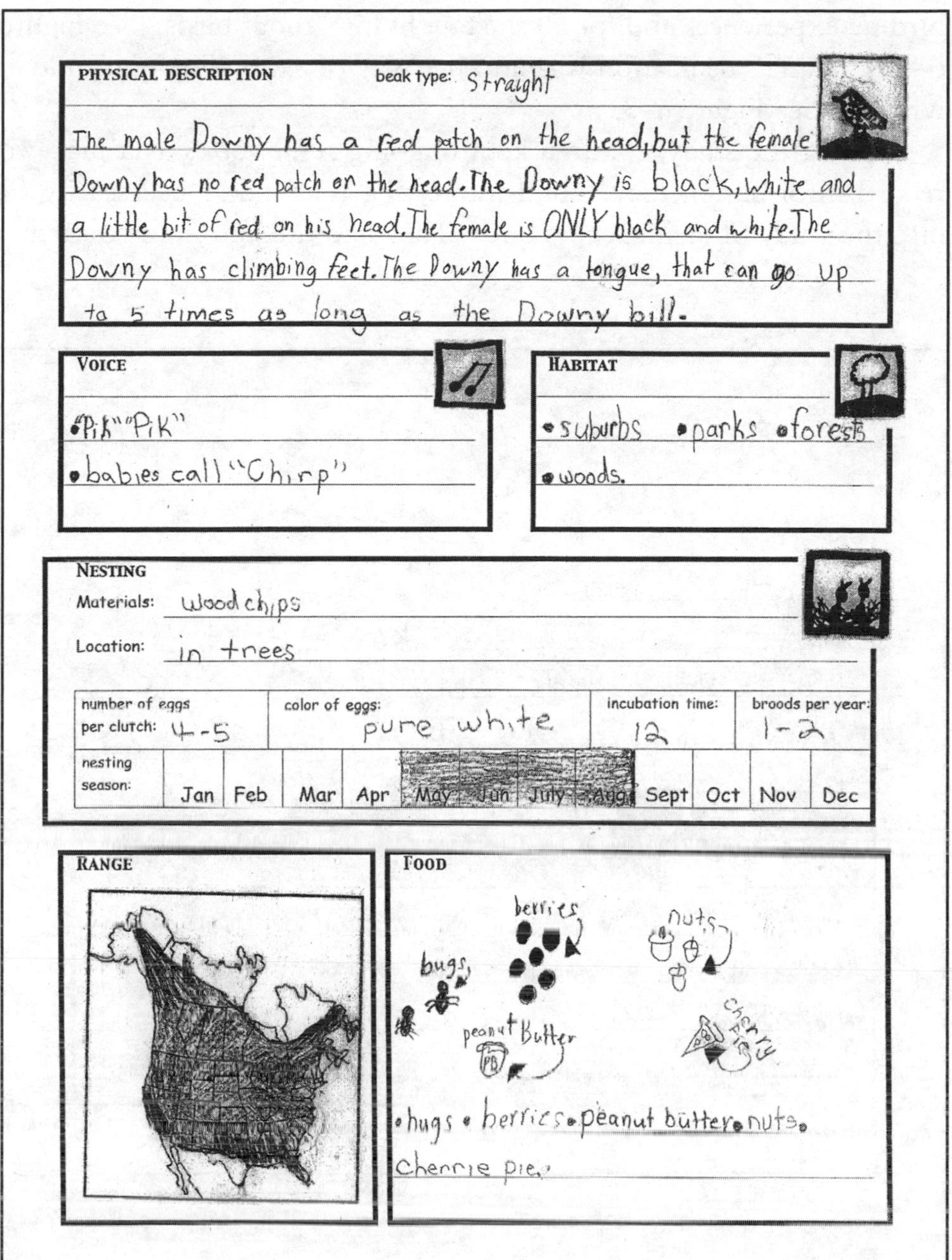

PHYSICAL DESCRIPTION beak type: Straight

The male Downy has a red patch on the head, but the female Downy has no red patch on the head. The Downy is black, white and a little bit of red on his head. The female is ONLY black and white. The Downy has climbing feet. The Downy has a tongue, that can go up to 5 times as long as the Downy bill.

VOICE

- "Pik" "Pik"
- babies call "Chirp"

HABITAT

- suburbs
- parks
- forests
- woods.

NESTING

Materials: wood chips

Location: in trees

number of eggs per clutch:	color of eggs:	incubation time:	broods per year:
4-5	pure white	12	1-2

nesting season:	Jan	Feb	Mar	Apr	May	Jun	July	Aug	Sept	Oct	Nov	Dec

RANGE

FOOD

- bugs
- berries
- peanut butter
- nuts
- cherrie pie.

Figure 6–29 *Part two of downy woodpecker field guide page*

birding experiences and for all she taught him about birds. (See Figure 6–30). Diana's dedication was another way of expressing gratitude in writing. (See Figure 6–31.)

During the study, children kept ongoing *scrapbooks* as a place to record information they found interesting that didn't necessarily fit into the study of their specific birds. They had full autonomy over this

June 8 2001

Dear Starr

Thank you for taking us Birding. There was Three birds that I liked Watching. One was The male northern cardinal. Because The Red is chiny and the sound is Beautiful. The second one is the Red Bellied WoodPecker. The PecKing made the sound Beautiful. The third is the Robin. Because the hopping made me lautgh.

From petrit

northern cardinal

Red Bellied Wood Pecker

Robin

Figure 6–30 *Petrit's letter*

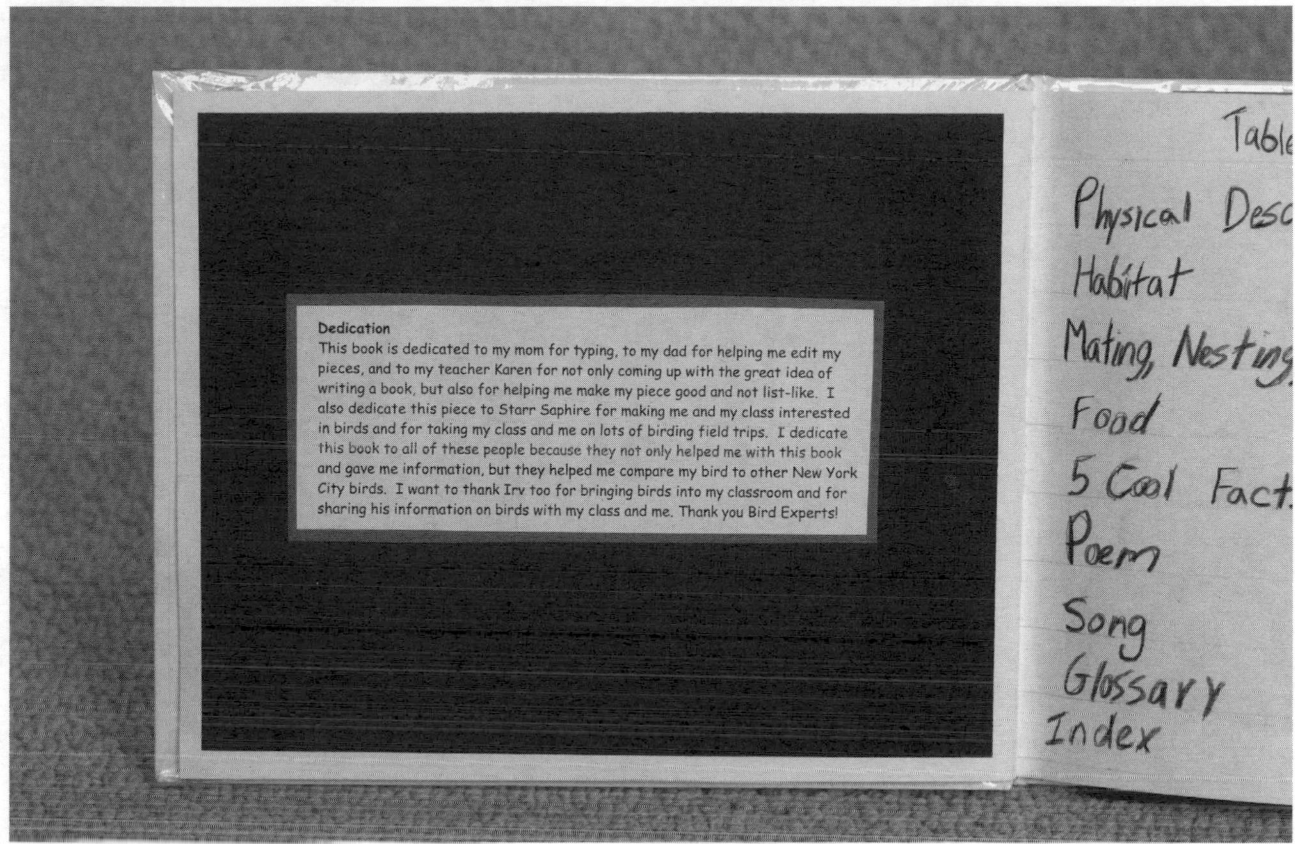

Dedication
This book is dedicated to my mom for typing, to my dad for helping me edit my pieces, and to my teacher Karen for not only coming up with the great idea of writing a book, but also for helping me make my piece good and not list-like. I also dedicate this piece to Starr Saphire for making me and my class interested in birds and for taking my class and me on lots of birding field trips. I dedicate this book to all of these people because they not only helped me with this book and gave me information, but they helped me compare my bird to other New York City birds. I want to thank Irv too for bringing birds into my classroom and for sharing his information on birds with my class and me. Thank you Bird Experts!
Physical
Habitat
Mating,
Food
5 Cool
Poem
Song
Glossary
Index

Figure 6–31 *Diana's dedication*

book. We did not teach into it or guide them in any way. They came to cherish these books because they belonged completely to them. Some children, of course, put more effort into them than others. It was a place where they sketched, wrote down facts, tried out nonfiction features such as graphs, did you know? boxes, internal thoughts, poems, and so on. (See Figures 6–32 and 6–33.)

In our research, we learned that serious birders keep a *life list*, which is essentially a running list of all birds they have seen while birding. This list is normally housed in a book that can be carried into the field. To be accurate, a birder would write down the name of the bird, the location in which it was spotted, and the date on which the bird was spotted. We, of course, wouldn't have considered thinking of ourselves as birders without keeping life list journals. We created our life list books in class and carried them with us while on class birding excursions. In addition, children updated their life lists on weekends as

Figure 6–32
Page from Diana's bird scrapbook

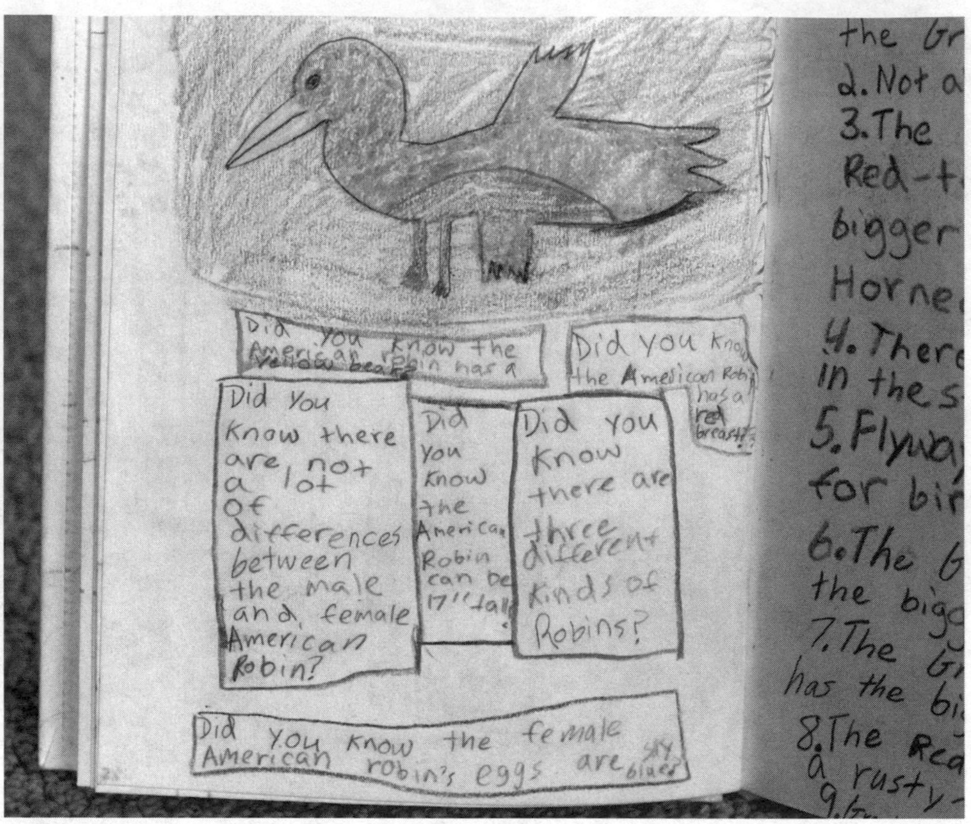

Figure 6–33
Page from James' bird scrapbook

they made their way to Grandma's country house outside of the city or stayed back home and spent time in Central Park. (See Figure 6–34.)

Aside from their life lists, our children became quite proficient in *list writing*. This form of writing came from a need to organize information. Our children made lists of birding vocabulary, words related to physical description, or words related to nesting and young. Our kids listed the contents of their bird books in tables of contents, a feature we had spent time studying while investigating nonfiction in the reading workshop (see Figure 6–35). In addition, our children wrote lists for what to bring when going birding and checklists for the field guide on which birds they spotted. They wrote materials lists that later supported procedural writing titled "How Birds Build Nests" and "How to Be a Good Bird Watcher." (See Figure 6–36.)

Lastly, the children produced acrostic *poems* modeled after some they had found in their research. The beginnings of these poems happened in their scrapbooks and they later made their way out of the scrapbooks and onto loose-leaf paper. Like the songs, these poems were another way of synthesizing what the children had learned. (See Figures 6–37 and 6–38.)

Figure 6–34 *Stephen's and Lauren's life lists*

Table of contents

.Physical Description.......1
.Habitat.......................2
.Nesting, young...............3
.Food..........................4
.5 cool facts..................5
.Acrostic poem...............6
.Song..........................7
.Glossary......................8

Figure 6–35 *Karla's table of contents*

It was the end of the school year, and the children pursued these projects not only because of their love for birds but because they had autonomy over their learning. They had come to internalize the many writing lessons that had taken place over the course of the year. This was a time to apply that knowledge and craft in forms outside of the class instruction. This was the culminating study, the one where all the lessons learned came together to produce high-quality reading and writing work.

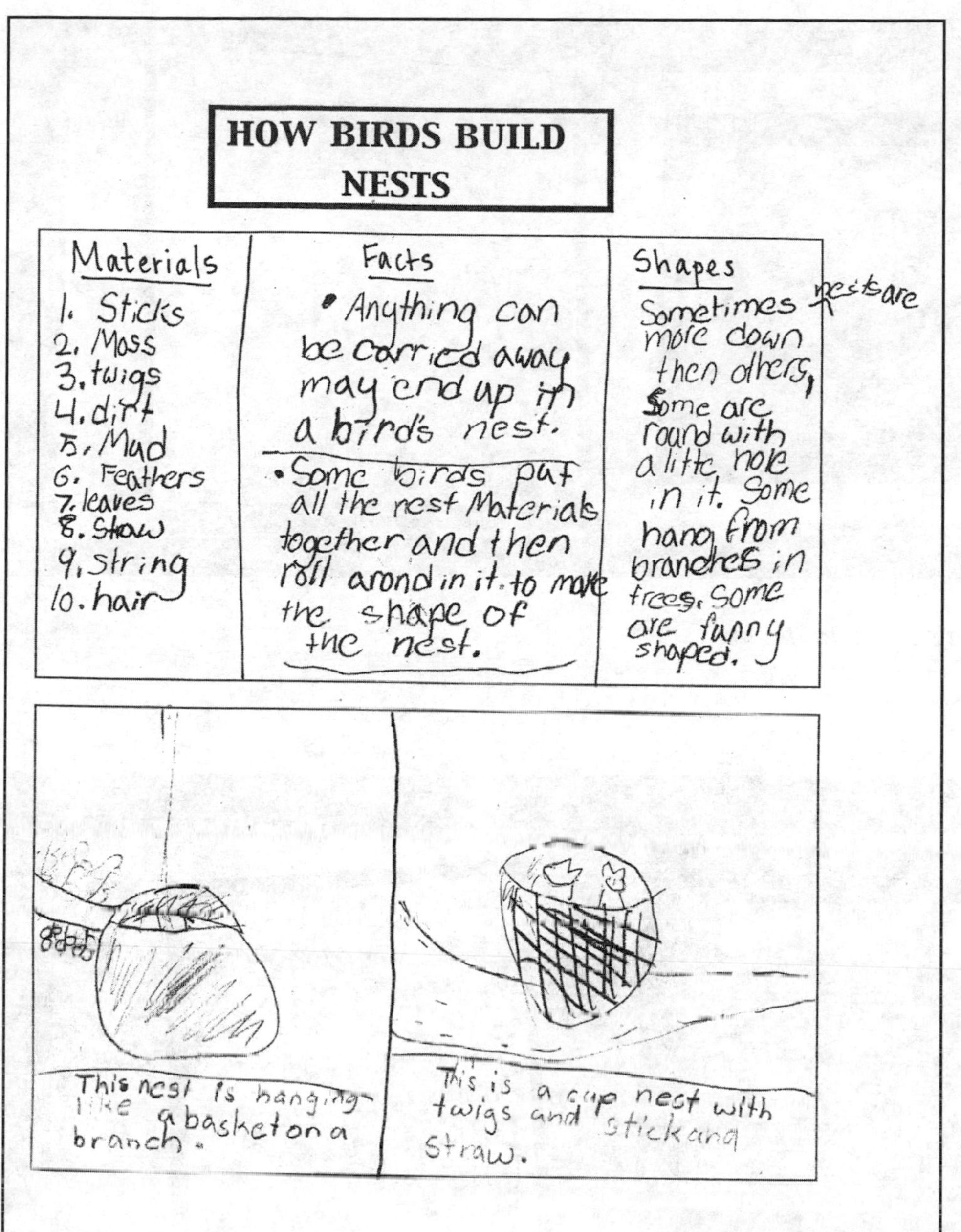

HOW BIRDS BUILD NESTS
Materials
1. Sticks
2. Moss
3. twigs
4. dirt
5. Mud
6. Feathers
7. leaves
8. Staw
9. String
10. hair
Facts
• Anything can be carried away may end up in a bird's nest.
• Some birds put all the nest Materials together and then roll arond in it. to make the shape of the nest.
Shapes
Sometimes nests are more down then others, Some are round with a litte hole in it. Some hang from branches in trees. Some are funny shaped.
This nest is hanging like a basket on a branch.
This is a cup nest with twigs and stick and straw.

Figure 6–36 *Lists that supported procedural writing*

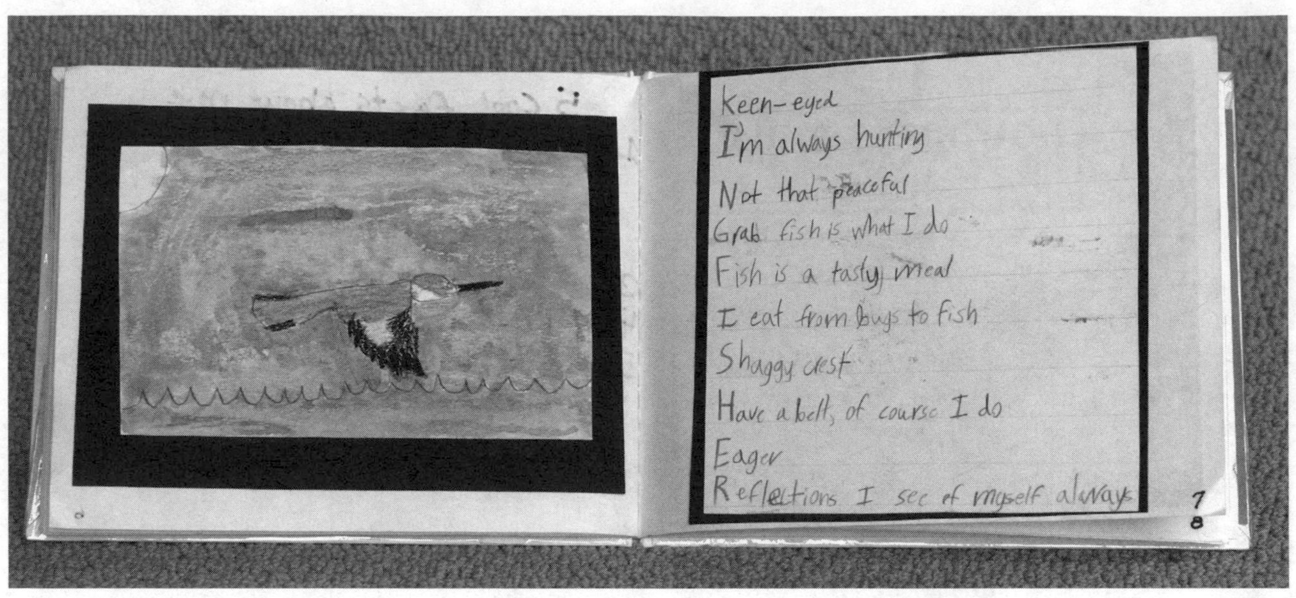

Keen-eyed
I'm always hunting
Not that peaceful
Grab fish is what I do
Fish is a tasty meal
I eat from bugs to fish
Shaggy crest
Have a belt, of course I do
Eager
Reflections I see of myself always
7
8

Figure 6–37 *Stephen's Acrostic poem*

Cheerful
Has a black cap
Insect eater
Chubby
Kind to People
Acrobatic
Delightful bird
Eats nuts
Eats seeds
7

Figure 6–38 *Caroline's Acrostic poem*

DEAR DIARY:

My son, who finished the second grade at P.S. 290 in Manhattan in June, completed a spring social studies project studying the birds native to New York City. For three months, the children researched every aspect of the birds assigned to them — migration, food, physical characteristics, habitats, etc. They loved the project, and were able to take bird walks through Central Park with professional bird-watchers.

I have never had any interest in birds, particularly New York birds. The only ones that are easy to spot have been pigeons, which I've never found appealing. That being said, one morning on the final day of school, my son heard birds calling outside our dining room window. We looked out and saw two birds carrying twigs and leaves onto the balcony for a nest. My son knew which was the male and which was the female and knew to call them mourning doves, not pigeons, as I assumed they had to be.

It was quite an exciting event. For the first week, we watched the nest being designed, the mother getting comfortable, the father bringing her what she needed. Then in a week or so, my son announced seeing the first egg.

For three weeks, we checked the mother (naming her Coo) mornings and evenings while we eagerly awaited the arrival of the first chick. And then, after becoming concerned about how long the mother had been nest-sitting, and wondering where dad was, the first baby's head appeared. As if on cue, dad returned. Male and female traded places on the nest and Coo stretched a bit and flew away.

For someone who was never interested in birds, I was elated by their appearance. And without my having to repeat second grade, I thank my son's all-encompassing bird study for helping me to find a whole new appreciation of our new balcony mates. *Claudia Bloom*

Figure 6–39 *Parent shares excitement over bird study in the* New York Times

Through Melissa's Eyes: A New Teacher's Voice

What I learned from this work

Having watched this study in action, I saw Mary Anne and Karen's minilessons and their interactions with the children firsthand. I was able to hear their questions, which resulted in thoughtful conversations among the group. I also watched them build a community around one subject, allowing children to become independent thinkers and researchers. I knew I had to ask questions to promote conversations in my class, leaving them open-ended enough to create meaningful learning experiences. After doing this same work, my children were reading and writing about birds for extended periods of time. For two years, my classroom buzzed each spring with young ornithologists—children who questioned, wondered, and found answers.

How I adapted this work to fit my classroom needs

I wanted to make room for individuality within a whole-class study. I wanted my children to have choice and room to grow on their own, all within certain boundaries so I could teach them about the content and about their writing. The children had learned a great deal about birds through research, so I constructed minilessons to support them as writers. For example, I used Joanne Ryder's book *Chipmunk Song* to model how to use the "you" voice to write about birds in general. Following the minilesson, the students used Ryder's structure and created sentences for their introductions. For example,

> Imagine you have no arms, but instead wings to fly.
> Imagine you have to leave your home, fly hundreds of miles away in search of food.
> Imagine you spend each day trying to survive in the wild.

As I become more comfortable as a teacher, I will continue to look for ways to expand on this study. Next year I will incorporate poetry, allowing the children to express their knowledge in a different form. Imagine the possibilities!

Study: ______________________ **Week:** ______________________

GOAL:

	OBJECTIVE	MINILESSON	STUDENT WORK	SHARE
DAY ONE				
DAY TWO				
DAY THREE				
DAY FOUR				
DAY FIVE				

Lines That Show Us the Time of Day

EARLY MORNING	MIDMORNING	NOON
AFTERNOON	**EVENING**	**NIGHTTIME**

Lines That Show Us the Time of Year

WINTER	SPRING

SUMMER	FALL

Book Title: ______________________________

Examples of no-*said* dialogue. One example per box.	How would a reader figure out who's talking? Strategies for figuring out who is talking. Two strategies per box.
	1. 2.
	1. 2.
	1. 2.

Names: ______________________________

Fiction	Nonfiction
Author:	Author:
Title:	Title:
What do you notice about your fiction book?	*What do you notice about your nonfiction book?*

Finding Possibilities for Explicit Teaching in Writing

TITLE	AUTHOR'S CRAFT/WRITING TECHNIQUE/TEXT STRUCTURE	TEACHING POSSIBILITIES	WAYS TO USE BOOK/ MINILESSONS

Planning Sheet—Study at a Glance

	WEEK 1	WEEK 2	WEEK 3	WEEK 4	WEEK 5	WEEK 6
GOAL						
LITERATURE						
MINILESSONS						
STUDENT WORK						

Homework Packet for Karen's Class and Mary Anne's Class, February 12

Note to Parents:

Children should bring a book home in their book baggies every night! **Parents**, please make sure classroom books are being returned to school. We've noticed several missing books—yikes! Please check inside couches and under beds—you'd be surprised where books may be hiding. THANKS!

Monday/12th	**Reading—Dialogue Study** Read chapters 4–6 (xeroxed copy) of *Pinky and Rex and the Spelling Bee*. Then reread story and underline the words spoken by Pinky and Rex using different color markers.
Tuesday/13th *Swim Day*	**Writing—Cynthia Rylant** 1. Reexamine the words Cynthia Rylant used to write *Scarecrow*. Underline parts where she shows you (the reader) time passing and where she describes seasons. **CHALLENGE:** Underline repetitive words in the story and anything else you notice in Cynthia Rylant's writing. 2. Write and illustrate your own story (fiction or nonfiction) and try to show how time passes. Ask yourself if your story takes place in one hour, one afternoon, one day, or longer? Use spelling try sheet to edit your spelling.
Wednesday/14th *Happy Valentine's Day*	**Math—100th Day of School!** Store problem
Thursday/15th	**Word Study** 1. Use the included letter cards to make as many words as you can. 2. Complete "Looks like—Sounds like" sheet for the "ea" spelling pattern.
Friday/16th	Homework due. Winter vacation begins.

Questions About Your Own Nonfiction Reading

Do you have more fiction or nonfiction books in your home library? ______________________

List your three favorite nonfiction books.

____

____

____

Other than books, what nonfiction reading materials do you have in your house?

______________________ ______________________

______________________ ______________________

______________________ ______________________

______________________ ______________________

Think about one nonfiction book/piece you read this week.

What was it?

Why did you choose to read it? ______________________

____

What did you learn from reading it? ______________________

____

____

____

Make a list of all nonfiction materials you read this week while out of school. This may include materials at home, at the doctor's office, on the bus, etc.

______________________ ______________________

______________________ ______________________

______________________ ______________________

What I Noticed About My Nonfiction

MONDAY

Title: ______________________ Author: ______________________

TUESDAY

Title: ______________________ Author: ______________________

WEDNESDAY

Title: ______________________ Author: ______________________

THURSDAY

Title: ______________________ Author: ______________________

Name: ______________________ Topic: ______________________

Facts I Know	Use your facts to craft a piece using what you learned from other writers.	Name the technique or style you tried. What writer taught you this technique/style?

Name: ______________________________ **Date:** ______________

HOME LIBRARY SEARCH FOR NONFICTION

Look through your home library. Choose three of your favorite nonfiction reading materials. It could be a book, magazine, baseball cards, map, or other things. Include the total (if it's a book) and author.

1. ______________________________

2. ______________________________

3. ______________________________

Choose one of the nonfiction materials and answer these questions.

Why do you enjoy it?

____

What did you learn from reading it?

____

How many times have you read it? How long have you had it?

____

MAKING A PAIR WITH NONFICTION AND FICTION BOOKS

Now look for two books—one nonfiction and one fiction—on the same subject, just as we did in class with *The Whales* by Cynthia Rylant and *How the Whales Walked into the Sea* by Faith McNulty. Bring the two books into class on Friday to share (if you can).

Subject: ______________________________

Titles and authors of the two books:

______________________________ Fiction

______________________________ Nonfiction

______________________'s Nonfiction and Fiction Reading Log

You need to read nonfiction twice and fiction twice this week.

Date	*Title*	*Nonfiction (NF) or Fiction (F)*	*Text Features I Noticed, for example: Diagrams, Dialogue, Maps, Table of Contents, etc.*
Monday			
Tuesday			
Wednesday			
Thursday			

Which text feature or features were the same with your fiction and nonfiction material?

______________________ ______________________ ______________________

Which were different?

______________________ ______________________ ______________________

Name: ______________________ Date: ____________

THE WHALES BY CYNTHIA RYLANT

QUESTIONS	NONFICTION INFORMATION	FICTION INFORMATION
Read through *The Whales* text again. Find *two* pieces of nonfiction information and *two* pieces of fiction. Underline them. Then write them down here.	1. 2.	1. 2.
From the lines you chose, what did the author teach you about whales?	1. 2.	1. 2.
Name one thing Cynthia Rylant does as a writer in a nonfiction way and one she does in a fiction way in her picture book *The Whales*.	1.	1.

SPELLING TRY SHEET

Name: ______________________

Date: ______________________

For copied spelling, use this strategy:

Look, Say, Name, Cover, Write, Check

Look at the word so that you have a picture of it in your head.

Say the word.

Name the letters.

Cover the word.

Write the word.

Check the word, letter by letter.

First Try	*Second Try*	*Correct Spelling*	*Copied Spelling*

Name: ______________________________ **Date:** ______________

Use the pages of Pinky and Rex to answer the following questions. You can have someone at home read the text to you, or you can read it alone. Remember, you need to answer all the questions.

PINKY AND REX BY JAMES HOWE

PAGE 1 **"Wake up, Wake up!"**

Who said that? ______________ How do you know? ______________

____

What reading strategy did you use to figure it out? ______________

____

PAGES 3–4 **"I can't decide what to wear to the museum today. Should I wear my tyrannosaurus T-shirt or my stegosaurus sweatshirt?"**

Who said that? ______________ How do you know? ______________

____

What reading strategy did you use to figure it out? ______________

____

PAGE 7 **"You should give me some."**

Who said that? ______________ How do you know? ______________

____

What reading strategy did you use to figure it out? ______________

____

Children's Books

Adler, David A. 1997. *Cam Jansen and the Scary Snake Mystery*. New York: Scholastic.

Allen, Judy, and Tudor Humphries. 2000a. *Are You a Butterfly?* New York: Kingfisher.

———. 2000b. *Are You a Ladybug?* New York: Kingfisher.

———. 2000c. *Are You a Spider?* New York: Kingfisher.

Arnosky, Jim. 1992. *Crinkleroot's Guide to Knowing the Birds*. New York: Simon and Schuster.

———. 1994. *All About Alligators*. New York: Scholastic.

———. 1999. *All About Deer*. New York: Scholastic.

Bailey, Jill. 1996. *Birds*. New York: Penguin

Bash, Barbara. 1990. *Urban Roosts. Where Birds Nest in the City*. Boston: Little, Brown.

Baylor, Bird. 1982. *The Best Town in the World*. New York: Simon and Schuster.

Boring, Mel. 1996. *Birds, Nests and Eggs*. Minocqua, WI: NorthWood.

Brenner, Barbara, and May Garelick. 1989. *Two Orphan Cubs*. New York: Walker.

Cannon, Janell. 1993. *Stellaluna*. San Diego: Harcourt Brace.

Cazet, Denys. 1999. *Minnie and Moo Go to Paris*. New York: HarperCollins.

Cherry, Lynne. 1997. *Flute's Journey: The Life of a Wood Thrush*. San Fransisco: Harcourt.

Cisneros, Sandra. 1994. *Hairs*. New York: Alfred A. Knopf.

Cowley, Joy. 1996a. *Sloppy Tiger and the Party*. Bothell, WA: Wright Group.

———. 1996b. *Old Grizzly*. Bothell, WA: Wright Group.

Curtis, Jamie Lee. 1993. *When I Was Little: A Four-Year-Old's Memoir of Her Youth*. New York: HarperCollins.

Danziger, Paula. 2001. *It's Justin Time, Amber Brown*. New York: G. P. Putnam and Sons.

Deluise, Dom. 1990. *Charlie the Caterpillar*. New York: Simon and Schuster.

Doyle, Malachy. 2002. *Cow*. New York: Margaret K. McElderry/Simon and Schuster.

Everett, Gwen, and National Museum of American Art Staff. 1992. *Li'l Sis and Uncle Willie: A Story Based on the Life and Paintings of William H. Johnson.* New York: Rizzoli International.

Fleischman, Paul. 1979. *The Birthday Tree*. New York: HarperCollins.

Fletcher, Ralph. 1997. *Twilight Comes Twice*. New York: Clarion.

Fox, Mem. 1994. *Possum Magic*. San Diego: Harcourt Brace.

French, Vivian. 2000. *Growing Frogs*. Cambridge, MA: Candlewick.

Galvin, Laura Gates. 2000. *Bumblebee at Apple Tree Lane*. Cambridge, MA: Soundprints.

Garelick, May. 1995. *What Makes a Bird a Bird?* New York: Mondo.

Garza, Carmen Lomas. 1990. *Family Pictures*. San Francisco: Children's Book.

George, Jean Craighead. 1959. *My Side of the Mountain*. New York: E. P. Dutton.

———. 1995. *There's an Owl in the Shower*. New York: HarperCollins.

———. 1997. *Look to the North: A Wolf Pup Diary*. New York: HarperCollins.

———. 1999a. *Frightful's Mountain*. New York: Scholastic.

———. 1999b. *On the Far Side of the Mountain*. New York: Putnam and Gossett Group.

George, William T. 1989. *Box Turtle at Long Pond*. New York: Greenwillow.

George, William T., and Lindsay Barrett George. 1998. *Beaver at Long Pond*. New York: HarperCollins.

Getz, David. 1997. *Floating Home*. New York: Henry Holt.

Gibbons, Gail. 1991. *Whales*. New York: Holiday House.

———. 1993. *Spiders*. New York: Holiday House.

———. 1999a. *Bats*. New York: Holiday House.

———. 1999b. *Pigs*. New York: Holiday House.

Graham, Ian S., and Geriant H. Jones. 2000. *All About Space: Amazing Cosmic Facts*. Anness.

Heinz, Brian. 2000. *Butternut Hollow Pond*. Brookfield, CT: Millbrook.

Himmelman, John. 1998a. *A Salamander's Life*. New York: Children's.

———. 1998b. *A Wood Frog's Life*. New York: Children's.

———. 2000. *A Hummingbird's Life*. New York: Children's.

Hirschi, Ron. 2000a. *When Morning Comes*. Honesdale, PA: Boyd Mills.

———. 2000b. *When Night Comes*. Honesdale, PA: Boyd Mills.

Howard, Arthur. 1996. *When I Was Five*. San Diego: Harcourt Brace.

Howe, James. *Pinky and Rex and the Dinosaur Game*. New York: Aladdin

———. 1991. *Pinky and Rex and the Spelling Bee*. New York: Simon and Schuster.

———. 1993. *Pinky and Rex and the New Baby*. New York: Scholastic.

———. 1995. *Pinky and Rex and the Double-Dad Weekend*. New York: Aladdin

Iverson, Diane. 1999. *My Favorite Tree: Terrific Trees of North America*. Nevada City, CA: Dawn.

Jackson, Ellen. 1994. *Winter Solstice*. Brookfield, CT: Millbrook.

Jenkins, Martin. 1997. *Chameleons Are Cool*. New York: Scholastic.

Jensen, Patsy A. 1997. *Johnny Appleseed Goes A'Planting*. New York: Troll.

Karas, Brian. 2002. *Atlantic*. New York: G. P. Putnam and Sons.

Kirk, David. 1995. *Miss Spider's Wedding*. New York: Scholastic.

Koch, Michelle. 1993. *World Water Watch*. New York: Greenwillow.

Langton, Jane. 1980. *The Fledgling*. New York: Scholastic.

Lasky, Kathryn. 1995. *Pond Year*. Cambridge, MA: Candlewick.

Legg, Gerald. 1998. *From Caterpillar to Butterfly*. New York: Scholastic.

Leonni, Leo. 1975. *A Color of His Own*. New York: Pantheon.
Lobel, Arnold. 1970. *Frog and Toad Are Friends*. New York: Harper and Row.
———. 1971. *Frog and Toad Together*. New York: Harper and Row.
Loewer, Jean, and Peter Loewer. 1998. *The Moonflower*. Atlanta: Peachtree.
London, Jonathan. 1993. *The Eyes of Gray Wolf*. San Francisco: Chronicle.
———. 1994. *Condor's Egg*. San Francisco: Chronicle.
———. 1995. *Honey Paw and Lightfoot*. San Francisco: Chronicle.
———. 1998. *Phantom of the Prairie: Year of the Black-Footed Ferret*. San Francisco: Sierra Club.
———. 1999. *Baby Whale's Journey*. San Francisco: Chronicle.
———. 2001. *Gone Again Ptarmigan*. Washington, DC: National Geographic Society.
Lyons, Dana. 2002. *The Tree*. Bellevue.
Marshall, James. 1987. *Red Riding Hood*. New York: Putnam and Gossett Group.
———. 1992. *Fox Outfoxed*. New York: Puffin.
McCurdy, Michael. 2000. *An Algonquian Year: The Year According to the Full Moon*. Boston: Houghton Mifflin.
McNulty, Faith. 1999. *How the Whales Walked into the Sea*. New York: Scholastic.
Micucci, Charles. 1992. *The Life and Times of the Apple*. New York: Orchard.
Miller, Debbie S. 1994. *Caribou Journey*. Boston: Little, Brown.
———. 1997. *Disappearing Lake: Nature's Magic in Denali National Park*. New York: Walker.
———. 2000. *River of Life*. Boston: Houghton Mifflin.
Nail, Jim. 1994. *Whose Tracks Are These? A Clue Book of Familiar Forest Animals*. Boulder, CO: Court Wayne.
Oates, Eddie Herschel. 1995. *Making Music: Six Instruments You Can Create*. New York: HarperCollins.
Parker, Steve. 1999. *It's a Frog's Life: My Story of Life in a Pond*. Pleasantville, NY: Reader's Digest Children's.
———. 1999. *It's an Ant's Life: My Story of Life in the Nest*. Pleasantville, NY: Reader's Digest Children's.
Park, Barbara. 2001. *Junie B. Jones Is a Graduation Girl*. New York: Random House.
Peterson. *Peterson Field Guides for Young Naturalists: Backyard Birds*. New York.
Pratt-Serafini, Kristin Joy. 2001. *Salamander Rain: A Lake and Pond Journal*. Nevada City, CA: Dawn.
Ridlon, Marci. 1996. *Sun Through the Window: Poems for Children*. Honesdale, PA: Boyds Mills.
Russell, Elizabeth. 2000. *Bats*. Thomson Learning.
Ryder, Joanne. 1982. *The Snail's Spell*. New York: Puffin.
———. 1987. *Chipmunk's Song*. New York: Dutton.
———. 1989. *Where Butterflies Grow*. New York: Puffin.
———. 1990. *Lizard in the Sun*. New York: William Morrow.
Rylant, Cynthia. 1982. *When I Was Young in the Mountains*. New York: Penguin.
———. 1985. *The Relatives Came*. New York: Bradbury.
———. 1986. *Night in the Country*. New York: Bradbury.
———. 1991. *Birthday Presents*. New York: Orchard.
———. 1995a. *Dog Heaven*. New York: Scholastic.

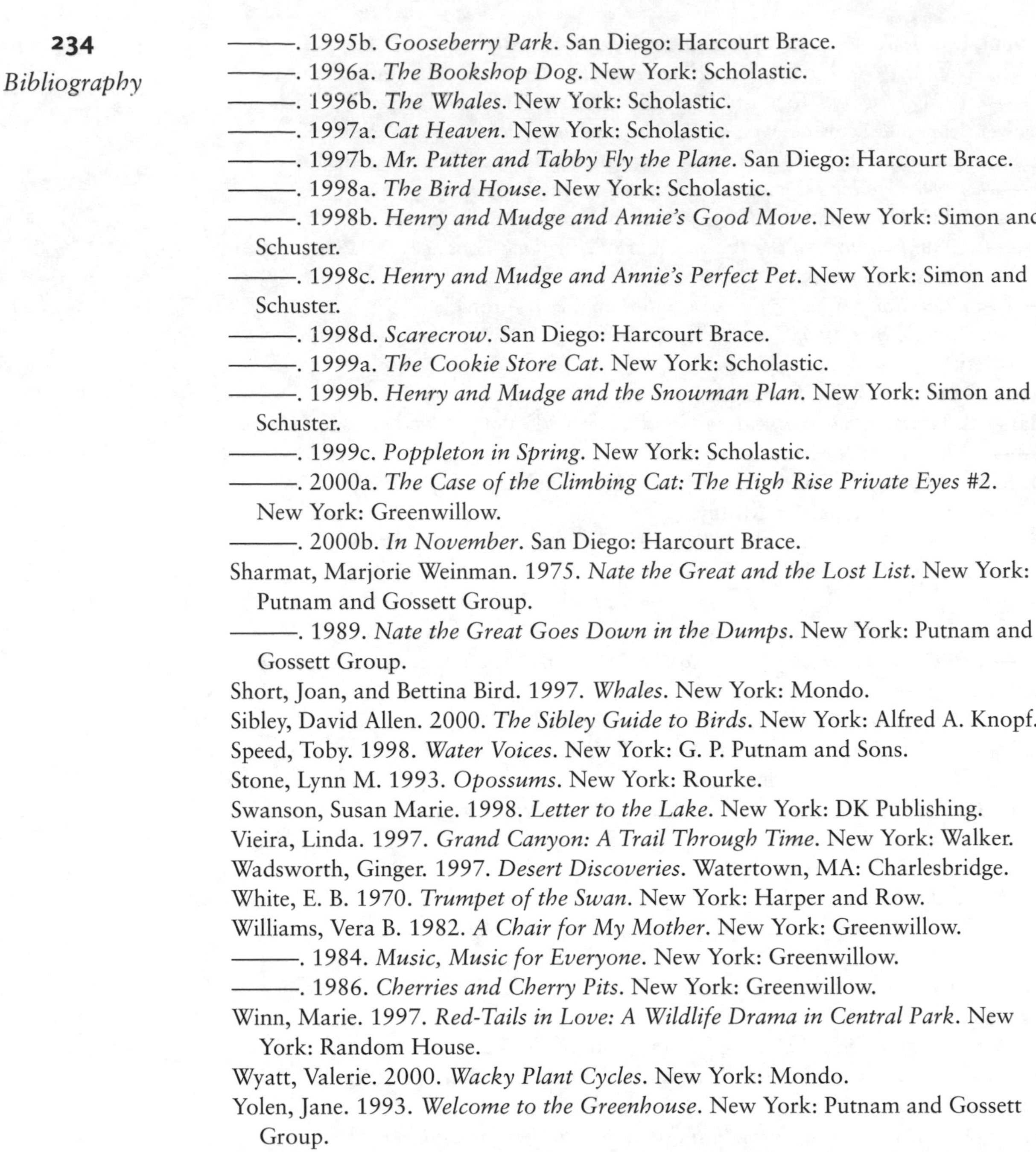

———. 1995b. *Gooseberry Park*. San Diego: Harcourt Brace.
———. 1996a. *The Bookshop Dog*. New York: Scholastic.
———. 1996b. *The Whales*. New York: Scholastic.
———. 1997a. *Cat Heaven*. New York: Scholastic.
———. 1997b. *Mr. Putter and Tabby Fly the Plane*. San Diego: Harcourt Brace.
———. 1998a. *The Bird House*. New York: Scholastic.
———. 1998b. *Henry and Mudge and Annie's Good Move*. New York: Simon and Schuster.
———. 1998c. *Henry and Mudge and Annie's Perfect Pet*. New York: Simon and Schuster.
———. 1998d. *Scarecrow*. San Diego: Harcourt Brace.
———. 1999a. *The Cookie Store Cat*. New York: Scholastic.
———. 1999b. *Henry and Mudge and the Snowman Plan*. New York: Simon and Schuster.
———. 1999c. *Poppleton in Spring*. New York: Scholastic.
———. 2000a. *The Case of the Climbing Cat: The High Rise Private Eyes #2*. New York: Greenwillow.
———. 2000b. *In November*. San Diego: Harcourt Brace.
Sharmat, Marjorie Weinman. 1975. *Nate the Great and the Lost List*. New York: Putnam and Gossett Group.
———. 1989. *Nate the Great Goes Down in the Dumps*. New York: Putnam and Gossett Group.
Short, Joan, and Bettina Bird. 1997. *Whales*. New York: Mondo.
Sibley, David Allen. 2000. *The Sibley Guide to Birds*. New York: Alfred A. Knopf.
Speed, Toby. 1998. *Water Voices*. New York: G. P. Putnam and Sons.
Stone, Lynn M. 1993. *Opossums*. New York: Rourke.
Swanson, Susan Marie. 1998. *Letter to the Lake*. New York: DK Publishing.
Vieira, Linda. 1997. *Grand Canyon: A Trail Through Time*. New York: Walker.
Wadsworth, Ginger. 1997. *Desert Discoveries*. Watertown, MA: Charlesbridge.
White, E. B. 1970. *Trumpet of the Swan*. New York: Harper and Row.
Williams, Vera B. 1982. *A Chair for My Mother*. New York: Greenwillow.
———. 1984. *Music, Music for Everyone*. New York: Greenwillow.
———. 1986. *Cherries and Cherry Pits*. New York: Greenwillow.
Winn, Marie. 1997. *Red-Tails in Love: A Wildlife Drama in Central Park*. New York: Random House.
Wyatt, Valerie. 2000. *Wacky Plant Cycles*. New York: Mondo.
Yolen, Jane. 1993. *Welcome to the Greenhouse*. New York: Putnam and Gossett Group.
Zoehfeld, Kathleen. 1994. *Seal Pup Grows Up: The Story of a Harbour Seal*. New York: Scholastic.
———. 1997. *Cactus Café: A Story of the Sonoran Desert*. Norwalk, CT: Soundprints.

Children's Book Series

Adler, David. Cam Jansen.
Cazet, Denys. Minnie and Moo.
Dadey, Debbie, and Marcia Thorton Jones. Bailey School Kids.
———. Triplet Trouble.
Danziger, Paula. Amber Brown.
Greenburg, Dan. Zack Files.
Howe, James. Pinky and Rex.
Hurwitz, Johanna. Riverside Kids.
Jane, Pamela. Winky Blue.
Kline, Suzy. Horrible Harry.
Lobel, Arnold. Frog and Toad.
Marshall, James. Fox.
Osborne, Mary Pope. Magic Tree House.
Park, Barbara. Junie B. Jones.
Preller, James. Jigsaw Jones.
Ross, Pat. M and M.
Rylant, Cynthia. Cobble Street Cousins.
———. Henry and Mudge.
———. High Rise Private Eyes.
———. Mr. Putter and Tabby.
———. Poppleton.
Sharmat, Marjorie. Nate the Great.

Professional Books

Clay, Marie. 1991. *Becoming Literate*. Portsmouth, NH: Heinemann.
Davis, Judy, and Sharon Hill. 2003. *The No Nonsense Guide to Teaching Writing*. Portsmouth, NH: Heinemann.
Harwayne, Shelley. 2000. *Lifetime Guarantees*. Portsmouth, NH: Heinemann.
———. 2001. *Writing Through Childhood*. Portsmouth, NH: Heinemann.
Harvey, Steph. 1998. *Nonfiction Matters*. York, ME: Stenhouse.
Hindley, Joanne. 1996. *In the Company of Children*. York, ME: Stenhouse Publishing.
Portalupi, Joann, and Ralph Fletcher. 2001. *Nonfiction Craft Lessons*. York, ME: Stenhouse.
Ray, Katie Wood. 1999. *Wondrous Words*. Urbana, IL: NCTE.
Snowball, Diane, and Faye Boylton. 1999. *Spelling K–8*. York, ME: Stenhouse.
Stead, Tony. 2002. *Is That A Fact?* York, ME: Stenhouse.
Szymusiak, Karen, and Franki Sibberson. 2001. *Beyond Leveled Books*. York, ME: Stenhouse.
Taberski, Sharon. 2000. *On Solid Ground*. Portsmouth, NH: Heinemann.

INDEX

acrostic poems, 207, 210
acting out lines
  with partners, 45
  using *said* alternatives, 29
Adler, David
  Cam Jansen and the Scary Snake Mystery, 31
  Cam Jansen series, 34
Algonquian Year, An: The Year According to the Full Moon (McCurdy), 136
All About Alligators (Aronsky), 108
All About Deer (Aronsky), 108
Allen, Judy
  Are You a Butterfly? (with Tudor Humphries), 185
alliteration, 146
alphabetization, of glossaries, 105–6
animals, as fictional characters, 77–78
apostrophe, 47
  Are You a Butterfly? (Allen and Humphries), 185
Aronsky, Jim, 106–8
  All About Alligators, 108
  All About Deer, 108
authors
  arranging nonfiction books by, 108–10
  knowledge about, 111

Baby Whale's Journey (London), 91
Bailey, Jill
  Birds, 94
Bash, Barbara
  Urban Roosts: Where Birds Nest in the City, 160
Bats (Gibbons), 111
Bats (Russell), 80, 82
Baylor, Byrd
  Best Town in the World, The, 116
Beaver at Long Pond (George and George), 131, 132, 135
Becoming Literate (Clay), 2
Best Town in the World, The (Baylor), 116
Beyond Leveled Books (Szymusiak and Sibberson), 11
biographies, 156–57
Bird, Bettina
  Whales (with Joan Short), 103
Birds, Nests and Eggs (Boring), 164, 195–96
Birds (Bailey), 94
Birthday Presents (Rylant), 116, 124
bold print, 103–4
book boxes, 14
book choice, 39
book covers
  back blurb, 52
  for student narrative books, 199, 200–201
books
  displaying pages on overhead projector, 36
  fiction/nonfiction text sets, 78–84, 112–13
  with first-and third-person narration, 35

gathering information about, 51–52
getting to know, 16–18
organizing, 16
with and without dialogue, 26
Bookshop Dog, The (Rylant), 88
Boring, Mel
Birds, Nests and Eggs, 164, 195–96
Box Turtle at Long Pond (George), 128–32, 135, 139, 147
Brenner, Barbara
Two Orphan Cubs (with Mary Garelick), 91
bulletin boards
for dialogue study, 49, 58, 60
for fiction/nonfiction comparisons, 91
Bumblebee at Apple Tree Lane (Galvin), 91
Butternut Hollow Pond (Heinz), 124–25, 134–39, 142–44, 149, 155, 193–95

Cactus Café: A Story of the Sonoran Desert (Zoehfeld), 136
Cam Jansen and the Scary Snake Mystery (Adler), 31
Cam Jansen series (Adler), 34
Cannon, Janell
Stellaluna, 80, 82
Caras, Brian G., 147
Case of the Climbing Cat (Rylant), 27
Cat Heaven (Rylant), 88
Chair for My Mother, A (Williams), 147
Chameleons Are Cool (Jenkins), 80
characters
changing voice to portray, 39
characteristics of, 77–78
determining who is talking, 23–24, 52–59, 66, 229
discussing characteristics of, 40–41
getting to know, 18–19, 20
knowledge of, as strategy, 58, 66
as narrators, 32–38, 40, 66
narrator vs., 24, 66
in nonfiction books, 93–94
student knowledge of, 58, 64–66
Charlie the Caterpillar (Deluise), 83
charts. *See also* T-charts
about tables of contents, 104
for comparing fiction and nonfiction, 77, 81
for dialogue study, 49
Cherries and Cherry Pits (Williams), 147
Chiou, Regina, 2
Chipmunk Song (Ryder), 212
choice
in reading books, 39
in reading spots, 13
Cisneros, Sandra
Hairs, 116
classroom, 15
Clay, Marie, 2
clue books, 180–86
Cobble Street Cousins (Rylant), 102
collaboration, 1, 2
Color of His Own, A (Leonni), 80
commas, 46, 53, 55
comparisons, using nonstandard measurements, 196
comprehension
dialogue and, 32
prereading and, 51–52
Condor's Egg (London), 193–94
content area research and writing study, 7, 156–212
classroom library, 173
creating narrative books, 197–201
drafting with attention to voice, 178–86
editing, 191–97
final draft, 197–99
folders, 173
general investigation, 162–66
general understanding of topic, 167–71
goals, 158–59, 162, 167, 171, 178, 186, 191, 197
illustrations, 197–99
minilessons, 158–59, 163, 169–70, 174–75
overview, 156–62
parents and, 179, 211
partnerships for, 167–68
related writing forms, 199–210
research process, 171–78
research sheets, 174–78
revision, 186–91
student work, 158–59
vocabulary for, 169–71
weekly schedule at a glance, 158–59
continuation dialogue
defined, 37
generalizations about, 43

identifying, 53
recognizing, 50
Cookie Store Cat, The (Rylant), 88, 130
cover-to-cover reading, 97–98, 108
Cowley, Joy
Old Grizzly, 28–29
Sloppy Tiger and the Party, 39–40
craft of writing, 144–45, 146, 157, 224
Curtis, Jamie Lee
When I Was Little, 116

Dandelion's Life, A (Himmelman), 97
Danziger, Paula
It's Justin Time, Amber Brown, 34, 69
day-by-day plans
for dialogue study, 30, 38, 48, 63, 71
form for, 213
dedications, writing, 201, 204, 205
Deluise, Dom
Charlie the Caterpillar, 83
Desert Discoveries (Wadsworth), 135
details
adding to writing, 120
for clue books, 180–81
dialogue, 20–72
acting out, 29, 45
comprehension and, 32
continuation, 37, 43, 50, 53
deepening understanding of, 39–47
determining who is talking, 23–24, 52–59, 66, 229
differentiating between narrator and character, 24
finding in books, 25–26, 27
generalizations about, 42–44
identifying, 27–28
indentations for, 43
listing books with and without, 26
marking text for, 41–43, 53–54
naming types of, 32, 36–37
in nonfiction books, 26, 87
no-*said,* 37, 50, 66, 67, 216
noticing types of, 36–37, 50
punctuation and, 21, 45–47, 51, 66–67
questions for understanding, 21–23
reading for meaning and, 44
said alternatives, 27–29, 31, 59
simple, 37, 43, 50
student understanding of, 6, 20, 24–25
styles of, 31–38
voice in, 31–38
written by students, 26–27, 59, 61–62, 69–70
dialogue strategies, 47, 54–60
rereading, 20–21
strategy chart, 54, 55
using *said* and *said* alternatives, 27–29
dialogue study
benefits of, 31
bulletin boards for, 49, 58, 60
charts for, 49
day-by-day plans, 30, 38, 48, 63, 71
first-person narration, 64–71
goals, 22, 24, 30, 31, 38, 39, 47, 48, 63, 64, 71
identifying dialogue styles, 31–38
identifying voice, 31–38
literature for, 22
minilessons, 22, 30, 38, 48, 63, 71
noticing dialogue in text, 24–30
objectives, 30, 38, 48, 63, 71
overview, 20–24
reading strategies, 47, 49–63
share time, 30, 38, 48, 63, 71
student learning from, 59–60
student work, 22, 30, 38, 48, 63, 71
teacher research on, 21–23
understanding how dialogue works, 39–47
understanding what students need to know, 23–24
weekly schedule at a glance, 22
dip in/out reading, 97–98, 108
Disappearing Lake (Miller), 136
Dog Heaven (Rylant), 88

editing, 145–47, 197–99
Esposito, Doreen, 8
Everett, Gwen
Li'l Sis and Uncle Willie: A Story Based on the Life and Paintings of William H. Johnson, 156–57
exclamation points, 46
experience, writing about, 138
Eyes of the Great Wolf, The (London), 108

Family Pictures: Cuadros de Familia (Garza), 120
fiction. *See also* dialogue; dialogue study

characteristics of, 78, 217
dialogue in, 26
goals for reading, 12
informational, 87–91
investigating for content area research and writing, 162
nonfiction vs., 76–86
predictable structure of, 75–76
writing style, 64–67
fiction/nonfiction text sets, 78–83, 112–13
forms for comparing, 217, 225
Venn diagram comparing, 84
field guides, 201, 202–3
first-person narration, 32–38
"I" voice in, 32
in nonfiction writing, 181, 185–86, 186–88
practicing strategies with, 64–71
student preference for, 186–87
Fledgling, The (Langton), 163
Fletcher, Ralph, 157
Twilight Comes Twice, 135
fonts, 104
forms
for analyzing informational fiction, 227
day-by-day plans, 213
dialogue strategies, 229
home library nonfiction, 225
homework packet, 220
nonfiction reading, 221, 223
no-*said* phrases, 216
questions about nonfiction reading, 221
reading logs, 226
spelling try sheet, 228
time of day phrases, 214
time of year phrases, 215
writing craft, 224
Freeman, Russell, 156
French, Vivian
Growing Frogs, 91
Frightful's Mountain (George), 163
Frog and Toad Are Friends (Lobel), 31
Frog and Toad Together (Lobel), 79–80
Frog and Toad series (Lobel), 34, 76
From Caterpillar to Butterfly (Legg), 83

Galvin, Laura Gates
Bumblebee at Apple Tree Lane, 91
Garelick, Mary
Two Orphan Cubs (with Barbara Brenner), 91
Garza, Caren Lomas
Family Pictures: Cuadros de Familia, 120
George, Jean Craighead
Frightful's Mountain, 163
My Side of the Mountain, 162
On the Far Side of the Mountain, 163
There's an Owl in the Shower, 162
George, Lindsay Barrett, 147
Beaver at Long Pond (with William T. George), 131, 132, 135
George, William T.
Beaver at Long Pond (with Lindsay Barrett), 131, 132, 135
Box Turtle at Long Pond, 128–32, 135, 139, 147
Gerstenhaber, Mindy, 39
Getz, Jacqui, 2
Gibbons, Gail, 107–11, 149
Bats, 111
Whales, 110
glossaries
alphabetization of, 105–6
in nonfiction books, 101, 104–6, 107
goals
for content area research and writing study, 158–59, 162, 167, 171, 178, 186, 191, 197
for dialogue study, 22, 24, 30, 31, 39, 47, 48, 63, 64, 71
for nonfiction study, 74, 76, 87, 92, 94, 101, 106
for reading, 11, 12
for reading fiction books, 12
for reading nonfiction books, 12, 74
for reading workshop, 11, 12
for setting study, 125, 127, 128, 129, 132, 141, 144, 145
for writing, 123–24
Gone Again Ptarmigan (London), 108
Gooseberry Park (Rylant), 19, 25, 28, 76, 77, 80, 96
grade-level collaboration, 2
Grand Canyon: A Trail Through Time (Vieira), 135, 155
Growing Frogs (French), 91

Hairs (Cisneros), 116
Harvey, Steph, 75, 156

Harwayne, Shelley, vii–x, 1, 121, 122, 123
Heinz, Brian J., 156
Butternut Hollow Pond, 124–25, 134–39, 149, 155, 193–95
as a mentor author, 124–25, 134–39, 142–44, 149
Henry and Mudge and Annie's Good Move (Rylant), 27
Henry and Mudge and Annie's Perfect Pet (Rylant), 33
Henry and Mudge and the Snowman Plan (Rylant), 36, 40
Henry and Mudge series (Rylant), 28, 32–38
High Rise Private Eyes series (Rylant), 20, 147
Himmelman, John
Dandelion's Life, A, 97
Hummingbird's Life, A, 164
Salamander's Life, A, 97, 108
Wood Frog's Life, A, 97, 108
Hindley, Joanne, 2
Hirschi, Ron
When Morning Comes, 155
When Night Comes, 155
home libraries, examining nonfiction in, 82–83, 225
homework packet form, 220
homework worksheets, 56
Honey Paw and Lightfoot (London), 91, 108
Horrible Harry series, 34
Howard, Arthur
When I Was Five, 116
Howe, James
Pinky and Rex and the Dinosaur Game, 53–54
Pinky and Rex and the Double-Dad Weekend, 56
Pinky and Rex and the New Baby, 40–46, 47, 50
Pinky and Rex and the Spelling Bee, 42, 51–52, 54–55, 59
Pinky and Rex series, 34, 51–52, 102, 229
How the Whales Walked into the Sea (McNulty), 89, 105, 106
Hummingbird's Life, A (Himmelman), 164
humor, in nonfiction writing, 188–90, 192
Humphries, Tudor
Are You a Butterfly? (with Judy Allen), 185

illustrations
for content area research, 197–201
in nonfiction, 87, 108
planning details with, 120
as reading strategies, 58
by students, 147–49
viewing before reading, 52
indentations, for dialogue, 43
indexes, 101, 106, 107, 174
informational fiction, 87–91
creating baskets of, 108
defined, 90
examples of, 91
form for analyzing, 227
In November (Rylant), 132
interviews, about nonfiction reading, 84–86
In the Company of Children (Hindley), 2
Investigations in Number, Data, and Space (TERC), 3
investigative design, 3
Is That a Fact? (Stead), 2
It's a Frog's Life (Parker), 79–80, 104–6, 187–89, 192, 193, 194
It's Justin Time, Amber Brown (Danziger), 34, 69
Iverson, Diane
My Favorite Trees of North America, 97–99, 101
"I" voice
in first-person narration, 32

Jackson, Ellen
Winter Solstice, 94
Jenkins, Martin
Chameleons Are Cool, 80
Jigsaw Jones series, 34
Johnson, William H., 156–57
Junie B. Jones Is a Graduation Girl (Park), 69
Junie B. Jones series (Park), 34

kindergarten students, reading with, 39–40

Langton, Jane
Fledgling, The, 163

Lasky, Kathryn
Pond Year, 91
learning, sharing passion in, 156–57
Legg, Gerald
From Caterpillar to Butterfly, 83
Leonni, Leo
Color of His Own, A, 80
Letter to the Lake (Swanson), 116, 121
letter writing, 121, 201, 204
life list journals, 205, 207
Lifetime Guarantees (Harwayne), 1
Li'l Sis and Uncle Willie: A Story Based on the Life and Paintings of William H. Johnson (Everett), 156–57
list writing, 207, 209
literature-based workshops, viii
Lizard in the Sun (Ryder), 183
Lobel, Arnold
Frog and Toad Are Friends, 31
Frog and Toad Together, 79–80
Loewer, Peter and Jean
Moonflower, The, 91
London, Jonathan, 106–8, 156
Baby Whale's Journey, 91
Condor's Egg, 193–94
Eyes of the Great Wolf, The, 108
Gone Again Ptarmigan, 108
Honey Paw and Lightfoot, 91, 108
Phantom of the Prairie: Year of the Black-Footed Ferret, *87–88, 108, 180*
Puddles, 147

M and M series (Ross), 34
Manhattan New School, vii–ix, 1–2, 3
back-to-school night, 10–11
McCurdy, Michael
Algonquian Year, An: The Year According to the Full Moon, 136
McNulty, Faith
How the Whales Walked into the Sea, 89, 105, 106
meaning, dialogue clues for, 44
meaning-based strategies, for dialogue, 58–59
measurements, nonstandard, 196
meeting area, for reading workshop, 13
memory collection notebooks, 122–23
encouraging writing with, 118
for writing about place, 134–36
memory writing, 115, 118
about place, 122–24, 134–39
books, 116–17
as letters, 121
mental images, 59
mentor texts
Butternut Hollow Pond (Heinz), 134–39, 142–44
for writing about setting, 124–32, 134–39
writing style in, 134
metaphor, 132
Miller, Debbie S., 156
Disappearing Lake, 136
River of Life, 192–93
minilessons
for adding detail to writing, 120
for changing writing form, 121
for content area research and writing study, 158–59, 163, 169–70, 174–75
defined, 4–5
for dialogue study, 22, 30, 38, 48, 63, 71
for establishing reading habits, 16
for getting to know characters in classroom books, 18–19
for getting to know characters in series books, 19
for getting to know series books in classroom, 18
for nonfiction study, 74, 81
for setting study, 129
for showing time of day and time of year, 133
on writing, 117, 119–20
ministudies
on adding detail to writing, 120
on changing writing form, 121
on establishing reading habits, 16
on establishing writing habits, 119–20
on getting to know characters in series books, 19
on getting to know series books in classroom, 18
on glossaries, 101, 104–6
on nonfiction tables of contents, 101–4
Moonflower, The (Loewer and Loewer), 91
Mr. Putter and Tabby Fly the Plane (Rylant), 26, 40
Mr. Putter and Tabby series (Rylant), 16, 17, 20, 28
dialogue study, 20

My Favorite Trees of North America (Iverson), 97–99, 101
My Side of the Mountain (George), 162

Nail, Jim, 183
  Whose Tracks Are These? A Clue Book of Familiar Forest Animals, 180, 186
narration. *See also* voice
  determining who is telling the story, 33–34
  distinguishing between first- and third-person, 35–37
  first-person, 32–38, 64–71, 181, 185–87
  reading approach and, 36
  second-person, 183–86
  third-person, 32–38
  time and setting provided in, 41
narrative nonfiction
  mentor texts, 125–32, 134–39, 142–44
  use of time in, 128–32
narrative nonfiction books. *See also* content area research and writing study
  covers for, 199, 200–201
  illustrations for, 197–201
  sharing content area research through, 197–201
narrators
  characters as, 32–38, 40, 66
  characters vs., 24, 66
  identifying, 32–38
Nate the Great and the Lost List (Sharmat), 65–70
Nate the Great Goes Down in the Dumps (Sharmat), 32
Nate the Great series (Sharmat), 18–19, 32–35, 38, 64–71, 76
New York Times, 211
Night in the Country (Rylant), 130
nonfiction. *See also* content area research and writing study
  authors of multiple books, 106–8
  characteristics of, 78, 217, 223
  classifying, 84–86
  dialogue in, 26, 87
  dip in/out vs. cover-to-cover reading, 97–98
  engagement in, 76
  examining home libraries for, 82–83, 225
  fiction/nonfiction text sets, 78–83, 112–13
  fiction vs., 76–86
  following two voices in text, 93–94
  glossaries, 101, 104–6, 107
  goals for reading, 12, 74
  illustrations in, 87
  informational fiction, 87–91
  interviewing family members about, 84–86
  investigating for content area research and writing, 162–66
  learning to read, 6, 73–113
  locating information in, 174
  predictability of, 75–76, 97
  questionnaires about, 85–86, 221
  questions to ask about, 98–99
  reading for information, 169, 172
  scheduling reading time for, 75
  strategies for reading, 73, 99–100
  student understanding of, 78, 97
  tables of contents, 101–4, 106
  text features and structures of, 75–76, 92–94, 101–6, 108–9, 164
  voice in, 105–6
  word choice in, 90
  writing style, 89–90, 94, 156
Nonfiction Craft Lessons (Portalupi and Fletcher), 157
Nonfiction Matters (Harvey), 75, 156
nonfiction study
  fiction *vs.* nonfiction, 76–86
  goals, 74, 76, 87, 92, 94, 101, 106
  information and support features, 101–6
  literature, 74
  minilessons, 74, 81
  overview, 73–76
  presenting information, 87–91
  reading strategies, 94–100
  reading workshop plan, 77
  reinforcement and practice, 106–11
  student work, 74, 81
  text features and structures, 92–94
  weekly schedule at a glance, 74
nonfiction writing
  entertaining and informative style, 188–97
  humor in, 188–90, 192
  revising, 191–97
nonstandard measurements, 196
no-*said* dialogue
  defined, 37

form, 216
recognizing, 50, 66, 67

Old Grizzly (Cowley), 28–29
On the Far Side of the Mountain (George), 163
onomatopoeia, 146
On Solid Ground (Taberski), 2

page layout, in nonfiction, 108
papier-mâché models, 198–99
parents
content area study and, 179, 211
questions about reading levels, 10–11
Park, Barbara
Junie B. Jones Is a Graduation Girl, 69
Parker, Steve
It's a Frog's Life, 79–80, 104–6, 187–89, 192, 193, 194
partner share, 5
partnerships, for research, 167–68
passions, sharing, 156–57
periods, 46
personal stories, 122–23
personification, 125–27, 132, 146
Peterson Field Guides for Young Naturalists: Backyard Birds, 164, 169, 170, 192
Phantom of the Prairie: Year of the Black-Footed Ferret (London), 87–88, 108, 180
Pinky and Rex and the Dinosaur Game (Howe), 53–54
Pinky and Rex and the Double-Dad Weekend (Howe), 56
Pinky and Rex and the New Baby (Howe), 40–46, 47, 50
Pinky and Rex and the Spelling Bee (Howe), 42, 51–52, 54–55, 59
Pinky and Rex series (Howe), 34, 51–52, 102, 229
place
focusing student writing on, 123–24
memory writing about, 122–24, 134–39
writing about, in a specific time, 134–41
writing about, in several time frames, 141–44
poetic writing, 126, 132
poetry, acrostic, 207, 210
Pond Year (Lasky), 91
Poppleton in Spring (Rylant), 76–77
Post-it Notes
for locating and extracting information, 164
for marking dialogue, 53–54, 57
for marking *said* alternatives, 29
for marking time phrases in texts, 130
organizing for class discussion, 164
uses of, 29
Pratt-Serafini, Kristin Joy
Salamander Rain: A Lake and Pond Journal, 92–94
predictability
of fiction, 75–76
of nonfiction, 75–76, 97
prereading
comprehension and, 51–52
for knowledge about characters, 65
pronunciation keys, 110
publishing celebrations, 149–52
Puddles (London), 147
punctuation
dialogue and, 21, 45–47, 51, 53, 55, 58
as reading strategy, 66

question marks, 47
questionnaires, about nonfiction reading, 85–86
questions
about nonfiction texts, 98–99
for research, 163–66, 168–69
quick practice exercises, 131–32
quotation marks, 27, 40, 46, 66–67

Ray, Katie Wood, 2
reading
goals for children, 11, 12
for information, 169, 172
nonfiction, 6
preparing students for independence in, 67–68
preparing students for longer books, 10
sharing preferences in, 13
thinking during, 11
transitional, 11
wonders of, 45–46
reading aloud
changing voice to portray characters, 39
fluency in, 39
practicing, 45

reading habits
establishing, 12–16
minilessons for, 16
reading levels
determining reading difficulty, 64
parent questions about, 10–11
reading logs
form, 226
noticing nonfiction features in, 93–94, 95
reading partners, 39–40
reading spots, 13, 14, 15
reading strategies, 47, 49–63
comprehension, 51–52
for determining who is talking, 52–59
for dialogue, 54–60
first-person narration and, 64–71
homework worksheets, 56
meaning-based, 58–59
for nonfiction books, 73, 94–100
punctuation, 66
reading the line before and the line after, 58, 66
strategy chart, 54, 55
student awareness and use of, 54–60, 67
visual, 58–59
reading workshop
book boxes for, 14
classroom for, 15
establishing habits, 12–16
getting started in, 6, 10–19
goals for, 11, 12
investigating differences between fiction and nonfiction, 81
investigating nonfiction, 77
meeting area for, 13
reading spots for, 13, 14, 15
sharing reading preferences in, 13
worktables, 13–14
yearlong plan, 7
Red-Tails in Love (Winn), 160
Relatives Came, The (Rylant), 124, 130
repetition, as writing technique, 125–27, 143, 146
rereading
own writing, 145, 196
for understanding dialogue, 20–21, 60
research. *See also* content area research and writing study
content area, 7
folders, 173
listing questions for, 163–66, 168–69
partnerships, 167–68
Post-It Notes for, 164
process, 171–78
reading for information, 169, 172
selecting books for, 164–66
selecting topics for, 167–70
research sheets, 174–78, 190
revision
craft lessons, 144–45, 146
of nonfiction writing, 191–97
rereading and, 196
Ridlon, Marci
"That Was Summer," 116
River of Life (Miller), 192–93
running records, 21
Russell, Elizabeth
Bats, 80, 82
Ryder, Joanne, 106–11, 183, 185, 186
Chipmunk Song, 212
Lizard in the Sun, 183
Snail's Spell, The, 183, 185
Where Butterflies Grow, 91, 183
Rylant, Cynthia, 128, 138
Birthday Presents, 116, 124
Bookshop Dog, The, 88
Case of the Climbing Cat, 27
Cat Heaven, 88
Cobble Street Cousins, 102
Cookie Store Cat, The, 88, 130
Dog Heaven, 88
Gooseberry Park, 19, 25, 28, 76, 77, 80, 96
Henry and Mudge and Annie's Good Move, 27
Henry and Mudge and Annie's Perfect Pet, 33
Henry and Mudge and the Snowman Plan, 36, 40
Henry and Mudge series, 28, 32–38
High Rise Private Eyes series, 20, 147
as a mentor author, 124, 130
Mr. Putter and Tabby Fly the Plane, 26, 40
Mr. Putter and Tabby series, 16, 17, 20, 28
Night in the Country, 130
In November, 132
Poppleton in Spring, 76–77
Relatives Came, The, 124, 130
Scarecrow, 124, 127, 130
Whales, The, 88–91, 126–27, 227

When I Was Young in the Mountains, 45, 124
writing style, 125–28, 143

said
as big clue for dialogue, 59
counting, 31, 32
identifying dialogue with, 27
said alternatives
acting out, 29
as big clue for dialogue, 59
finding, 27–29, 31
interpreting text with, 28–29
Salamander Rain: A Lake and Pond Journal (Pratt-Serafini), 92–94
Salamander's Life, A (Himmelman), 97, 108
Scarecrow (Rylant), 124, 127, 130
scrapbooks, 118, 204–5, 206
second-person narration, 183–86
series books
getting to know, 16–18
getting to know characters in, 18–19
setting. *See also* place; time of day; time of year
creating, 7
establishing in writing, 122–55
setting study
editing, 145–47
final work, 153–54
goals, 125, 127, 128, 129, 132, 141, 144, 145
illustrating, 147–49
literature, 129
minilessons, 129
overview, 122–25
publishing celebration, 149–51
revising, 144–45
student work, 129
using time as a structure, 128–32
weekly schedule at a glance, 129
writing about a specific place, 125–28
writing about place through several time frames, 141–44
writing about time of day, 132–41
share time
defined, 5
for dialogue study, 30, 38, 48, 63, 71
for nonfiction study, 81
partner share, 5
whole-group share, 5
Sharmat, Marjorie Weinman
Nate the Great and the Lost List, 65–70
Nate the Great Goes Down in the Dumps, 32
Nate the Great series, 18–19, 32–35, 38, 64–71, 76
Short, Joan
Whales (with Bettina Bird), 103
showing *vs.* telling, 133
Sibberson, Franki, 11
Sibley, David Allen
Sibley Guide to Birds, The, 179, 186
Sibley Guide to Birds, The (Sibley), 179, 186
similes, 132, 146
simple dialogue
defined, 37
generalizations about, 43
recognizing, 50
Sloppy Tiger and the Party (Cowley), 39–40
Snail's Spell, The (Ryder), 183, 185
Snowball, Diane, 145, 197
Snyder, Clara Hemphill, 179
song writing, 201
Speed, Toby
Water Voices, 132, 133, 136
Spelling K-8 (Snowball), 145
spelling try sheet, 145, 148, 197, 228
Stead, Tony, 2
Stellaluna (Cannon), 80, 82
strategy chart, for dialogue, 54, 55
strong verbs, 146
student work
for content area research and writing study, 158–59
defined, 5
for dialogue study, 22, 30, 38, 48, 63, 71
for nonfiction study, 74, 81
setting study, 129
summer memories. *See also* memory writing
writing about, 115, 118, 137–38
surprising language, 146
Swanson, Susan Marie
Letter to the Lake, 116, 121
Szymusiak, Karen, 11

Taberski, Sharon, 2
tables of contents
bold print in, 103–4

charts for comparing, 104
for content area studies, 208
in nonfiction books, 101–4, 107, 174
prereading, 52
visual qualities of, 102–4
Tallat-Kelpsa, Kevin, 2
T-charts
for adding voice and humor to writing, 188–89
for listing books with and without dialogue, 26
for listing what we know and what we want to know, 163–64, 168
teachers
collaboration by, 1
introducing literature-based workshops to, viii
professional books for, 2
study groups, ix
text features, 92–94, 101–6, 108–9, 164
text sets
fiction/nonfiction, 78–84, 112–13
"That Was Summer" (Ridion), 116
There's an Owl in the Shower (George), 162
thinking, during reading, 11
third-person narration, 32–38
time
in narrative nonfiction, 128–32
phrases about, 130–34
writing about a specific time, 132–41
writing about passage of, 141–44
as a writing structure, 128–32
time of day
comparing to time of year, 130–31
descriptive phrases about, 130, 133, 135, 214
form, 214
marking in texts, 130
noticing use of, 131–32
quick practice exercises, 131–32
showing *vs.* telling, 133
writing about, 124
writing about place and, 134–41
Time of Day chart, 134, 135
time of year
comparing to time of day, 130–31
descriptive phrases about, 133, 215
form, 215
noticing use of, 131–32
quick practice exercises, 131–32
showing *vs.* telling, 133
writing about, 124
titles, in nonfiction, 108
transitional readers, 11
Trumpet of the Swan (White), 163
"try sheets," for misspelled words, 145, 148
Twilight Comes Twice (Fletcher), 135
Two Orphan Cubs (Brenner and Garelick), 91

Urban Roosts: Where Birds Nest in the City (Bash), 160

Venn diagrams, comparing fiction/nonfiction text sets with, 84
verbs, strong, 146
Vieira, Linda
Grand Canyon: A Trail Through Time, 135, 155
visual strategies, for dialogue, 58–59
vocabulary, for research topics, 169–71
voice. *See also* narration
determining who is telling the story, 33–34
entertaining and informative writing style, 188–97
following two voices in text, 93–94
identifying, 31–38, 51
in nonfiction, 105–6, 108
second-person, 183–86
writing with attention to, 178–86

Wacky Plant Cycles (Wyatt), 93, 105
Wadsworth, Ginger
Desert Discoveries, 135
Water Voices (Speed), 132, 133, 136
weekly plans
for content area research and writing study, 158–59
for dialogue study, 22
for nonfiction study, 74
for setting study, 129
Welcome to the Greenhouse (Yolen), 91
Whales, The (Rylant), 88–91, 126–27, 227
Whales (Gibbons), 110
Whales (Short and Bird), 103
What Makes a Bird a Bird?, 166
When I Was Five (Howard), 116
When I Was Little (Curtis), 116
When I Was Young in the Mountains (Rylant), 45, 124
When Morning Comes (Hirschi), 155
When Night Comes (Hirschi), 155

Where Butterflies Grow (Ryder), 91, 183
White, E. B.
  Trumpet of the Swan, 163
whole-class studies. *See also* content area research and writing study
  benefits of, 160–62
whole-group share, 5
Whose Tracks Are These? A Clue Book of Familiar Forest Animals (Nail), 180, 186
Wigdor, Melissa, viii, 8–9
  content area study response, 212
  dialogue study response, 72
  nonfiction study response, 112–13
  setting study response, 155
Williams, Vera B.
  Chair for My Mother, A, 147
  Cherries and Cherry Pits, 147
Winn, Marie
  Red-Tails in Love, 160
  Winter Solstice (Jackson), 94
  Wondrous Words (Ray), 2
  Wood Frog's Life, A (Himmelman), 97, 108
  word choice
  in nonfiction, 90
  surprising language, 146
workshops. *See also* reading workshop; writing workshop
  format of, 4–5
  minilessons in, 4–5
  share time in, 5
  student work time in, 5
worktables, for reading workshop, 13–14
writing. *See also* content area research and writing study; memory writing
  about experiences, 138
  about place, 122–24
  about setting, 7, 122–55
  about summer memories, 115, 118
  about time, 128–44
  acrostic poems, 207, 210
  adding detail to, 120
  celebrating, 149–52
  changing form of, 121
  craft of, 144–45, 146, 157, 224
  dedications, 201, 204, 205
  dialogue, 26–27, 59, 61–62, 69–70
  editing, 145–47
  entertaining and informative, 188–97
  establishing writing habits, 115, 118, 119–20
  explicit teaching of, 117
  field guides, 201, 202–3
  goals for, 123–24
  illustrations for, 147–49
  to inanimate objects, 121
  letters, 121, 201, 204
  lists, 207, 209
  minilessons, 117, 119–20
  personal stories, 122–23
  practicing specific skills, 122
  quick practice exercises, 131–32
  rereading, 145
  revision, 144–45, 146
  songs, 201
  voice and, 178–86
writing folders, 119, 134–36
writing spots, 118
writing style
  clue books, 180–86
  encyclopedia-like, 193, 194
  entertaining and informative, 188–97
  listlike writing, 193
  of mentor authors, 125–28, 134
  modeling, 181–83
  nonfiction, 89–90, 94, 156
  in nonfiction, 108
  repetition, 125–27, 143
  student awareness of, 64–67
  word choice, 90, 146
Writing Through Childhood (Harwayne), 2, 121, 122
writing workshop
  getting started in, 6, 114–21
  planning and setting goals for, 115–21
  showing time of day and time of year, 133
  yearlong plan, 7
Wyatt, Valerie
Wacky Plant Cycles, 93, 105

Yolen, Jane
  Welcome to the Greenhouse, 91

Zoehfeld, Kathleen Weidner
  Cactus Café: A Story of the Sonoran Desert, 136